WITHDRAWN

Borderless Borders

Borderless Borders

U.S. Latinos, Latin Americans, and the Paradox of Interdependence

edited by

Frank Bonilla, Edwin Meléndez, Rebecca Morales,
and María de los Angeles Torres

Temple University Press
Philadelphia

Temple University Press, Philadelphia 19122
Copyright © 1998 by Temple University
All rights reserved
Published 1998
Printed in the United States of America

Text design by Anne O'Donnell

∞ The paper used in this publication meets the requirements of American
National Standard for Information Sciences—Permanence of Paper for
Printed Library Materials, ANSI Z39.48-1984

Library of Congress Cataloging-in-Publication Data
Borderless borders : U.S. Latinos, Latin Americans, and the paradox
   of interdependence / edited by Frank Bonilla . . . [et al.].
        p.   cm.
   Includes bibliographical references (p.) and index.
   ISBN 1-56639-619-0 (cloth : alk. paper). — ISBN 1-56639-620-4
(paper : alk. paper)
   1. Hispanic Americans—Politics and government. 2. Hispanic
Americans—Social conditions. 3. Hispanic Americans—Economic
conditions. 4. United States—Ethnic relations. 5. United States—
Relations—Latin America. 6. Latin America—Relations—United
States.   I. Bonilla, Frank.
E184.S75B674 1998
305.868073—DC21   97-41270

Contents

Acknowledgments

This volume culminates more than a decade of effort by Latinos in a Changing U.S. Economy, a working group operating under the umbrella of the Inter-University Program for Latino Research (IUPLR). Along with others, this team pioneered a now-established mode of collaboration across academic institutions, disciplines, communities, and policy specialties. The Bellagio Conference on which the book is based provided a setting in which to explore the most recent trends in global restructuring. This opportunity, unique perhaps for a Latino-centered enterprise, was generously supported by the Rockefeller Foundation's Bellagio Study and Conference Center, by the Andrew W. Mellon Foundation, and by the Ford Foundation. Key staff persons at these institutions who helped to guide and monitor the project include Susan Garfield, Stephanie Bell-Rose, Mahnaz Isprahani, Antonio Romero, Linda Triangolo, Pasquale Pesce, and Aida Rodriguez. The volume editors coordinated four groups of writers (corresponding to the four sections of this book) who addressed the principal themes of the conference throughout the planning phase and the completion of this book and the associated video, a task stretching over nearly four years. (The video is available from IUPLR, University of Texas at Austin, P.O. Box 8180, Austin, TX 78713-8180.) Details of day-to-day coordination for the conference were efficiently managed by Ana LoBiondo, then part of the IUPLR headquarters staff. Michele Miller Adams helped in the preparation of the manuscript. Bibiana Suárez coordinated the images and text.

Preface

Changing the Americas from Within the United States

Frank Bonilla

Over the past several decades, Latinos in the United States have emerged as strategic actors in major processes of social transformation. This new reality—the Latinization of the United States—is driven by forces that extend well beyond U.S. borders and asserts itself demographically and politically, in the workplace and in daily life. The perception that Latinos are now positioned to bring about change in the Americas from within the United States has taken hold, prompting hemispheric governments to cultivate new forms of relationships with emigrant communities.

In December 1994 the Inter-University Program for Latino Research (IUPLR) convened a conference at the Rockefeller Foundation's Bellagio Center in northern Italy. Scholars, policy specialists, community advocates, and cultural workers came together to take stock of pertinent research and policy on the present condition and promise of Latino peoples, with a special focus on the transnational dimension. During the past decade, IUPLR has promoted a substantial body of research on the significance of the binational and global processes of the major Latino communities in the United States—Mexicans, Puerto Ricans, Cubans, and Central Americans. Four themes were highlighted in sessions extending over three days:

- Emergent forms of global and transnational interdependence
- The negative impact and demographic repercussions within the United States, especially in Latino communities, of economic and political restructuring
- Changing concepts of and social bases for community formation, citizenship, political participation, and human rights as individuals are obliged to construct identities in more than one sociopolitical setting
- Fresh pathways into international relations and issue-oriented social movements and organizations among these highly mobile populations

A primary objective of the conference was the formulation of a long-term research, policy, and organization-building agenda linking the intellectual and political resources generated by Latinos in the United States with counterparts in their countries of origin. The following sketch is meant to convey what was accomplished on each front and some of the common ground between the conference's four main themes and the work presented in this volume.

Global Interdependence. Complex and interlocking forms of interdependence are emerging between the United States and Latin America, involving the movement of capital, modes of industrialization, trade, migration, and growing inequality. As fluid movement across political boundaries interacts with the continued assertion of national, regional, and community controls over economic processes, Latinos throughout the hemisphere are in strategic positions to define and assert new interests, identities, and voices in economic and foreign policy. Two days before the Bellagio meeting, Latin American presidents at the Miami "Summit of the Americas" embraced a broad array of reformist strategies—a show of unanimity that belied the objective indeterminacy of the outcomes of these measures and the potential roles of social actors not represented at the summit. This tension between the premises and projections of those committed to specific neoliberal policies and those wishing to withhold judgment while pursuing further inquiries surfaced repeatedly in the Bellagio deliberations.

The Reconfigured United States. Parallel processes of restructuring within the United States, some tied directly to transnational dynamics, are shaping the incorporation of Latinos into the work force and other institutional domains. National origin weighs heavily in these adaptations via the formation of networks, enclaves, shared social capital, and distinctive forms of social performance. At the same time, inequality is growing, reinforced by institutionalized exclusion, selective incorporation, and heightened hostility against newcomers, all documented among the principal Latino populations and similarly situated communities. Defensive empowering strategies put into place over the past few decades, however, now position Latinos to claim a place in the policy-making apparatus at every level.

Community, Identity, and Civil Rights. Diaspora communities identify themselves according to national origin, while political demands call for or seek to impose an overarching Latino identity. The tensions between community processes and the structures through which people can participate in politics are particularly complicated. Moreover, homeland and host country interact in the lives of most Latinos, who must address events as diverse as the 1994 Chiapas uprising, Central American peace processes, the effects of NAFTA, Proposition 187, changing patterns of border crossings and their policing, and shifts in refugee and immigration law, in terms of their human and legal dimensions. There are few analytical or practical approaches, and even fewer legal constructs, through which people can understand and act upon these disparate and often conflicting relationships. Conventional models of assimilation deal with only a narrow segment of these problems. The encounters in this session among community organizers, lawyers, human rights advocates, artists, and academics from the humanities and social sciences were encouraging and productive. The successful integration of these perspectives foreshadowed at the conference is a distinctive feature of this volume.

International Dialogue. Participants offered sharply contrasting views of the conditions and prospects for a more inclusive and productive international dialogue that is responsive to human needs and rights. An optimistic vision (stimulated by the recent Miami Summit) emphasized steps toward full democratization of formally elected governments, accompanied by commitments to government reforms, renewed social initiatives, and a revitalized partnership between the United States and Latin America. However, detailed treatment of the political situation in Cuba, as well as "bottom up" perspectives articulated by labor organizers, feminists, environmentalists, and human rights advocates, documented persistent inequalities and limited progress in advancing popular interests in the transnational setting, despite the increasing activity of nongovernmental organizations. In addition, an overview of competing models for regional integration and development (European, Asian, and Western) found them all deficient, especially in their capacity to deal with persistent and growing inequality and popular discontent. These judgments reaffirmed the complexity of the task ahead and its long-term character. Yet participants' experiences on the cutting edge of these issues provided realistic hopes for mapping a Latino path through this maze of contradictions.

Ironically, the perception that Latinos and other minorities in the United States are destined to play an increasingly active role in U.S. foreign and domestic policy crystallized in the 1980s, the very decade that dealt them the most serious material setbacks since the depression of the 1930s.[1] With the national and international policy establishments in disarray, Latinos are claiming enhanced readiness and practical capacity to enter these policy domains in a context of authoritatively declared crises in the social and natural sciences and pervasive disjuncture between social scientific endeavors and technocratic policy management. In 1992 a Gulbenkian Foundation commission called for a comprehensive "restructuring of the social sciences," signaling a widespread concern about the bounds of traditional disciplines and distinctive scientific "cultures." "Scholars," the commission noted, "feel dismayed at the state of the social sciences, but very little is being done collectively to change the situation."[2]

The centrality of Latino and Latin American Studies in this connection and the linking of these intellectual resources to the challenges of analyzing global and hemispheric changes has become a salient theme in these contentious debates.[3]

This is a far cry from the reigning mentality some three decades ago, when Daniel Bell, speaking for the National Commission on the Year 2000, declared confidently that there would be no foreseeable economic or political challenge in what remained of the century that the U.S. economy and political structure could not resolve. More recently, however, Bell has come to see the work of essaying projections into the next century as akin to "lighting a small candle in the middle of a hurricane to see if there is a way out."[4] Uncertainty has penetrated even the natural sciences. Physicist Murray Gell-Mann, a 1969 Nobel prize winner who is currently probing the dilemmas of reconciling the adaptive strategies of human communities with those driven by natural evolution on a planetary scale, echoes Bell's imagery. Immanent contradictions in the adaptive schemata of the biosphere over some four billion years are, in Gell-Mann's view, now poised to converge destructively in a not-too-distant future with cognate processes of human adaptation over some 100 million years. Speaking of Project 2050, recently launched to map paths toward "sustainable" development—that is, a future in which both human communities and the natural environment may prosper—he says, "We are all in a situation that resembles driving a fast vehicle at night over unknown terrain that is rough, full of gullies, with precipices not far off. Some kind of headlight, even a feeble and flickering one, may help to avoid some of the worst disasters."[5]

The Gell-Manns among scientists see poverty-stricken, tropical nations as prime settings for the unfolding of this apocalyptic vision. In this light, they can construe ongoing debt swaps between the United States and Latin American nations that include some provisions for environmental measures as "planetary bargains."[6] However, equally pressing planetary bargains remain to be undertaken within the United States, especially in communities along the U.S.-Mexican border and in major cities across the country where Latino peoples are highly segregated and subject to environmental hazards.[7]

Other, less abstruse forms of U.S.-Latin American interdependence have been widely acknowledged for some time, but their implications in terms of U.S. policy, especially with successive changes in U.S. national administrations, remain obscure. Experts are realizing that there is now no clearly framed U.S. policy toward Latin America and that whatever stances are improvised will depend mainly on how the United States manages its own internal social crisis. Abraham Lowenthal, a seasoned Latin Americanist and executive director of the Inter-American Dialogue, has stated the matter forthrightly: "The single greatest factor that will define U.S.–Latin American relations in the decade of the 1990s will be whether and how the United States confronts its own economic and political agenda."[8]

Should these insights prove accurate, they add to the conditions under which significant contingents of U.S.-based Latinos will be drawn into social movements across national boundaries. The limited democratization that has been part of more than a decade of neoliberal economic reform in most of Latin America has done little to cushion the impact of deepening absolute poverty and undiminished inequality and even less to muster hopes and popular support for reforms by government decree.[9] The inefficacy of traditional left and labor organizations in the present circumstances seems also to have set in motion a combined movement of ethnic, gender, and regional resistance partly modeled on and readily linked with its counterparts in the United States, as John Brown Childs has observed:

> As ethnic and gender demands come into Latin America's social consciousness, positive outcomes can fortify the future of tridimensional alliances (ethnicity, gender, class) on a basis of equality. . . . From this communal point of reference, and in association with a set of political commonalities, movements can become transnational indeed. It is in this communal space where there are clear bases for creating transcommunal cadres as answers to transnational attacks.
>
> To not develop such transcommunal cadres for the 21st century is to risk a weakened, divided and conflicted marginalized general population confronted by a well-united ruling social bloc that is actually quite demographically diverse but which is separated by class and privilege from the rest of the America[s].[10]

At the Bellagio conference and in this volume we chronicle in a critical spirit the structural processes and active interventions taking place within and outside U.S. Latino communities. These have produced a complex of challenges and opportunities for resistance and constructive action in social policy, some of which are explored in the chapters that follow.

Chapter 1

Dependence or Interdependence: Issues and Policy Choices Facing Latin Americans and Latinos

Rebecca Morales

Over the last decade, the Western Hemisphere has become progressively integrated economically. This is particularly evident among the industrialized and advanced industrializing countries of North and South America. Here, as elsewhere worldwide, regional blocs are gaining prominence, each shaped by unique developmental paths. The term "interdependence" has been used to convey the way in which the welfare of each country within the region affects that of others. In the Americas, this path has been guided by liberal economic policies, combining economic growth with high rates of poverty and income inequality and a heightened mobility of people and capital. However, interdependence extends well beyond economics. The interpenetration of societies has changed political systems, the nature of social relationships, and forms of cultural expression. In the midst of this transition, the status of Latinos in the United States and of disadvantaged Latin Americans has become more tenuous and at the same time increasingly central to understanding the broader implications of interdependence.

Latinos are now so prominent that they are expected to make up 15 percent of the population by the year 2020, thereby becoming the nation's largest minority. Yet they are for the most part poor and disenfranchised, even though the growth of the U.S. economy has become the envy of other industrialized countries. Latin America has also seen escalating poverty and inequality, despite such growth-stimulating policies as monetary devaluation, fiscal deficit reduction, and increased trade. The lives of U.S. Latinos and Latin Americans are becoming increasingly interlinked through a process of economic, political, and social integration. The purpose of this volume is to examine the nature of the ties that are being forged in order to understand the meaning of interdependence for Latinos and the growing number of disadvantaged Latin Americans.

The four parts of this volume take up the key issues in turn. Part I examines the process of global interdependence. Although the period from the end of the Cold War to the present has seen the rise of free trade and the spread of democratization—two elements associated with the modern state—there has been no corresponding improvement in social justice. Income inequality and poverty are pervasive throughout the hemisphere. Will interdependence ultimately be accompanied by a decline in disparity, thereby leading to individual economic *independence*? Or will it instead lead to the disenfranchisement of whole segments of society, which will then become even more *dependent* on social intervention? This dilemma has become the center of a major policy debate across the hemisphere, and is critical to the well-being of Latinos and Latin Americans.

The difficulty of determining policy outcomes is exacerbated by the limitations of national sovereignty. Transnational movements of firms, nongovernmental organizations, multilateral institutions, capital, and people are eroding traditional spheres of influence associated with nation-states. Rules governing inclusion and exclusion are under constant challenge—not only issues of citizenship and immigration, but also such far-reaching questions as the role of the state versus that of the firm in the market, and the changing boundaries of the firm. Borders of all kinds, not just those delineating the physical boundaries of a nation-state, are being penetrated and in many instances replaced by new intersections, resulting in what we have termed "borderless borders."

Part II concerns the way interdependence affects the economic well-being of Latinos in the United States. Despite Latinos' long history in this country and their many contributions to its founding and growth, the large wave of recent immigrants, migrants, and refugees makes the overall Latino population relatively young and new. From this complex mosaic of generations and backgrounds come people with vastly different expectations and outcomes. The heterogeneous category "Latinos" comprises political refugees from left- and right-wing dictatorships, the wealthy and the disinherited, fourth-generation citizens and recent immigrants. Despite variations, the largest and fastest-growing groups are those who are falling behind economically; for them, the benefits of economic integration seem particularly remote. These groups are learning new ways of coping and developing their communities. Rather than embracing the questionable image of the United States as a melting pot, they are looking to community networks and the development of social capital as sources of strength. In so doing, they are reopening debates about growth versus development, and how development occurs cross-culturally.

The changing nature of culture and identity during this period is the theme of Part III. As previously noted, "Latinos" are by no means homogeneous. Individuals may identify with different nationalities, such as Puerto Rican, Dominican, or Salvadoran, and be further distinguished by immigrant status, class, language, or color, but they understand the use of "Latino" as a societal identifier. Use of either a more specific self-descriptor or the broad label of "Latino" depends on the circumstances. Although Latinos may appear to enter society through a few avenues, a more nuanced examination reveals a number of complex dimensions. Furthermore, despite international ties, transnational connections have failed to emerge uniformly. Rather, the rise of a highly international Latino population, combined with an economy having strong international links, is creating contradictions among Latinos and dividing those who are favored from those who are not. Similar contradictions surface across the generations. The result is a concept of *Latinismo* that is in many ways richer than in the past, but also filled with ambiguity. In this context, civil institutions have generally not come to terms with the demands of the new polity.

Part IV focuses on the need to redefine both frameworks for analyzing trends and methods for collective action to influence policy outcomes. Here, "borderless borders" refers to disciplinary boundaries and traditional approaches for influencing decision-makers. The integration of economy, society, and polity in the Americas is bringing together the previously distinct fields of Latino Studies and Latin American Studies, in spite of deeply ingrained opposing forces. At the same time, it is uniting unexpected allies in the struggle to address problems despite a context in which national efficacy has been seriously eroded and often supplanted by interventions at the local and multistate regional levels. Tensions between global decisions and local consequences are challenging both theory and action as the process of integration deepens. Latinos and Latin Americans are now in the forefront of defining new disciplines and shaping the rise of a new transnational citizens' diplomacy.

Although the process of interdependence has resulted in greater opportunity for some, it has led to persistent and growing social and economic imbalances for others. The imbalances have had a disproportionately negative effect on Latinos in the United States and on the poor in Latin America, resulting in a growing sense of urgency. These groups have only recently entered into sustained discussions of sufficient intensity to alter policy,[1] but the 1997 annual meeting of the National Council of La Raza, which featured Mexican President Ernesto Zedillo, testifies to their emerging strength. The current challenge is to understand how the opportunities created by interdependence can be used to benefit Latinos and disadvantaged Latin Americans. This volume is a contribution to that dialogue. Toward this end, we begin by briefly examining the status of Latinos and Latin Americans.

Growing Poverty and Income Inequality: The U.S. Experience

Latinos in a Changing U.S. Economy: Comparative Perspectives on Growing Inequality, published in 1993, warned of a growing economic, social, and political isolation of Latinos in the United States.[2] Historically, Latinos enjoyed an economic standing midway between Anglos and African-Americans. Given current indicators, the authors argued, the situation could easily worsen. Change was evident just four years later. In January 1997 the *New York Times* ran a front-page article under the headline "Hispanic Households Struggle as Poorest of the Poor in the U.S." As the article noted:

> While other groups are staying ahead of inflation, Hispanic families, whether American born or newly arrived, are falling behind. . . . Census data show that for the first time the poverty rate among Hispanic people in the United States has surpassed that of blacks. Hispanic residents now constitute nearly 24 percent of the country's poor. . . . Of all Hispanic residents, 30 percent were considered poor in 1995, meaning they earned less than $15,569 for a family of four. That is almost three times the percent of non-Hispanic whites in poverty. Of the poorest of the poor, those with incomes of $7,500 or less for a family of four, 24 percent were Hispanic. . . . Overall, income for Hispanic households has dropped 14 percent since 1989, from about $26,000 to under $22,900, while rising slightly for blacks.[3]

U.S. census statistics further document that the "Hispanic population is experiencing an almost across-the-board impoverishment." According to one commentator, "It is the American nightmare, not the American dream."[4]

What went wrong? Several factors contribute to the problem:

- Structural changes in the economy that have drastically reduced the number of well-paid blue-collar jobs
- Institutional failures, particularly the failure of schools to retain Hispanic students and provide them with a marketable education (Hispanics have the highest high school dropout rate of any group in the nation)
- Discrimination, especially among employers who see Hispanic immigrants and others who are not proficient in English as disposable workers
- Policy shifts resulting in the reduction of social services—during the Reagan and Bush administrations (1980–92), federal aid as a proportion of city budgets fell nearly 64 percent below the 1980 level.[5]

Of these contributing factors, structural changes are the most pervasive.[6] During the 1980s and 1990s, international influences prompted companies to downsize, outsource to low-cost suppliers, and turn to part-time workers, while simultaneously upgrading technologically and seeking out highly skilled workers. Throughout the period, industries and occupational structures became increasingly bifurcated, resulting in a growing divide between the "haves" (those employed in secure, high-paying jobs) and the "have nots" (the unemployed, working poor, and unskilled workers). Goods-producing industries that had provided high wages for low-skilled workers were supplanted by services and high-technology manufacturing. The new, bifurcated occupational structure comprised high- value-added jobs demanding college graduates and low-wage jobs requiring less-educated workers. Lost were occupational ladders between the two extremes along with those workers who had previously made up the middle class.

When work is redefined as complex problem-solving, the highly educated are generously rewarded, while those with little education are unable to keep pace.[7] In the 1970s, men with some college experience earned an average 20 percent more than those with only a high-school education; by 1980, the gap had grown to between 40 and 50 percent. College-educated men (between the ages of twenty-five and fifty-four) realized a 7 percent increase in their incomes between 1979 and 1989, while those with a high-school diploma suffered an 11 percent decrease, and those without a diploma a 23 percent decrease. The gap widened throughout the 1990s, not because college graduates earned significantly more, but because high school graduates earned so much less.[8]

In contrast to the period from 1947 to 1968, when family income inequality declined by 7.4 percent, the years from 1968 to 1994 saw an actual increase in inequality, amounting to 16.1 percent for the 1968-92 period and 22.4 percent for 1992-94.[9] Between 1973 and 1993, the percentage of those living below the poverty level nationwide grew from 8.8 to 12.3 percent. Among whites, the poverty rate rose from 6.6 to 9.4 percent, while the percentage of blacks living in poverty rose from 28.1 to 31.3 percent. However, the proportional increase was greatest for Latinos, whose poverty rate grew from 19.8 to 27.3 percent.[10] While median incomes (using constant dollars) rose for all households from 1980 to 1993, including those of whites and blacks, Latinos' average income actually dropped.[11] Ironically, the rise in poverty occurred in the midst of an expanding economy. It was not a lack of jobs, but the quality of jobs, that accounted for the deterioration.

From 1980 to 1990, Latinos became more prominent in the economy as their numbers rose from 6.5 percent to 11.4 percent of the nation's population. From 1980 to 1994, the Latino population grew by 44 percent nationwide, with much of this growth coming from immigration. In 1990, over one-third of all Latinos were immigrants. The economic conditions described above intersect with a demographic profile that shows a largely young and immigrant Latino population with a high dropout rate, a low level of educational attainment, and lack of English proficiency:

- Nearly half of all Latinos over the age of twenty-five are high school dropouts. Only 51 percent of Latinos have completed high school (compared with more than 80 percent of the general population and nearly 67 percent of blacks). Fewer than 10 percent of Latinos have completed four or more years of college (compared with more than 22 percent of the general population and nearly 12 percent of blacks).
- Between 25 and 45 percent of Latinos lack English proficiency.
- Among Latinos, more than 19.0 percent of households are headed by females, compared with 11.4 percent for the nation as a whole. Among Puerto Ricans, the proportion of female-headed households is nearly 34 percent; for Central and South Americans, the figure is 22 percent. In the Americas, this path has been guided by liberal economic policies that combine economic growth with high rates of poverty and income inequality and a heightened mobility of people and capital (the comparable rate for blacks is 47.8 percent).[12]

Despite their circumstances—or perhaps because they have few alternatives—Latinos have shown a strong attachment to work. Most Latino subgroups (with the exception of Puerto Ricans) have higher-than-average labor force participation rates. Trapped in a revolving door of low-wage jobs and frequent unemployment, Latinos exit from and reenter the labor market relatively rapidly, often circulating among poorly paid jobs lacking benefits, security, or full-time employment.[13] For the most part, Latinos constitute the "working poor."

Latinos also fuel the growth of metropolitan economies. Nearly 92 percent of Latinos live in urban areas, compared with about 73 percent of the general population. Furthermore, 90 percent of Latinos are located in six states, with approximately 54 percent situated in fourteen major metropolitan areas. Since many Latinos are poor, the poor are also concentrated in cities. In contrast to the 34 percent of impoverished whites who live in cities, 59 percent of poor Latinos (and 60 percent of poor blacks) are urban residents.

Although the United States has become a major job generator compared with other advanced industrialized countries, the economy is becoming extremely skewed. Inadequate social programs have left the working poor and the unemployed exposed to the harsh forces that flow from economic openness and structural change. According to one 1992 account, "the direct and indirect cost to society of tolerating an underclass of urban poor is at least $230 billion annually and mounting."[14] A careful

assessment would also reveal a society held back by underutilized resources and unnecessarily low productivity.

Economic Liberalization and Declining Trade: The Latin American Experience

During the 1980s and 1990s, most Latin American countries undertook
a process of economic liberalization. Within a relatively short period, they
made the transition from inward-oriented to outward-oriented trade and
investment policies. The transformation was motivated by an effort to
raise productivity and reduce inefficiency by exposing domestic producers
to international standards. Following traditional economic theory, the
countries devalued their currencies and reduced tariffs and other trade
restrictions. In return, they expected to realize a cost reduction in imported capital goods and intermediate inputs, and a shift in relative prices
to favor exports. Consistent with the neoliberal model, they also mini-
mized the role of government through privatizing, financial and industrial
deregulation, labor market reform, and cutbacks in social programs. After
more than a decade of sacrifice, however, the results have been disappointing.

Most Latin American countries have yet to reach the export growth
rates achieved during the decade of import substitution industrialization
(roughly 1970–80). By 1992, their export performance was still only
one-half to one-third of the level attained throughout the 1970s.[15] In just
four years of rapid economic liberalization, Latin America's trade balance
actually dropped from a $26 billion surplus (1989) to a $13 billion deficit
(1993).[16] Some of the most serious deterioration in the trade balance
occurred in Argentina and Mexico, two leaders in liberalization. In contrast, Brazil and Venezuela, which had far more nuanced liberalization
programs, experienced trade surpluses.

Trade declined steadily for two decades beginning in 1974, despite
increased trade worldwide. When the trade of manufactures rose globally,
Latin America realized significant growth only in food and fuel exports.
Because it did not keep pace technologically with the rest of the world,
most of its manufactured exports have been in basic input industries,
traditional industries, or semimanufactures, and not in the new growth
industries. As a result, those sectors of the economy most exposed to
outside forces, such as small and medium-sized businesses and unskilled
workers, have experienced increasing economic hardship.

Throughout the 1980s, gross national product growth rates fell
below population growth, while poverty escalated.[17] By 1990, the incidence of poverty had reached nearly 50 percent (compared with 41 percent in 1980). The rise in poverty was coupled with an increase in income

concentration.[18] Income inequality in Argentina, Brazil, Chile, Panama, Peru, and Venezuela in particular worsened throughout the 1990s relative to the previous decade.

Frustrated by the lack of a Latin American counterpart to the East Asian "miracle," a number of economists began to argue that liberal economic policies emphasizing macroeconomic stabilization and economic stimulation while neglecting political and social issues actually invite economic losses. Numerous studies began to show that trade liberalization strategies applied without concurrent distributional policies damage growth.[19] Even the United Nations Economic Commission for Latin America and the Caribbean concluded that "excessive reliance on the 'automatic' effectiveness of macroeconomic price signals and reform has led to a tendency to underestimate the weakness of institutions and the failures of markets."[20]

The Overall Picture

Growing poverty and income inequality make it critically important to understand the premises underlying interdependence. One assumption is that liberal economic policies and increased trade will stimulate economic growth throughout the hemisphere. Neoclassical theory predicts that lower tariffs should lead to greater internationalization. Yet, historically, the decline in tariffs and increase in trade have been accompanied instead by a rise in quantitative restrictions on imports. Worldwide, approximately 40 percent of trade is believed to be managed.[21] Rather than broadly diffused international trade, we have seen a rise of regional trading blocs since the 1980s. In fact, it was the desire to protect regional markets that led to adoption of the North American Free Trade Agreement (NAFTA). NAFTA essentially codified a process of regionalization that was already taking place. Yet if NAFTA were to be extended to all of Latin America, it is not clear that the benefits of hemispheric integration would exceed those associated with the emergence of regional trade blocs.

Furthermore, numerous studies show that liberal economic strategies emphasizing macroeconomic stabilization and economic stimulation through increased trade, when applied without concurrent distributional policies, have a negative effect on income distribution. An ambivalence about inequality lies at the core of the economic development literature. Traditional economic theory views development as a tradeoff between economic growth and equality. Economist Arthur Okun argues that in a world of limited resources, redistribution comes at the expense of efficiency, while diminishing incentives for work and investment.[22] Sociologist Charles Murray and others have applied this logic to social theory by claiming that policies aimed at income redistribution have far greater negative social consequences than those directed at stimulating growth.[23] Coalesced into conventional wisdom, these ideas justify dismantling social welfare systems while tolerating poverty and inequality.

More recent studies have challenged the notion of a tradeoff between economic growth and equity. One study of seventeen industrialized nations reported that the countries with the most unequal income distribution at the beginning of the 1980s, like the United States and Switzerland, showed slower productivity growth during the subsequent decade than did Japan, Belgium, and Sweden, where incomes are the least unevenly distributed.[24] In another study of fifty-six countries, the authors found a distinct correlation between inequality and slow growth.[25] The conclusion of these scholars and others is that there is no growth–equity tradeoff per se; rather, institutional and political environments determine the relationship between growth and equity. Poverty and inequality arguably hinder growth because they create a drag on the economy: resources are underutilized, costly social programs prevail, and consumption—the engine of a healthy economy—is suboptimal. Under ideal conditions, converging incomes give rise to a growing middle class, which then stimulates consumption and facilitates economic growth.

The second assumption predicts a positive result from unrestrained market relationships between more and less developed countries. This assumption is not shared by everyone. A different philosophy, for example, underpins the European Union. Tied together by the Single Europe Act of 1986, the EU creates a unified internal market (it is a customs union) in which goods, services, and labor move with relative ease, on the assumption that countries with well-developed economies make better trading partners than those with accentuated disparities. Thus, in Europe, regional development programs aimed at upgrading lagging regions or countries are important components of the overall integration plan.

NAFTA, on the other hand, is propelled by the objective of lowering the costs of trade and foreign investment. NAFTA intentionally links less developed countries, which offer advantages associated with low-cost production, with advanced nations that provide markets and high-value-added products. The agreement reinforces existing strengths and exacerbates weaknesses. The *Washington Post* put it this way: "From Mexico's vantage point, NAFTA marks the foundation of a common market in which it could never be more than a secondary power. By codifying Salinas' economic liberalization program, NAFTA gives American companies privileged access to the [previously] fast growing Mexican market."[26] Not surprisingly, neither the working-class population nor small firms in either the United States or Mexico have benefited from NAFTA. According to Arthur D. Little Mexicana: "Ninety percent of the labor force and 90 percent of the companies in Mexico are outside of NAFTA."[27]

This leads us to the third assumption behind interdependence in the Americas: that macroeconomic policies and economic stabilization programs alone can rebuild economies. Clearly, this assumption ignores the microeconomic policies and supportive institutions that must accompany macroeconomic policies. Political scientist Robert Wade relates this omission to the difference between a "framework" and an "ingredients" approach to industrialization. In the framework approach, "the emphasis is on correcting distortions in price signals, so that individual agents can make investments and innovation decisions that are as close to optimal as possible," where the key actors are individual firms acting autonomously in the market. By contrast, the ingredients approach focuses "on the tangible structure of the economy, defined as a *set* of industries and organizations already in place (the ingredients), and especially on the desirable future structure of the economy."[28] Whereas trade policy alone is central to industrialization in the framework approach, in the ingredients approach it is only one of several policies making up an industrial strategy; equally important are technology and educational policies, as well as those aimed at strengthening links between firms.

With the advent of the high-technology revolution and pressures to innovate, industrial organization has changed to resemble "global industrial networks with highly integrated, but remarkably stable, regional nodes."[29] These industrial networks require more rather than fewer government initiatives, including "worker training; technology transfer; competition policies; export and investment promotion; and specific policies targeted at micro and small enterprises."[30] The shift in the technological basis of industrialization, by favoring the highly educated, is arguably one of the most important factors behind the trend toward growing income inequality worldwide.[31]

Finally, the fourth assumption is that policies of economic openness should permit the mobility of factors of production. In the Americas, however, this assumption has not extended to labor. Under NAFTA, flows of labor are tightly controlled, so that labor markets are far more constrained in their ability to adjust to external pressures. The dislocations created by capital and the de facto movement of people following the trail of jobs have resulted in a vast, clandestine migratory stream. Migrants' vulnerable status makes them the object of economic and political abuse. This distortion of the liberal agenda results in a perverse class structure and exclusionary problems that can be resolved only by addressing issues of citizenship and individual rights in a transnational society.

Jointly, these four assumptions—that the Americas are moving toward a free multilateral trading system; that unrestrained market relations between more and less developed nations will have positive outcomes; that macroeconomic policies and economic stabilization programs are sufficient for rebuilding economies; and that economic openness does not need to include labor mobility—underlie policies contributing to the poverty traps and second-class citizenship that plague Latinos in the United States and impoverished Latin Americans. As recent peasant uprisings in Mexico and Peru have illustrated, such imbalances cannot be sustained without negative political consequences.[32]

However, a free market philosophy is only one reason for the U.S. tolerance of increased social degradation. Social and democratic exclusion and limited economic possibilities have combined to create an environment in which blaming the victim has become acceptable for governments and citizens alike. Latinos are seen as the problem rather than as those who are shouldering the costs of economic policies. Harsh policies are acceptable as long as Latinos and poor Latin Americans are criminalized or viewed as outside the social, political, and economic mainstream and, therefore, unentitled to its benefits. Policy interventions aimed at shifting the process of economic growth from unbalance to one of broadly shared wealth and well-being offer a starting point for reversing this situation.

Policy Choices in an Interdependent World

Latinos and Latin Americans have several policy options. First, they can attempt to influence regional trade agreements like NAFTA, the Caribbean Basin Initiative, and their counterparts in Central America (Caricom) and South America (MERCOSUR). The goal is to ensure that microeconomic policies associated with regional integration will facilitate the intended economic transitions with a minimum of domestic disruption. However, gaining a seat at the table has never been easy. Some policy analysts have called for special hearings aimed at:

> (1) having the General Accounting Office investigate the underrepresentation and assignment patterns of Latinos in the State Department; (2) examining the funding available for promoting Latino participation in U.S.-Latin American assistance; and (3) advising the Agency for International Development that Latino businesses and nonprofit organizations are ideal agencies for promoting AID programs in Latin America.[33]

Such hearings are only a beginning. Latinos also recognize that additional visibility and influence may be achieved through better utilization of the media and more Latino-elected officials.

A second area of concern is labor migration and citizen rights. If labor is not allowed to migrate as freely as capital, then labor markets will remain constrained in their ability to adjust to changes in supply and demand, and job migration will force people into an illegal status. True transnationalization should permit more fluidity for workers. Thus, it may be appropriate to visit the idea of extended citizenship rights among countries engaged in multilateral trade agreements. Extended citizenship would restore democratic due process and confer legal rights on the thousands of undocumented persons who have become both politically and economically disenfranchised. Such thinking recently prompted Mexico to adopt dual nationality, allowing millions to seek U.S. citizenship without losing their rights as Mexicans.

A third policy area involves developing an urban agenda that reflects the perspectives and priorities of Latinos and Latin Americans. With the devolution of federal policy to the state and local levels in the United States, and general downsizing of government at all levels, it is sometimes hard to know who is in charge of making urban policy. Yet urban areas have emerged as the engines of economic growth in most countries, and the sites where the new economically based international relations are being forged.[34] An integral part of an urban agenda is an economic development strategy. Economic development programs that most effectively address the needs of disadvantaged people are those which build on their own social institutions, or "social capital."[35] Successful economic development strategies also combine educational enrichment and skill enhancement with social support for the working poor. In the United States, early waves of Cuban refugees made a relatively successful transition into the economic mainstream, but their success may be hard to replicate. This group required substantial financial investment and technical assistance to make the adjustment,[36] suggesting that too often the real costs of economic development are vastly underestimated.

Lastly, a new type of citizen diplomacy has begun to emerge through cross-border coalitions.[37] Artists, labor unions, environmental groups, and human rights organizations in particular have taken the lead in forging transnational links among U.S. Latinos and Latin Americans. In the process, new cultural identities are being created along with new voices that reflect cross-cutting loyalties and interests. National boundaries do not begin to contain the emerging sociopolitical dimensions of greater integration. Yet the potential for developing policies through these avenues remains largely untapped.

On all these fronts, the experiences of Latinos and Latin Americans have become a common lens for identifying broader societal issues and defining appropriate solutions. Interdependence brings these groups closer together. Despite real differences, U.S. Latinos and Latin Americans are tied together by similar economic pressures and multilateral policies. These ties have forced a reexamination of disciplines at the academic level, while stimulating a cultural renaissance. Thus, although the crisis of growing inequality and poverty may call into question current economic policies, emerging solutions may lead to outcomes that transcend existing societal bonds. This could well be the ultimate legacy of interdependence.

Looking Ahead

Addressing these issues, the individual contributors to this volume perceive the notion of interdependence as paradoxical for Latinos and Latin Americans. The weight of sheer numbers and the numerous cross-border connections unleashed by the integration process make Latinos at home and abroad a potentially powerful voice even if current circumstances effectively marginalize them. It remains to been seen whether the process of interdependence can ultimately be changed to their benefit through direct political and economic routes, if not through the spread of culture and the values of a transborder people.

Part One

Global Interdependence

Chapter 2

Interdependence, Inequality, and Identity: Linking Latinos and Latin Americans

Manuel Pastor, Jr.

Over the past several years, researchers in the fields of Latino/Chicano Studies and Latin American Studies have been struck by a remarkable convergence of themes and issues. Many scholars who began their work in the area of Latin American political economy are now contributing key insights into issues of Latino political identity and economic advancement. At the same time, scholars originally rooted in the field of Latino Studies have recognized the need to understand the dynamics of Latino countries of origin, particularly as the Latino experience in the United States has continued to resist neat categorization within traditional "immigrant" or "underclass" paradigms.[1] We are truly on the eve of defining a new agenda for research, one that blends the international and the domestic into a fuller picture of the situation of Latino-origin individuals in the Americas.

What explains this convergence of interests and research? While a range of factors are at work, including scholars' personal histories and agendas, the basic dynamics are rooted in the very themes explored in this volume. First, economic globalization has meant that "external" events and patterns have a deep impact on domestic policy choices. Latin Americanists, of course, always have recognized the need to take into account the dynamics of the U.S. economy and polity in order to understand Latin America development. Now scholars in the United States concerned with the economic situation of Latinos are increasingly aware that international arrangements like the North American Free Trade Agreement (NAFTA) will have quite specific effects on the kind of low-wage labor that characterizes the barrios of the United States.

Second, the fact that Latinos will soon be the largest minority group in the United States—itself partly a result of international trends that have globalized the demand for labor and helped push the Latin American work force northward—means that this group will soon "reconfigure" the United States. To understand this "Latinized" U.S. future, researchers in Latino Studies and other fields must look carefully at the patterns of urban living, labor force participation, health, and family structure that immigrants carry with them from their home communities.

Finally, the search for Latino identity and the defense of Latino civil rights have forced a crossing of jurisdictional and disciplinary borders. Cultural production aimed at understanding the Chicano experience is rooted increasingly in the notion of *frontera* (border).[2] Moreover, the key political issue to emerge for Latinos in recent years is the defense of the rights of undocumented immigrants, an agenda based implicitly on a notion of transnational (or noncitizen) human rights.

Against this backdrop, it is appropriate to stand back and ask what, aside from the focus on Latino-origin people, really links these two fields of study. Is there a way to place Latinos in the context of Latin American Studies that goes beyond the obvious cultural linkages and instead stresses the sort of structural parallels familiar to those in the social sciences? And can this be done in a way that incorporates the phenomenon of internationalization, which is both central to this volume and apparent to any observer of current events?

In this chapter I address these questions by stressing four political economy issues that cross disciplinary and physical borders and are rooted in the unifying themes of internationalization, inequality, and identity. In the order of the argument, they are as follows:

- The inequality that faces both Latin Americans and Latinos, particularly urban residents, is partly a result of internationally induced economic restructuring. In this sense, integration into global society has had uneven effects for both Latin and Latino Americans.
- Much of this inequality is, in fact, unproductive in the sense that it actually impedes any resolution of the economic difficulties facing Latin America or the areas of the urban United States where most Latinos reside. Indeed, a new body of research on both the international and domestic fronts suggests that measures to improve the distribution of income would help economic growth. This research may serve to promote a pro-Latino, pro-equality agenda.
- Reversing inequality might especially enhance Latino and Latin American economic well-being because the sort of inequality that typically affects both groups challenges the usual models or explanations of poverty. In particular, poverty in this context does not emerge from a lack of economic energy: in the United States, high rates of Latino labor force participation are coupled with low wages; in Latin America, a thriving informal sector receives poor remuneration. This concurrence of high poverty levels and significant work effort suggests the presence of misused or

underutilized resources that might appropriately be redirected toward growth.

- The emergence of an egalitarian but pro-growth agenda is constrained by the political disenfranchisement of Latinos in the United States and the lack of political power of the poor within Latin America. As a result, feasible technical solutions to the problem of poverty are dependent upon the achievement of a sense of Latino community, identity, and empowerment, particularly among the poor. Bridging the gap between Latinos and Latin Americans—and between the fields of Latino and Latin American Studies—may help in this task of identity-building.

Each of the four main sections that follow flows directly from one of the propositions above. In illustrating specific points, I often focus on the city of Los Angeles, partly because it has been the subject of much of my research, but also because Los Angeles serves as a unique reality and metaphor in the meeting of Latin and Latino America. My propositions about internationalization, inequality, and identity are generalizable beyond U.S. Latinos and their Latin American counterparts. In a sense, then, the experiences of Latinos and Latin Americans are particular reflections of broader structural trends; the fields of Latino and Latin American Studies therefore are linked not only to each other but to the work of scholars in other fields.[3] I conclude by noting that globalization is likely to continue, and that we had best be prepared to understand and reverse its unproductive and disequalizing consequences. To do so will require the further theoretical linking of the seemingly bifurcated concerns of area and ethnic studies.

Internationalization and Inequality

The notion that internationalization might contribute to either international or domestic inequality may seem surprising to mainstream economists and political scientists. After all, the view that internationalization has an equalizing effect across nations is both conventional and seemingly logical: when goods, capital, or labor can move freely, it is argued, the poorer (capital-scarce/labor-abundant) countries should see their economies and income move in the direction of the more advanced countries. Enhanced mobility should also ensure that the returns to each productive factor within any particular country will more closely parallel those in world markets; for the labor-abundant countries, this should imply improvement in the domestic distribution of income. Finally, to the extent that internationalization is a consequence of (or promotes) trade liberalization, isolated islands of a tariff-protected labor aristocracy should be swept aside by a tidal wave of less protected and poorer workers, enhancing outcomes for the latter and thereby reducing domestic inequality.

So why has the recent period of internationalization been accompanied by a worsening distribution of income in both Latin America and the United States? While some of the factors in this disequalization are specific to these regions and the current time period, we should first stress that such a result is not as novel as mainstream social scientists might think. The standard models of growth and trade are sometimes too limited in their assumptions and reasoning. Recent developments in growth theory, for example, make it clear that the failure of incomes to converge across the developed and developing world is rooted in a bottling up of technological innovations in the richer countries;[4] when capital flows to the developing world are oriented primarily toward setting up the Fordist production lines of the past (as seems to be the case for much of today's globalization), poorer countries are unlikely to accomplish the sort of "catch-up" expected from internationalization.[5] Moreover, the notion that internationalization will improve the domestic distribution of income in poorer countries by raising demand for abundant labor is based on a simple two-factor model of the economy in which capital and labor compete as inputs, and any shift toward a labor-intensive comparative advantage will favor the latter. There is, however, a new group of three-factor models in which labor is broken up into its skilled and unskilled components. Given the quality and technological demands of the tradable (or exportable) sector, skilled labor can benefit from internationalization while unskilled labor, which is substitutable and in nearly endless supply from the rural sector, sees little change in wages.[6]

Turning to more historically specific factors behind the worsening inequality, we should first recognize the importance of the debt crisis and its legacy in Latin America. While evidence on poverty and inequality is difficult to obtain, partly because of the reluctance of Latin American governments to collect "smoking gun" data on distributional issues, the general trends in average wages, quintile distributions, and other measures point to a redistribution of income away from the poorest groups and toward the richest. Gary Dymski and I, for example, offer estimates suggesting that debt outflows have worsened the distribution of income both *between* North and South and *within* Latin America itself (that is, workers have lost more relative income than was needed to fund debt obligations).[7] Eva Paus has conducted a careful analysis of postcrisis adjustment policies and suggests that the recent wave of liberalization has probably made the picture worse.[8] The reason for the likely redistribution of income relates directly to the alternative three-factor model sketched above: as the foreign exchange crisis broke out, capital increased its scarcity value and hence its power; as trade was opened up to bridge the foreign exchange gap, skilled labor became similarly scarce; in both processes, unskilled labor, which makes up the bulk of Latin America's working population, was the unqualified loser.

In the United States, Latinos also have been sharply affected by the process of economic internationalization.[9] One key trend in this regard has been "deindustrialization"—the relative shrinkage of basic industries such as automobiles and steel in the face of international competition and multinational mobility.[10] This phenomenon has likely had larger effects on Anglo and African-American workers than on Chicano and Puerto Rican workers, primarily because the former groups had been more successful at obtaining jobs in the traditional blue-collar unionized industries that were hard-hit by increasing trade penetration and the export of production jobs. Of more importance to Latinos has been the "reindustrialization" phenomenon: that is, the reemergence in the United States of "old" industries, such as garment assembly, based on the use of newer and cheaper immigrant labor increasingly available because of economic difficulties in Latin America. While such reindustrialization has occurred in many areas of the United States, its most dramatic manifestation may have been in Los Angeles and in other areas of the Southwest.[11] In Los Angeles, for example, the growth in reindustrialized sectors managed to mask the employment loss in traditional manufacturing. Many of these low-wage "gains" involved the increasing use of Latino labor.[12]

Los Angeles, in fact, represents a unique nexus of the various pressures of economic internationalization. Here, the inequality of Latin America and Latino America come together—in part because this is a region where the poor of both groups meet face-to-face.[13] The population of Los Angeles County is now around 40 percent Latino, up from only 18 percent in 1970.[14] Nearly half of that group is immigrant, having been pushed northward by growing inequality and poverty within Latin America itself. Most importantly, the bulk of the poor in Los Angeles are Latino, including the vast majority of those living below the poverty line and an even larger percentage of those living "near poverty" (defined as those in households where income hovers between one and two times the poverty line; see Figure 2.1).[15]

The pattern outlined above suggests why any analysis of Latinos and globalization might choose to focus on the seemingly nonethnic issues of urban poverty and inequality: these economic outcomes are central to determining life opportunities for Latinos. A focus on poverty and inequality is equally important for Latin America as it seeks finally to move past the "lost decade" of the 1980s and create a sounder basis for economic growth and stable politics. Note also that focusing on inequality takes us beyond the

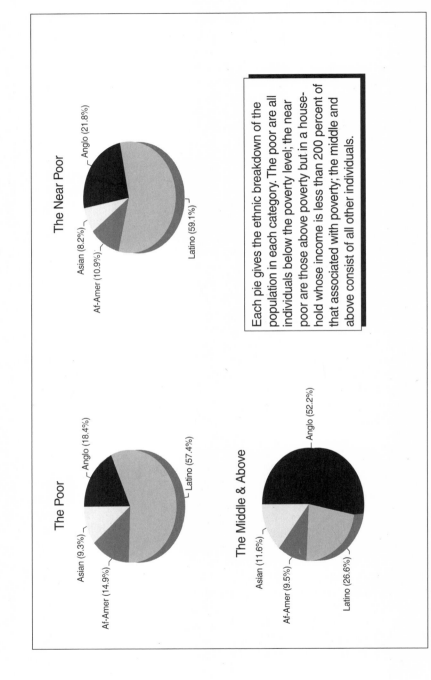

The Poor

Asian (9.3%)

Af-Amer (14.9%)

Anglo (18.4%)

Latino (57.4%)

The Near Poor

Asian (8.2%)

Af-Amer (10.9%)

Anglo (21.8%)

Latino (59.1%)

The Middle & Above

Asian (11.6%)

Af-Amer (9.5%)

Anglo (52.2%)

Latino (26.6%)

Each pie gives the ethnic breakdown of the population in each category. The poor are all individuals below the poverty level; the near poor are those above poverty but in a household whose income is less than 200 percent of that associated with poverty; the middle and above consist of all other individuals.

Figure 2.1. The Color of Poverty in Los Angeles County

usual boundaries of ethnic and area studies and into the territory of comparative political economy. Such an analytical opening may also broaden the terrain of ethnic studies by incorporating the work of those social scientists interested in studying the broader structural linkage between international trade and the distribution of income: Latinos are one key "subject" of those trends and hence an appropriate focal point for empirical work and policy. Below, I bring together some of that broader research to suggest that the growing inequality noted above may be counterproductive for economic recovery, and to argue that this insight could inspire a key part of a positive agenda for Latino and Latin American empowerment.

Inequality and Growth

Even if internationalization has contributed to the inequality affecting Latinos and Latin Americans, it remains unclear what, if anything, should be done about it. Reversing economic globalization is, after all, nearly impossible and probably undesirable: increased international intercourse can, if properly harnessed, promote growth, technological development, and domestic income. The challenge then is finding mechanisms to ensure that internationalization is consistent with distributional improvement and the alleviation of poverty. However, the first step in this process involves offering reasons for social justice that go beyond the usual normative claims. Moral reasoning can, for example, be easily rejected by those who claim that efforts to improve distribution take a large toll on overall economic well-being. Specifically, many analysts and political actors feel that inequality is "productive" in a Kuznets-like sense: policies to promote a more progressive income distribution may erode market incentives and hence slow economic growth, while harsh and sometimes regressive adjustment measures may position the economy for future growth that eventually will benefit even low-income individuals.[16]

Interestingly, a new wave of academic research is rejecting the old consensus in favor of a view that more egalitarian distributions of income are better for macroeconomic stability and restructuring, as well as for long-term growth. This "pro-equality" argument remains a bit elusive, but some general lines of reasoning can be discerned in the literature. For example, some authors argue that more equal distributions of income lead to fewer political struggles over relative prices, such as conflicts between farmers and city-dwellers, between exporters and producers for the domestic markets, or between workers and the owners of their firms; these reduced sectoral tensions mean less "rent-seeking" for sectorally favorable government policies that tend to suppress growth.[17] Other analysts suggest that more equitable distributions of income mean less conflict-driven inflation and fewer stabilization delays, caused when various classes "out-wait" each other in the hope that the costs of any eventual stabilization will be imposed on another group;[18] the resulting macroeconomic stability is generally thought to help investment and output growth. Finally, political economy frameworks suggest that a less skewed distribution of income will lead to policies such as investment in basic health and education;[19] one can conclude from the "endogenous growth" literature[20] that this sort of reorientation of government spending is likely to yield a relatively high return in terms of economic growth.

Anyone familiar with Latin America, where sectoral conflicts, policy favoritism, failed stabilizations, and under-investment in human capital are closely associated with dampened economic performance, can see immediately the possible relevance of these propositions. Establishing their validity, however, has required the generation of empirical work that at least suggests the plausibility of a positive relationship between improved social and income equality and more rapid economic growth. While the first efforts in this direction were often simple comparisons of inegalitarian Latin America and the more distributionally progressive nations of East Asia,[21] recent efforts have involved more sophisticated econometric exercises. One strand of research demonstrates that countries with a more problematic distribution of income were more likely to run into foreign debt problems.[22] The newest empirical research is a more direct test of both outcomes and the chain of causation. Specifically, Torsten Persson and Guido Tabellini offer a model of policy formation suggesting that more equal societies will tend to favor investment in the sort of broad educational development most conducive to growth. Running growth regressions for a sample of fifty-six countries, the authors find the expected negative link between inequality and growth; moreover, the implied positive effects of equality on growth are most pronounced in democratic regimes, where the poor presumably have better access to public policy making and hence a better opportunity to push for growth-enhancing basic education.[23]

The argument that inequality makes for bad economics as well as bad politics can easily be extended to the situation of U.S. Latinos, particularly in urban areas. To do so, we must first acknowledge that internationalization has, perhaps surprisingly, diminished the importance of national economies and elevated the role of the region as the basic economic unit. In a world in which tariff barriers are falling and national economic policy has less latitude, business and political networks and alliances are what matters; these networks, however, tend to emerge at the level of the region, a scale at which production economies can still be realized (particularly given access to a world market), but within which economic actors also can maintain the face-to-face contacts that build trust. As a result, the dynamic manufacturing areas of the world are not countries but specific regions like northern Italy, Silicon Valley, and the Monterrey industrial works in Mexico.[24]

Does equality matter for regional performance? A recent flurry of research on the United States (in which the focus on a single national political unit helps control for cross-country differences in national policy and societal tolerance of inequality) has found that more equal metropolitan regions perform better. Specifically, those regions with the widest income gaps between city and suburb were more likely to suffer regional stagnation, meaning that even suburban incomes, while still above those of the inner city, were lower than they might otherwise have been.[25] The explanation commonly offered for this result is parallel to that offered for nations: equality facilitates cooperative relationships among classes, ethnic groups, and public and private actors, and this, in turn, allows a region to forge a common agenda for growth.[26] In short, on both international and domestic levels, a growing body of evidence suggests that it makes economic as well as moral sense to reduce inequality.[27]

Again, Los Angeles stands as reality and metaphor. Battered harder than almost any other U.S. region in the early 1990s, the L.A. economy has only recently joined in the national recovery. While international competition and cutbacks in U.S. military spending are certainly factors, so are the L.A. basin's tremendous inequality and the resentment and policy stalemate it has produced. The most evident example, of course, is the L.A. uprising of April–May 1992, a social upheaval that poisoned the investment climate and produced little in the way of positive repair initiatives. To restore regional growth, policy-makers will need to rebuild investor confidence, a task requiring a regional approach that addresses seriously the issues of poverty alleviation and development in low-income communities. Little has been accomplished in this direction, because of analytical blinders that hide the equality–growth nexus and political and ethnic divisions that often preclude the realization of an egalitarian strategy. To improve Latino life in Los Angeles, however, such a strategy is essential and may also be uniquely powerful in promoting regional recovery, primarily because of the particular nature of Latino poverty in the urban Southwest—a topic addressed below.

Working and Poor

In the previous section, I argue that the poverty and inequality confronting much of Latino and Latin America may be "unproductive" in the sense that they are neither necessary nor good for growth. This argument is strengthened if we consider the type of poverty suffered by Latinos and Latin Americans—a poverty caused primarily by structural barriers that prevent full returns from very high levels of economic energy and entrepreneurship.

Beginning with the United States, we observe that the usual categorization of the urban poor does not neatly fit the situation confronting urban Latinos. In most analyses of urban poverty, the dominant paradigm is the "underclass" framework popularized by William Julius Wilson. In this model, poverty is largely a function of joblessness, itself caused by spatial and skill mismatch and the changing family structure. The mismatch is connected to the internationalization/deindustrialization process explored earlier: the disappearance of basic industry in the United States, especially from older industrial cities (or areas within cities, such as the neighborhoods of South Central Los Angeles) is said to leave residents both geographically isolated and lacking in new skills. The resulting unemployment is so persistent that inner-city residents eventually drop out of the labor force altogether, further reducing the opportunity to acquire new skills. This phenomenon of joblessness, coupled with a simultaneous exit of the middle class, creates both a shortage of "marriageable men" and a lack of role models; this, in turn, contributes to a shifting family demographic that includes a rise in the number of female-headed, children-present households in which poverty is a frequent guest.[28]

Although this model may resonate with the experience of African-Americans in the United States, it is generally a poor fit for Latinos.[29] It is especially inappropriate for Los Angeles, where Latinos, while the poorest of the major ethnic groups, also exhibit both high rates of male labor force participation and high rates of traditional family formation (Latino households, for example, are 60 percent more likely than non-Latino households to consist of married couples with children). The contrast is perhaps most stark in South Central Los Angeles (52 percent African-American and 45 percent Latino, according to the 1990 census). Here, 82 percent of Latino males were in the labor force, as opposed to 58 percent of non-Latino males; nearly 60 percent of Latino households were made up of married couples with children, as opposed to 20 percent of non-Latino households.[30] As for the "spatial mismatch" explanation, many of the bustling "reindustries" that employ immigrant labor are directly to the east of South Central (in areas like Vernon and Commerce); some of the "Latinization" of South Central Los Angeles (from around 20 percent in 1980 to around 45 percent in 1990) is connected to the desire to be close to this burgeoning employment base.

Essentially, the poverty of Latinos is rooted not in joblessness but rather in low wages. Latino poverty is, in fact, that of the working poor, who work hard every day, keep families intact, and are still unable to succeed economically. This pattern of low returns for labor is partly a reflection of the entry experiences of immigrants; we expect new labor market entrants with few skills and limited English to enter at the bottom of any labor scale. However, many Latinos who were born in the

United States or immigrated many years ago find that discrimination and lack of appropriate social networks limit them to the low-wage, low-security jobs typical of a secondary labor market. The situation presents both a challenge and an opportunity. The challenge is straightforward: being trapped in bad jobs leads to frustration, a phenomenon evident in studies showing that juvenile delinquency and other negative social characteristics increase the longer Latino immigrants stay in the United States.[31] The opportunity relates to a point made earlier: we have in the Latino population a source of energy that can generate economic success once obstacles to its full realization are removed. In short, Latinos constitute a perfect "subject" for the general analytical argument that enhancing equality could promote economic growth.

Latin America is similarly fertile ground for such an argument. There, too, segmented labor markets (and the failure of land reform) have contributed to a burgeoning informal sector. This informal sector, once projected to disappear with modernization, has instead persisted, changing the locus of regional politics and organizing.[32] In it live Latin America's working poor, struggling full-time to eke out a living in the absence of social welfare supports. The barriers to improvement in this sector include discrimination by national credit systems and the difficulties associated with organizing in the highly decentralized small enterprises typical of informal production. As with the situation of Latinos in the United States, improvements hinge upon gaining access to primary sector employment and improving conditions for those in secondary labor markets.[33]

In short, the two areas under discussion exhibit similar patterns of frustration as high levels of labor and entrepreneurial energy yield low market returns. These patterns present an indictment of social organization, particularly given the paramount value attributed to the work ethic in capitalist societies. More importantly, they suggest that efforts to channel this energy better could improve both allocation of resources and economic output. Measures that promote equality in such settings are entirely consistent with improving economic growth.

Politics and Policy

The current pattern of internationalization has contributed to disequalization, inequality is "unproductive," and the economic energy of the poor suggests that a more egalitarian social organization could yield improvements. What, then, should be done, and where can we look for the political will to do it?

We should recognize first the general constraints on a more progressive policy framework, not the least of which is internationalization itself. Essentially, globalization has limited (but not eliminated) the scope of government action. For Latin America, this has happened in two ways. First, the enhanced mobility of capital and goods, particularly in the Western Hemisphere, is not likely to be reversed. This, in essence, gives both domestic and foreign capital a veto over domestic policy, since few countries will now be willing (or able) to embark on courses that are perceived to threaten the rights of investors or create a less profitable environment.[34] The resulting constraint on policy is exacerbated by a second international factor: a homogenization of policy thinking so severe that nearly all Latin American policy initiatives emerge from, or speak the language of, the Bretton Woods institutions (BWIs).[35] In the United States, fear of international competition—not to mention the political drift to the right—likewise constrains attempts to help the poor.

Interestingly enough, the BWIs themselves are beginning to recognize the damage caused by inequality. While they are still unwilling to condition resources on distributional improvement, there is increasing agreement at the highest levels of the International Monetary Fund and World Bank that the alleviation of poverty and the reduction of income disparities, particularly in Latin America, must be the focus of future action. Within the United States, the rightist drift narrows the policy opening. In another example of the growing relevance of regional groupings at the expense of the nation-state, however, local policy-makers seem to be recognizing that excessive inequality is bad for business and are pushing for ameliorative measures.[36]

Even in light of the policy homogeneity alluded to above, a range of activities could target poverty and reduce disparity without widespread government intervention or rising fiscal expenditures. In Latin America, the key policies would be the acceleration of land reform where this is still crucial (as in El Salvador); shifts in credit allocation toward smaller firms in the informal sector; improvement in the conditions and regulations governing union organizing in both formal (including transnational) and informal arenas; the involvement of nongovernmental organizations in the task of community development; a reallocation of government spending in the direction of basic education, housing, and community services; and an attempt to think seriously about what kind of industrial policy interventions would be necessary to promote the development of important sectors and bring workers up to speed in those areas.[37] In the United States, a not-too-dissimilar list is both necessary and feasible. It includes eliminating residential and business "red-lining" to promote minority-owned business; encouraging unionization in the reindustrialized sectors; raising the minimum wage; using community development corporations to enhance neighborhoods; and linking together low-income and low-skill workers with specific training that will let them take advantage of opportunities in emerging regional industries.

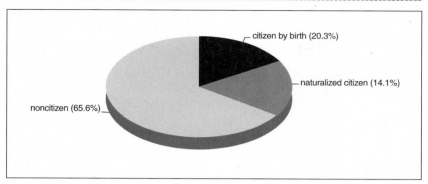

Figure 2.2. Citizen and Noncitizen Adult Latinos in the City of Los Angeles, 1990

Little of the latter urban agenda is specific to Latinos. We would certainly want to add ethnically oriented policies, such as the protection of bilingual education, but many of the policies that will enhance Latino well-being are universal enough to achieve general political acceptability. But here is where the question of *who* is poor inevitably raises its head: the subjects of our analysis are not those who dominate the political mechanisms needed to develop and implement new policy.

The contrast is especially stark in our metaphor and exemplar, Los Angeles, where Latinos constitute nearly 60 percent of the poor and near-poor and 40 percent of the population, but only 10 percent of the voters.[38] The reasons for these startling figures are complex and include the age profile of the population, the traditional reluctance of Mexican immigrants to go through the citizenship process, and the alienation many feel from the political system. But an additional, and perhaps crucial, factor is the residency and citizenship status of many of the Latinos in question.

Figure 2.2 explores this issue for the City of Los Angeles. Note first that more than 65 percent of L.A. Latinos of voting age are not citizens; only 20 percent are citizens by birth. Breaking down the citizen/noncitizen distinction by age and including those not yet of voting age yields what may be an even more important fact: the vast majority of those under 18 are citizens by birth, while the vast majority of the group that most likely contains their parents (18–35) are noncitizens (see Figure 2.3).[39] The general pattern suggests what Jorge Castañeda has termed the "de-democratization" of Southern California: many of those who work cannot vote and thus have little influence over the public policies that determine their lives and those of their citizen children.[40]

While the particular difficulties of noncitizenship generally do not

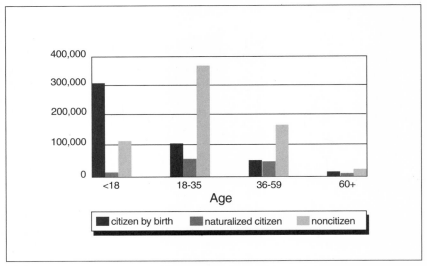

Figure 2.3. Latino Citizens and Noncitizens by Age in the City of Los Angeles, 1990

afflict Latin Americans in their own countries, representation remains a problem.[41] Despite a wave of regional democratization in the 1980s, one need look no further than Mexico to question the depth of commitment to reforms designed to make the electoral process transparent and fair. The problem is even more daunting when one defines democracy as a process that includes more than an occasional vote. Democratic participation in policy making is lacking throughout most of Latin America, and the prospect of democracy has become even more remote as Bretton Woods officialdom and Washington analysts insist that insulating policymakers from "populist" pressures (as the United States insulates the Federal Reserve) is necessary for responsible macroeconomic management.

But democratic participation is the *sine qua non* for achieving the sort of equalizing measures that even the BWIs see as essential for Latin American economic development. As long as the poor lack resources and a voice, the message of "more equality, more growth," however well documented, is unlikely to become a government priority.

Given these goals and constraints, how can constituencies that favor change recognize and pursue their interests? One key ingredient is the affirmation of identity: by Latinos in the United States and the poor in Latin America. An important element in this new politics of identity is the emergence of community as a unit for social organizing and activity. In Latin America, political energy seems to have moved from the working class and the workplace to the community and neighborhood, particularly with regard to struggles for government services and clear title to land.[42] For Latinos, community also plays a special role in political struggles; for example, labor organizers working with immigrants in Los Angeles have begun to marry the two arenas, organizing workers in their neighborhoods, not just in their workplaces, in order to pursue their own objective of increased unionization as a vehicle for improving economic outcomes for Latinos.

Of course, not all self-labeled calls to "community" are the same. The state-dominated corporatist-style organizing in Mexico and elsewhere in Latin America may play on themes of a national community, but the actual practices have often tended to (and been intended to) stifle organic notions of community-building. Ethnic politics and politicians in the United States have sometimes manipulated common "identity" to build coalitions that elevate elites to electoral office but otherwise have little impact on the public policies that harm the poor. Grassroots mobilization has also been constrained by institutional barriers to civic participation, including the lack of voting rights for noncitizens in the United States and undemocratic practices in many countries of Latin America. Against this backdrop, there has nonetheless been a significant rise in community movements on both sides of the border, ranging from the relief efforts organized by Mexico City residents after the 1986 earthquake to the anti-Pinochet struggle based in the shantytowns of Chile to the successful fight for a 1988 increase in the California minimum wage, led not by unions but rather by an Alinsky-style community group based in East Los Angeles.[43] In all of these struggles, the "community" has been a key locus of organizing, and identity formation at this level has had a special motivating effect on social actors.[44]

Meeting the new challenges posed by a globalized economy and society will require social movements to build on notions of community even as they simultaneously forge a broader sense of identity that crosses borders and recognizes the links between the experience of the poor in Latin America and in the Latino communities of the United States. This is not an easy task. While I have stressed the commonalities of the Latin American and Latino experiences, particularly with regard to the economic position of the working poor, this very experience can lead to antagonistic interests. Massive waves of Latin American immigration may have only modest effects on the general wage level, but any negative effects are usually felt most sharply in the secondary labor markets, where both immigrant and native-born Latinos congregate. In this light, it is unsurprising that, prior to the late 1970s, many mainstream Latino organizations were wary of relaxing immigration restrictions: their leaders felt that they were defending the interests of those who were already here.[45]

Contemporary Latino political groupings derive much deeper sympathies and bonds with immigrants from the links of culture and family. Yet the bonds also reflect a growing realization that, given the overwhelming forces of labor demand and supply, immigration is not likely to be deterred, and the policies flowing from the anti-immigrant stance emerging in California and the rest of the United States will exacerbate whatever damage immigrant competition causes to native-born or long-term immigrant Latinos. Consider the consequences of California's Proposition 187, which sought to deny public education and services to the undocumented but did not restrict their employment. While legal challenges have impeded implementation of this measure, further attempts to restrict social welfare for immigrants, both legal and illegal, may swell the secondary labor markets occupied jointly by Latinos and Latin Americans even as their "social wage" (or access to government resources) falls, adding fuel to the fire of inequality. Latinos will fall victim to this poverty trap unless their identity politics includes the memory of their immigrant and transnational experience and uses this to counter the current trend of immigrant-bashing. In short, a broader sense of Latin American and Latino community and identity is needed to confront—*y sobresalir*—the complex challenges posed by globalization and internationalization.

Conclusion

In years past, the topic of this volume might have seemed a bit obscure: how could Latinos, a minority group in the United States, have an experience of globalization distinct from that of the rest of the U.S. population? Yet it is clear that their experience is different: Latinos themselves are formed culturally, socially, and economically by the international flows of labor and deeply affected by the continuing internationalization of the U.S. economy, particularly as it is filtered through the segmented labor markets typical of cities.

Moreover, there is both room and reason for merging the seemingly disparate agendas of Latino and Latin American Studies. The subjects of these fields—Latin and Latino Americans—have cultural patterns and economic experiences in common. More importantly, their experience illustrates some generalizable propositions: that internationalization has contributed to widening inequality within countries; that this inequality is unproductive and constrains future development; that some straightforward policy changes would remove the blockages that prevent the poor from using their energy to further national and regional growth; and that the real barriers to these policies lie in the contemporary disenfranchisement of the poor, particularly of Latinos in the United States and of the *barrios marginador* (shantytowns) and rural communities of Latin America.

What, then, is the prognosis? The successful conclusion of the most recent round of the General Agreement on Trade and Tarriffs (GATT), the increasing connections of international financial markets, and the continuing revolution in communications all signal that globalization will continue. With it will come the stresses and strains of adjustment. The resulting disequalization will have significant effects on Latin and Latino Americans. To counter such trends, more research of the sort detailed here will be required, along with a political project committed to deeper democratization of public and private life.

The bifurcated research agenda of many of us who work in Latino and Latin American Studies presents an opportunity to contribute to this issue. It is time to cross disciplinary lines as Latinos historically have crossed borders, to go beyond traditional ethnic and area study agendas and deploy the analytic tools of political economy. If we do this, we will help advance both social science research and the interests of the Latino-origin peoples of the Americas.

Chapter 3

Trading Places: U.S. Latinos and Trade Liberalization in the Americas

Manuel Pastor, Jr., and Carol Wise

Just as the 1980s stand out as the decade of the debt crisis in Latin America, the 1990s have become the decade of free trade. After a number of failed attempts at trade liberalization during the 1970s, many states in the region began, by the second half of the 1980s, to make dramatic progress in reducing tariffs and eliminating quantitative trade restrictions.[1] While the strongest evidence of this new open approach to hemispheric integration was reflected in Mexico's 1994 entry into a North American Free Trade Agreement (NAFTA) with the United States and Canada, the trends also include the commitment to develop hemispheric free trade growing out of the 1994 Miami Summit of the Americas and the ongoing consolidation of subregional trade pacts like South America's MERCOSUR (see Table 3.1).

Of course, the movement toward free trade has not been without delays. Mexico's 1994 currency crisis took some of the shine off the notion of trade liberalization. The "tequila effect" meant that foreign investors' worries about the Mexican experience negatively influenced flows to other countries such as Argentina and Brazil, and some observers and policy-makers queried the value of open (and volatile) capital accounts. Meanwhile, the striking contradiction between the U.S. encouragement of Latin America's liberalizations of goods and capital and the increasingly restrictive U.S. attitude toward immigration have triggered anger and frustration among Latin Americans and U.S. Latinos alike.

However, while U.S. Latinos and Latin Americans may share a concern about that contradiction and a general agreement on the need for a less restrictive immigration policy, the rationales for their respective positions differ. Latin American leaders and policy-makers, for example, seem to hope to maintain a location for labor export (in the case of Mexico) or a base for worker remittances (in the case of El Salvador) while U.S. Latino leaders (political and otherwise) are more worried about the racial discrimination likely to spill over from enhanced enforcement of immigration regulations. Given this divergence, it is perhaps unsurprising that

Table 3.1. Recent Commercial Policy Reform in Latin America

Country	Reform Period	Prereform Policies	Accomplishments of Trade Reform
Chile	1975–79 1985–88	Multiple exchange rate system; QRs[a] and prohibitions on imports; average tariff 94%, maximum tariff 220%; prior import deposits	Unified exchange rate; QRs removed; uniform tariff of 10% (excluding automobiles), increased to 35% in response to 1982 crisis but since reduced to a uniform rate of 11%; prior import deposits and most tariff exonerations eliminated
Mexico	1983–85 (mild) 1985–88 (strong) 1994–Accession to NAFTA	In 1982, QRs covering 100% of tariff positions and 92% of domestic production; average tariff 27%; official reference prices covering 19% of domestic production; export controls covering 60% of total exports	QR production coverage 20% in 1990; production-weighted average tariff 12.5%; maximum tariff 20%, with most items 10–20%; most export controls removed; official reference prices removed; GATT joined in 1986; further liberalization of trade under NAFTA with 10–15 year timeline
Argentina	1988–92 1995 MERCOSUR[b] implemented	Dual exchange rate; QR coverage in manufacturing more than 30%; maximum tariff over 100%; additional specific duties and quasi-tariffs; import prohibitions, advance notice requirements, etc.	Unified exchange rate; QR coverage in manufacturing reduced to approximately 5%; progressive reduction in levels and dispersion of tariffs, with 3 rates and 22% maximum; 12.2% production-weighted average; no specific duties, but some quasi-tariffs remain; buy-Argentina and sectoral regimes still in place; further tariff and nontariff reductions under MERCOSUR

Country	Reform Period	Prereform Policies	Accomplishments of Trade Reform
Colombia	1984-86 1990-94	QRs covering 61% of tariff positions and 82% of domestic manufacturing; tariff range 0–200%, plus 18% surcharge; average tariff including surcharge 45%	By end of 1990, QRs virtually eliminated, now covering 3% of tariff positions; maximum tariff 100% (excluding luxury automobiles at 300%); tariff surcharge 13%; average tariff including surcharge 33.5%. Targets for 1994: most tariffs 5–15%, with automobiles at 100%; tariff surcharge 8%; average tariff including surcharge 12%
Peru	After 1990	Multiple exchange rate system providing high protection to nonessential imports; widespread import licensing; maximum tariff 155%, average 67%	QRs eliminated overnight; tariffs reduced to two levels: 15% and 25%
Brazil	After 1990 1995 MERCOSUR implemented	Foreign exchange licensing and negative import lists resulting in discretionary control of virtually all imports; in 1988, maximum tariff 80%	Foreign exchange licensing virtually eliminated; no negative import lists. Tariff reform initiated in February 1991, setting maximum tariff target of 40% for end of 1994; tariff reduction accelerated to 14% in 1993; further tariff and nontariff reductions under MERCOSUR

[a] Quantitative Restrictions.

[b] MERCOSUR, or the Southern Cone Common Market, came into effect January 1, 1995, when its four member countries (Argentina, Brazil, Paraguay, and Uruguay) ended tariffs on most of their exports to each other and set a Common External Tariff on imports coming into this free trade area.

Sources: Kirsten Hallberg and Wendy Takacs "Trade Reform in Colombia: 1990–1994," in Alvin Cohen and Frank Gunter, eds, The Colombian Economy: Issues of Trade and Development (Boulder, Colo.: Westview Press, 1992), pp. 286–87; Judith Dean, Seema Desai, and James Reidel "Trade Policy Reform in Developing Countries Since 1985: A Review of Evidence," World Bank Discussion Papers no. 267 (Washington, D.C.: World Bank, 1994).

attitudes regarding trade policy and the ongoing hemispheric integration of goods and capital markets differ even more.

Once again the strongest evidence in this area involves NAFTA. In the national debate prior to U.S. adoption of the treaty, different Latino interest groups took quite different positions. In the final vote, only nine of the seventeen Latino members of Congress supported the treaty. Sub-ethnicity accounted for some of the difference—for example, all three Cuban-American congresspeople cast negative ballots because of concerns about Mexican–Cuban relations—but support was not unanimous even among Mexican-American congresspeople, and came only after significant arm-twisting and deal-making with the Clinton administration.[2] This surprised many Latin American leaders and technocrats, who had expected a groundswell of Mexican-American support. After all, it was suggested, U.S. Jews have generally induced legislators to be supportive of Israel; why should there be such sharp disagreements within the Mexican-American community freer trade with the "home" country?

Although this question may make sense from a Latin American perspective, it reveals a failure to understand the complex nature of the U.S. Latino communities.[3] Many Latinos are, or are the descendants of, people who left "home" because of political disagreements or limited economic opportunities, often attributed to the failure of governments to generate employment and growth; supporting the economic policy of Mexico or other Latin American countries requires them to suspend a historic distrust. Moreover, many U.S. Latinos are working in the very secondary labor markets most likely to be hit by low-wage competition from the South; as workers, they have no immediate interest in more open markets.[4] Of course, Latino businesses and professionals may be especially well placed to gain from the expansion of hemispheric trade because they may have a comparative advantage at managing the interchange between Latin American and U.S. firms. However, the occupational structure of U.S. Latinos, particularly of Mexican-Americans, is heavily skewed toward working-class and secondary sector jobs. Given this class composition, particularly the thin layer of professionals and managers, a unified Latino position supporting freer trade in the Americas is a remote possibility.

Many of these tensions were revealed in the NAFTA debate. A variety of early research efforts noted that while the United States. might experience aggregate gains from further integration with Mexico, among the likely losers were Latino workers in the United States.[5] Latino trade unionists and community groups were deeply concerned and often expressed opposition to the coming trade treaty.[6] Meanwhile, business groups were early and firm supporters for the reasons noted above; in the words of Jose Nino, then president of the U.S. Hispanic Chamber of

Commerce," Hispanic entrepreneurs are a natural bridge for the economic integration of North America."[7]

Concerned about the growing disunity, some Latino-based groups spearheaded an attempt to discuss the NAFTA issue in various communities and arrive at a single Latino position. While this "Latino consensus" was not complete—as reflected in the continuing debate among Latinos and the voting pattern of Latino members of Congress—many in the Latino policy community were induced to support the treaty when the Clinton administration agreed to create a North American Development Bank (NADBank), guaranteed Trade Adjustment Assistance, and offered a series of side agreements to safeguard the interests of displaced Latino (and other) workers.[8] The attention to the interests of Latino workers in this key policy episode suggests what it will take to garner Latino support for further hemispheric integration, a point to which we return in the Conclusion.

In this chapter, we examine the movement to free trade in the Americas and the implications for U.S. Latinos. The focus is on the Latin American side, in part to fill the information gap that has so often plagued this debate. While we begin by examining the powerful trends that have been driving trade liberalization in Latin America, we suggest that, even within Latin America, challenges are emerging that could be properly addressed through some rethinking of trade theory and policy. Such new policy could include: (1) a departure from the recent tendency in Latin America to link macroeconomic stabilization with both trade liberalization and fixed exchange rates; (2) the design of effective industrial policy to facilitate the adjustment of small firms to open trade; (3) the opening of political and policy-making processes; and (4) the construction of social compensation packages to buffer free trade's "losers" as well as institutional reforms to promote equitable development. We argue that such a reworking of trade and stabilization policy would not only benefit Latin Americans; by propping up wages and creating more democratic and more supportable governments, it would also lead U.S. Latinos to be more favorably disposed toward increased trade openness, resolving the apparent divergence of class and other interests noted above.

The Origins of Free Trade in the Western Hemisphere

While economists have long extolled the virtues of free trade—sometimes with less than compelling evidence[9]—a nation does not relax trade restrictions because of a sudden awareness of potential economic and social welfare gains. Rather, external pressures and domestic political dynamics conspire to loosen the grip of one group over trade policy and prepare the way for the entrance of another set of interests and associated policy makers. Below, we examine the kinds of international and domestic influences that fostered a more open trade regime in Latin America.

External Influences

Several international factors stand out as necessary, although not entirely sufficient, to explain Latin America's receptivity to a liberal commercial policy. The first is the impact of the 1982 debt crisis. One might suppose that a region facing Latin America's situation in 1983—declining terms of trade, developed country protectionism, an abrupt drop in external capital flows, and severe macroeconomic disarray—would be unlikely to proceed with the reduction of tariff and nontariff barriers. On the other hand, the drastic foreign exchange crunch gave international creditors and multilateral agencies more leverage in promoting an open trade regime, a long-term goal.

Moreover, the sheer force of the 1982 debt shocks shattered economic and political models in most of Latin America. The resulting destabilization led to increasing inflation, and it proved difficult to balance the need to contain inflation and the need to generate foreign exchange. The problem was that most of Latin America sought to promote exports through a strategy of rapid currency depreciation—a strategy that fueled domestic inflation as rising prices from intermediate imports quickly permeated Latin America's productive structure. In frustration, Argentina, Peru, and Brazil launched a series of heterodox experiments in the mid-1980s, geared toward reducing inflation via wage and price controls. Unfortunately, each of these alternative programs backfired, as all three governments succumbed to fiscal laxity and thus failed to rein in excess demand.

Having witnessed these earlier failures, Mexican policy-makers devised their own version of heterodoxy in 1987, combining an orthodox commitment to fiscal austerity and tight monetary control with a more open trade regime. The latter was also coupled with a targeted exchange rate, which, in effect, constituted a second level of price controls: domestic producers were not able to set prices above competitive foreign substitutes that were now entering the country more freely. Mexico's success in reducing inflation from nearly 160 percent in 1987 to below 10 percent in 1994 prompted other countries (such as Argentina, Peru, and El Salvador) to follow suit. Thus, the twists and turns of macroeconomic management in the region eventually led to the coupling of macroeconomic stabilization and trade liberalization: the identification of free trade with reduced inflation widened the circle of beneficiaries from liberalization and gave it a new basis for political support.

A second international-level factor in Latin America's recent economic opening was the increasing importance of intraindustry trade. By 1990, intraindustry trade, or the mutual exchange of goods across borders in a certain product category, accounted for as much as 50 percent of manufacturing trade activity for Argentina, Brazil, and Mexico.[10] Since open borders reduce the costs of imported inputs while trade protection complicates cross-border production, those Latin American manufacturing interests that are tied into this trade network (which often amounts to multinational intrafirm trade) tended to constitute a domestic force favoring trade liberalization.[11]

A third factor propelling free trade was the end of the Cold War. On one hand, near-universal rejection of state-centered economic models led Latin America, which had its own set of disappointing experiences with state intervention, to accept more readily the market policies being heavily prescribed in both the East and the West. Perhaps more importantly, the post-Cold War era prompted U.S. policy-makers to refocus on international economic as well as military matters. In doing so, Washington increasingly recognized that its own trade balance had been harmed by the formidable competition emanating from the European Union in the West and the Asian regional economic bloc to the East.

One way to respond to the growth of regional bloc competition was to launch a regional counterinitiative. Thus, the United States announced "Enterprise for the Americas" in June 1990, promising debt reduction and a small private investment fund while extending an open invitation for Latin American countries to sign bilateral Free Trade Agreements (FTAs) with the United States. From the standpoint of U.S. policy-makers, the initiative fell on unexpectedly receptive ears, as many adjustment-weary Latin American states rushed to sign such agreements.[12] Because of its geographical proximity and close economic ties with the United States, Mexico was predictably the first in line. With the launching of the NAFTA negotiations in 1991, what had been absolutely unthinkable in 1982— Mexico's entrance into a highly competitive and legally binding free trade agreement with the United States and Canada—became a political reality by 1994.

In sum, the regional shift to free trade emerged from the scramble to find a new macroeconomic adjustment strategy to counter the lasting shocks of the debt crisis. When export promotion via exchange rate depreciation worsened the domestic problem of inflation, countries sought to solve their external and internal problems by linking macroeconomic stabilization with trade liberalization. The rise of intraindustry trade— with its attendant creation of domestic interests who could only benefit from lower tariffs—and the U.S. attempt to respond to the "regionalization" of the world economy via the consolidation of its own hemispheric bloc also provided "external" impulses for trade liberalization.

⊠⊠⊠

Internal Influences

Those external influences do not explain fully how a domestic alliance was crafted to reject Latin America's protectionist past. One important factor here was simply the decline in the strength of older import-substitution industrialization (ISI) producers, whose industries were battered by the prolonged recession that followed the debt crisis; another was the afore-mentioned strategy of linking import competition with inflation reduction, an approach that helped enhance the positive consequences, and image, of free trade.[13]

While free trade worked its way into policy circles throughout the region, at least two broad patterns of institutional policy-making change had to occur in order to cement a new political coalition. The first, characteristic of Chile, Colombia, and Mexico, involved a wide range of institutional innovations and new business–state alliances. Institutional innovations included the establishment of an autonomous central bank in various countries; in Mexico, moreover, trade policy was extracted from its traditional base in the Ministry of Industry and dispersed to other state agencies that were much less susceptible to interest group pressures.[14] As for business-state alliances, all three countries have created links between well-trained technocrats and the "commanding heights" of the business community. Interestingly, all three have also developed compensatory programs to quell potential protest and help facilitate the adjustment to an open economy.

In a second group of countries—Argentina, Brazil, and Peru—coalitional strategies have been less prominent; instead, the reform effort has been pushed from above, often with a certain ideological fervor, and executive politics and presidential decrees have assumed the role played by institutional overhaul in the first group of countries. The result has been free trade without a safety net: officials within the main trade and finance ministries have played second fiddle to elite, executive-level decision-makers, state–business relations remain underdeveloped, and these countries lag far behind in terms of devising credible compensatory policies for the hardest-hit sectors and income groups. As a result, the free trade process in Argentina and Peru has a thin social and institutional base, while Brazil's commitment to commercial opening remains lukewarm.

Although we include Chile in our first group of institutional innovators, it is important to note that Chile's open trade policy actually emerges from a much longer sequence of external economic shocks interacting with intense domestic and political conflict that produced nearly twenty years of authoritarian rule. A decade (1973–82) of groping in the dark with market-oriented policies driven largely by ideology and political force was followed by a second set of external shocks in the early 1980s, which forced public authorities and private economic actors to regroup. A number of institutional reforms and a more flexible set of policy approaches to correct for previous macroeconomic errors resulted. By the early 1990s, a sophisticated state–business alliance was consolidated, along with a shared commitment to the more successful macro policy management of the late 1980s.[15]

While this torturous path might offer some hope for our second group of reformers—given enough time, policy-makers can eventually hit upon the right set of policies and then build the necessary political coalitions—it is important to stress that the authoritarian nature of the Chilean reform process is both undesirable and unacceptable in the current political atmosphere. Indeed, both groups of reformers have unfortunately tended to rely on a policy-making approach based on technocratic expertise and bureaucratic insulation, the key difference being whether the insulation has been institutionalized and used to build new alliances with capital. While this less-than-democratic approach may have been functional for the initial phases of reform, it likely has negative implications for the sustainability of a new policy regime.

The Challenges to Western Hemispheric Free Trade

The Latin American embrace of free trade has gratified international financial institutions and many outside observers. Yet both the path ahead and the sustainability of liberalization face a series of emerging challenges. Following the format used above, we explore those issues at first the international and then the domestic level; we then briefly consider what sorts of policies and politics might best address these difficulties.

External Challenges

The negotiation and eventual approval of NAFTA both delighted and worried the rest of Latin America. Many leaders—eager for heightened access to the large U.S. market and anxious to obtain the "seal of approval" NAFTA entry symbolizes in order to attract greater capital flows—were relieved that some mechanism for accession to NAFTA had been included in the final agreement. On the negative side, many observers feared that U.S. congressional and public resistance—evident in the NAFTA debate and reflected in the discord over trade policy even within the U.S. Latino community—would render accession of further Latin American partners a long and tedious endeavor.[16]

The Clinton administration announced after the signing of NAFTA in 1993 that it would host a December 1994 Summit of the Americas in

Miami to discuss the broader hemispheric agenda, including trade and investment, the environment, and other issues. Worried about securing passage of the implementing legislation for the Uruguay Round of GATT, the Clinton team publicly emphasized other elements of the Miami agenda (effective governance and sustainable development) to avoid inflaming the anti-NAFTA forces that had lost in Congress. Latin American policy-makers most interested in the trade agenda groused; to maintain good relations and enthusiasm for the summit, U.S. policy-makers made the interim gesture of offering bilateral accords on investment and intellectual property rights.[17]

In the meantime, Latin American governments pushed ahead on subregional free trade agreements such as MERCOSUR and the Andean Pact (a customs union made up of Bolivia, Ecuador, Colombia, Peru, and Venezuela).[18] Chile, viewed as the next likely entrant into NAFTA, moved in mid-1994 to negotiate an affiliation with the MERCOSUR bloc as a whole and signed a number of bilateral free trade accords in the region. Colombia, initially considered another probable candidate for NAFTA, also pursued a "G-3" arrangement (with Mexico and Venezuela)[19] and a series of other bilateral deals (with Chile, for example). Meanwhile, Brazil indicated that it did not want to become "an appendix of NAFTA" and instead lobbied to combine MERCOSUR and the Andean Pact into a powerful South American Free Trade Area (SAFTA) over the next ten years—a group that could well compete with NAFTA for intraregional market access.[20]

Fearful that it might be dropping the ball on hemispheric free trade and worried about the dynamics that could emerge if a patchwork of subregional pacts were to evolve with no overall coordination, the United States eventually engaged in a serious discussion of free trade at the Miami Summit. The results were a long-term commitment to complete a Western hemispheric free trade area by 2005 and an agreement to begin immediate negotiations for Chile's entry into NAFTA. Yet U.S. policy-makers remain vague about whether hemispheric trade should be extended through direct accession of a given state to the actual NAFTA document or through the negotiation of bilateral "interim" FTAs between the United States and individual Latin American countries.

As a result, the institutional framework for the expansion of free trade is still murky, especially since the administration was unable to secure fast-track negotiating authority from the U.S. Congress, even after heavy lobbying in late 1997. Ironically, since NAFTA's implementation, most of the thrust for deepening trade liberalization has come from Latin America, in the context of the Free Trade Area of the Americas (FTAA) working groups created after the Miami Summit. While these groups are making considerable progress in gathering and disseminating data and hammering out technical details, doubts over the depth of the U.S. commitment continue to cast a shadow over the FTAA process.[21]

Added to the external challenge of perceived U.S. ambivalence and free trade's unclear institutional path are the interrelated problems of external capital flows and macroeconomic instability. As noted above, several recent macroliberalization episodes (in Mexico, Argentina, and Peru) have been marked by the use of the exchange rate as an anti-inflation tool. The resulting real overvaluation has rendered this set of recent adjusters hungry for the foreign exchange needed to prop up their currencies and sustain their inflation reduction victories; as a result, their dependence on short-term portfolio capital flows has increased.

In stark contrast, countries like Chile and Colombia have, for diverse reasons, recognized the importance of maintaining competitive exchange rates and have been willing to live with the slightly higher inflation rates that depreciation can provoke.[22] The result of these policy differences is a paradox: those recent reformers (Argentina and Peru) which most need the capital- and confidence-enhancing endorsement of a free trade pact seem to be further back in the NAFTA queue than those countries (Chile and Colombia) which have pursued less fragile economic policies and therefore could survive *sans* NAFTA.[23]

Internal Challenges

Within Latin America itself, the failure thus far of trade reform to reverse regressive distributional trends threatens political consensus on reform. We suggest in the Conclusion that addressing these distributional issues is the key to enhancing sustainable growth as well as reducing the ambivalence many U.S. Latinos have shown about further economic integration in the hemisphere.

Reform usually proceeds in stages. Initially, reform is blocked by a status quo arrangement of political forces. An external shock can loosen the structure (as when the debt crisis diminished the power of old ISI producers) and create the space for reform. Policy-makers need to be insulated from lobbying pressures during this early, unsettled phase. In a final period of consolidation, the "winners" from the reform effort are persuaded or induced to develop a collective voice to maintain the new policy regime. Such a sequence is tricky, requiring both political skills and the ability actually to deliver expected gains in growth, productivity, and distribution.

Although policy-makers enjoy a "honeymoon" during which memories of high inflation and other disruptions create a social tolerance for austerity, public patience with models that do not eventually ameliorate adjustment burdens wears thin. Technocratic insulation, including the redesign of state institutions to make them less susceptible to pressure from special interests, can extend the testing period for policy reform.[24] Yet there are also drawbacks to such insulation. Technocrats may develop a disdain for politics (as when Mexico's new generation of technocratic policy-makers distanced themselves from traditional forces within the ruling Institutional Revolutionary Party), failing to acquire the political skills needed for the task of organizing "winners" and crafting the broader political coalitions that can weather longer-term adjustment challenges. Insulation also can work against the kinds of policy debates that could serve to resolve adjustment problems before they explode into full-blown crises. Mexico again is an example: the lack of significant debate over exchange rate policy prior to the December 1994 crisis, as well as the ability of President Carlos Salinas and Treasury Secretary Pedro Aspe to resist the pro-devaluation entreaties of incoming President Ernesto Zedillo, speaks volumes about the difficulties associated with closed policy-making systems. In countries like Argentina and Peru, exaggerated patterns of bureaucratic insulation have blinded policy-makers to the more pragmatic interventions and politicking that have rendered equally difficult adjustments more acceptable in contemporary Chile and Colombia.

Underlying the political difficulties in Latin America are distributional pressures that either stem directly from trade liberalization or are the residue of past policy errors still unaddressed by neoliberal reform. Economic models generally suggest that free trade can be quite progressive in distributional terms: shifting toward labor-intensive comparative advantage should raise wages, and eliminating protection should shrink monopoly rents. The real world of economic adjustment has proved much more complex. For one thing, trade liberalization can disrupt traditional agricultural relations, triggering a mass exodus from the countryside, swamping urban labor markets, and dampening any upward trend in wages.[25] Second, the demands of production for a world market generally raise the relative demand for skilled labor, widening the income gap within the labor force. Finally, the scale of operations needed to compete successfully in world markets can induce a rise in the concentration of industrial assets, damaging the small business sector, often a major source of employment.[26]

In the country we have studied most extensively, Mexico, the distributional pattern thus far gives cause for concern. Surveys of household income and spending recently released by the Mexican government suggest that income inequality (as measured by the distribution of monetary income to households) rose from 1984 to 1989—logically enough, given the tremendous debt-related adjustments of this period—and then worsened during the period of intense liberalization between 1989 and 1992.[27] Real monetary income for the poorest Mexicans actually fell in the latter period (down 2.6 percent for the poorest tenth and 1.2 percent for the next-poorest decile).[28] According to the most recent survey, distribution remained roughly the same between 1992 and 1994, and real incomes were basically flat over the period; although the data are fragmentary, most observers agree that the post–peso crash economy, in which unemployment rose and real wages fell, made distribution more unequal.

In Mexico, these income disparities are exacerbated by the continued concentration of industrial assets. Trade liberalization worsened this underlying problem in Mexico's business structure,[29] partly because smaller producers have lacked access to the credit needed to modernize their productive structure.[30] Again, the problem became worse after the peso crash, as larger firms have been better able to export out of the depressed local markets, and smaller firms have been hit harder by skyrocketing interest rates.

Are these distributional strains common to other recent reformers? Argentina's distributional picture has gotten worsen over the post-1989 reform period, and unemployment ticked up from around 5 to around 17 percent between 1990 and 1996; Peru, also following the neoliberal model, has been faced with crushing poverty statistics and continued social tension. Meanwhile, Chile, with its jump start on the reform process, succeeded in restoring rapid growth rates beginning in 1994; the elected civilian government has also expanded its social spending. Colombia has been moderate in its policy approach and is the only major Latin American country whose Gross Domestic Product (GDP) grew every year of the 1980s and 1990s. It is interesting to note that these two most robust reformers have worked hardest to preserve their reform trajectory with credible social compensation schemes; in contrast, Mexico's social compensation scheme has been replaced by charges of inadequacy and political manipulation.[31]

Making Reform Work

What would make reform more successful and sustainable in Latin America? A key task for policy-makers—and one highlighted by the Mexican peso crisis—is to reassess the macroeconomic sustainability of recent liberalization approaches. Some of today's strategies have coupled liberalization with fixing the exchange rate, mostly to tame inflation. Characteristic of Argentina, Peru, and pre-crash Mexico, such a strategy leads to increasing overvaluation, rising trade deficits, and a growing reliance on external flows to cover the deficits and prop up the currency. Chile went through this in an earlier era (the late 1970s) until macroeconomic disaster led to more responsible management of the exchange rate, as well as a number of impressive institutional reforms within key economic entities. Colombia has long believed in maintaining a competitive exchange rate and living with the slightly higher inflation that often results. Mexico is now learning to do the same; whether others, such as Argentina, can follow suit will depend in part on whether they can convince investors that credibility is not as thin as the exchange rate band they are currently following.

As for industrial concentration, it is useful to recall that some contraction of firms is to be expected; if the old system really was protectionist, both bankruptcies and complaints are part of a healthy adjustment. However, the end goal of reform is not simply to disrupt the old order, but to create a more efficient and internationally competitive industrial base. In this light, it is important to note that successful industries are based on "clusters" of economic activity, with numerous vertical and horizontal ties between large firms capable of competing effectively in world markets and smaller companion firms that provide innovative backup and serve as "just-in-time" suppliers to their larger parent enterprises.[32] The current liberalization approach, which often has condoned the collapse of small firms as an example of a "survival-of-the-fittest" commitment to market discipline, has failed to recognize that small- and medium-sized firms are an essential element of a successful export drive. Hence, there is a need to provide adequate transitional financing, job training, and other support to small innovative firms, a policy that Latin America has lacked sorely during the 1990s.[33]

On the political front, the key question is whether certain countries can go beyond insulated technocrats and tepid democracies and create opportunities for more citizen participation in the policy-making process. States as diverse as Argentina, Brazil, Mexico, and Peru have relied on a highly insulated executive ruling by legislative decrees; this has streamlined the policy process but done little to incorporate congress, political parties, and the citizenry into everyday politics. In contrast, countries like Chile and, to some extent, Colombia are now expanding the reform backdrop to include political parties, congress, and other nonstate actors. One sign of this more encompassing model of reform is the current Chilean government's willingness to place tariffs under the jurisdiction of the legislature—an arrangement that Brazilian and Peruvian technocrats would surely view with fear. This incipient trend toward greater transparency, participation, and accountability in the policy-making process needs to be encouraged.

Finally, the Achilles heel of Latin American reform remains the region's regressive distribution of income. Economic liberalization generally has failed to reverse, and may have contributed to, the polarization of income in the region. While common wisdom has it that such regressive impacts are temporary and will be corrected once growth begins anew, we are more pessimistic about the medium-term (five- to ten-year) distributional benefits of economic opening in Latin America, especially in the absence of in-depth reform of the underlying structural factors that have led to persistent income inequality throughout Latin America's modern history.

Correcting this inequality, particularly in light of the impact of liberalization, is not simply a matter of "social justice." An emerging body of literature suggests several positive linkages between income equality and economic growth: more equal societies are less likely to postpone adjustment in response to short-term macroeconomic shocks; a better distribution of economic opportunities helps build the consensus for supporting property rights and thus encouraging economic innovation and long-term growth; and societies with both equal distribution and widespread access to political power tend to invest more in the sort of basic education necessary to create a productive base of human capital.[34]

The relevance of these arguments for Latin America—a region long characterized by slow growth, high inequality, volatile politics, and subsidies tilted away from primary education—is obvious. If restoring growth is the real object of trade reform, then an equally important policy imperative is the reduction of poverty and regressive income distribution within the region. The positive impact on growth would be dual: a direct boost for economic output, for the reasons sketched above, and an indirect benefit as greater equality averted or softened potential political challenges to economic liberalization.[35]

There are, of course, risks. Countries may simply pursue compensation schemes as a sort of payoff for political support during the adjustment process, and government efforts to encourage equity could deteriorate into the budget-breaking subsidies and antimarket interventions of the past. The road to good intentions, it seems, is lined with potential detours to the economic hells of the past.

Yet something more than the current laissez-faire attitude must be adopted. As we have noted, alleviating Latin America's longstanding patterns of inequality is necessary for the ultimate sustainability of market reforms within the reforming countries. It is also required to sustain free trade coalitions across the borders of North and South. As we suggest below, distributional improvement within Latin America could minimize the threat open trade with the region has seemed to pose to lower-wage workers in the United States. This, along with the more open political systems that we also advocate for "home" countries, could cause U.S. Latinos to abandon their cautious attitude toward NAFTA and other free trade efforts and become the champions of hemispheric integration that Latin American policy-makers once hoped for.

Conclusion

The past decade of reform in Latin America has been truly historic. Faced with unprecedented external pressures, Latin American policy-makers abandoned old economic models and adopted both new kinds of macroeconomic stabilization plans and new strategies for international integration. Gone was the protectionism of ISI; in was the openness of trade liberalization. By the early 1990s, NAFTA was proposed and signed, subregional trade blocs were gaining prominence, and hemispheric free trade had become a distinct possibility.

In this chapter, we review the trends toward, and challenges facing, the trade liberalization and reform processes in Latin America. While the turn to free trade seems irresistible, there are nonetheless key obstacles to the further consolidation of reform. These include the need to reconsider three features of the current period: (1) the linkage, in several cases, of trade liberalization with exchange rate targeting; (2) the tendency of reformist governments to ignore the needs of the poor, lower-skilled workers, and small business; and (3) the continuation of closed policy-making processes.

Addressing these issues would not only benefit the continent but would also tend to create a basis of common interest for U.S. Latinos and Latin Americans. We have noted Latinos' ambivalence about free trade pacts like NAFTA. The reasons are less opaque than many Latin American decision-makers believe: worries about competition at the low end of the labor markets, the fact that only a thin group of Latino businesses stands poised to benefit, and the historic resentments of immigrants and their descendants at less-than-democratic governments in "home" countries. Moreover, these reasons are also better rooted in reality than many free trade proponents might think: a recent report indicates that "NAFTA's burdens have fallen disproportionately on Latino and other minority workers," leading Latino congresspeople who had voted both for and against NAFTA to warn the Clinton administration that they would not support extending free trade agreements across the hemisphere without major improvements in federal adjustment programs.[36] Adopting the same view were leaders of several major Latino groups that had provided critical support for a "Latino consensus" in favor of NAFTA. Clearly, allegiances regarding free trade are once again in doubt.[37]

A Latin American shift to the sort of approach outlined above might moderate Latinos' concerns. For example, promoting smaller businesses and integrating them within Latin America's export chain could help U.S. Latino businesses, many of which are also small and would therefore be useful partners to their Latin American counterparts. Democratizing the policy process could enhance the political image of Latin American reformers and lead to the political solidarity with U.S. Latinos many Latin American governments desire. Finally, distributional improvements within Latin America itself could diminish legitimate worries among U.S. Latinos that reducing trade barriers with the region's reformers constitutes a "race to the bottom," with U.S. minorities likely to suffer most in the competition.

In their pathbreaking work on the labor market effects of NAFTA, Albert Fishlow, Sherman Robinson, and Raúl Hinojosa-Ojeda sketched the hemispheric dilemma quite clearly.[38] Focusing on the United States and Mexico, they argued that protectionist strategies were likely to diminish each nation's potential for GDP growth and consumer welfare. Free and unfettered trade could represent an improvement—and, in any case, was already under way in fact as production was becoming increasingly integrated under the authority of transnationals and their subsidiaries and suppliers. Given this, the best alternative—the one most likely to raise production and interindustry trade growth and help those in the lower reaches of labor—is to create a planned integrative process that includes strong doses of social policy to drive up the wage floors in both the United States and Mexico.

While modest elements of that approach were embodied in NAFTA via side agreements on labor and the environment and creation of NADBank to help burdened communities, it is safe to say that too little was done initially and that the implementation of NADBank and other NAFTA bandaids has been slow and uneven.[39] Moreover, as is evidenced by the inclusion of such concerns in side agreements and parallel institutions, these efforts were largely an afterthought for both the U.S. and the Mexican governments. Unless more is done, and done intentionally, U.S. Latino support will be an afterthought as well. U.S. Latinos are, as noted elsewhere in this volume, exceptionally open to transborder flows of ideas and culture, and have frequently defended the rights of border-crossing individuals. As hemispheric commerce expands as well, the position of U.S. Latinos will depend on the concrete form such economic integration takes.

Chapter 4

The Transnationalization of Immigration Policy

Saskia Sassen

When it comes to immigration policy, states under the rule of law confront a range of rights and obligations from both outside and inside the state, from universal human rights to not-so-universal ethnic lobbies. The overall effect is to constrain the sovereignty of the state and undermine old notions about immigration control. We see emerging a de facto regime, centered in international agreements and conventions as well as in various rights gained by immigrants, that limits the state's role in controlling immigration even when the rhetoric of sovereignty proceeds as if nothing had changed.

Further, states have relinquished some of their sovereignty in matters concerning the cross-border circulation of capital and have formally recognized this partial relinquishing. A growing consensus among states supports lifting border controls for the flow of capital, information, and services, and, more broadly, for furthering globalization. Insofar as the state has been transformed by its participation in the implementation of laws and regulations necessary for economic globalization, we must accept the possibility that sovereignty itself has been transformed. Elsewhere I have argued that exclusive territoriality—a marking feature of the modern state—is being destabilized by economic globalization: we are seeing the elements of a process of denationalization of national territory, although in a highly specialized institutional and functional way.[1] With denationalization under way, what does it mean to assert that the state has exclusive authority over the entry of non-nationals?[2]

The analysis here focuses largely on immigration in the highly developed receiving countries.[3] I use the notion of immigration policy broadly to refer to a wide range of distinct national policies, some of which involve resident refugees. (It is often difficult to distinguish between immigrants and refugees.) The first section focuses on the constraints faced by the state in highly developed countries in making immigration policy and the second on the constraints arising from the transformation of the state and the interstate system in the furthering of a global economy. In the ensuing sections I discuss the implications of these two types of constraints for immigration policy making and implementation.

Beyond Sovereignty: Constraints on States' Policy Making

Today a de facto, loosely articulated regime has the capacity to limit the state's control over immigration in various ways.[4] One component of this regime is represented by the International Convention adopted by the United Nations General Assembly in December 1990 to protect the rights of migrant workers and their families (Resolution 45/158).[5] Another component is a set of rights of resident immigrants that have been upheld widely by legal authorities; these rights and their enforceability will vary for different countries. We also have seen the gradual expansion over the past three decades of civil and social rights to marginal populations, whether women, ethnic minorities, or immigrants and refugees in most states under the rule of law.

The extension of rights, which has taken place mostly through the judiciary, has confronted states with a number of constraints in the area of immigration and refugee policy. For instance, legislative attempts in France and Germany to limit family reunification have been blocked by administrative and constitutional courts on the grounds that such restrictions would violate international agreements. The courts have also regularly supported a combination of rights of resident immigrants that have the effect of limiting government power over them. Similarly, courts have limited governments' ability to restrict or prevent asylum-seekers from entering a country.[6]

Finally, the number and kinds of political actors involved in immigration policy debates and policy making in Western Europe, North America, and Japan are far greater than they were two decades ago. These include the European Union (EU); anti-immigrant parties; vast networks of organizations that represent immigrants (or claim to do so); immigrant politicians, mostly second-generation; and, especially in the United States, so-called ethnic lobbies.[7] The policy process for immigration is no longer confined to the narrow governmental arena of administrative and ministerial interaction. In some European countries, political parties may even position themselves wholly in terms of their stand on immigration. At the other end of the spectrum is an emerging debate about the whole notion of nation-based citizenship.[8] Public opinion and political debate have become part of the realm in which immigration policy is shaped.

These developments are particularly evident in the case of the EU. Europe's single-market program has brought to prominence various issues associated with the free circulation of people as an essential element in creating a frontier-free community. Europe-wide institutions initially lacked the legal competence to deal with many of these issues but gradually have become more deeply involved in visa policy, family reunification, and migration policy—all formerly the exclusive domain of individual nation-states. National governments have resisted this involvement, but now both legal and practical reasons have made it acceptable and inevitable, notwithstanding many public pronouncements to the contrary.

In practice, the EU is assuming an increasingly important role as it becomes clear that many aspects of immigration and refugee policy intersect with EU legal competence. The monetary union proposed for the future will require even greater flexibility in the movement of workers and their families, thereby posing new problems for national immigration laws regarding non-EU nationals in EU member states. There is growing recognition of the need for an EU-wide immigration policy—a need denied for many years by individual states. The matter has become even more urgent with the collapse of the socialist bloc and the rapid increase in refugees. Although progress is slow, the general direction has been toward a closer union of member states' immigration policies.

In the case of the United States, the combination of forces at the governmental level is different, yet it has similar implications regarding constraints on the state. Immigration policy in the United States is largely debated and shaped by Congress; hence, it is highly politicized and subject to a multiplicity of local interests.[9] This has made immigration a very public process, in marked contrast to other policy arenas.[10]

The fact that immigration in the United States historically has been the preserve of the federal government, particularly Congress, assumes new meaning in today's context of radical devolution of powers to the states.[11] Conflict is emerging between several state governments and the U.S. government over federal mandates concerning immigrants—such as access to public health care and schools—that come without mandatory federal funding. States with disproportionate shares of immigrants are asserting that they are burdened disproportionately by the putative costs of immigration.[12] At the heart of this conflict is the fact that the federal government sets immigration policy but does not assume responsibility, financial or otherwise, for many aspects of its implementation. The extent of the conflict is illustrated by several state lawsuits against the federal government for costs incurred in recent fiscal years for the handling of undocumented immigrants.[13] The ongoing devolution of federal power to the states will accentuate these conflicts.

The developments described above have important implications for immigration policy. The question is not so much the effectiveness of a state's control over its borders—we know it is never absolute. Rather, what is the substantive nature of state control over immigration given international human rights agreements, the extension of various social and political rights to resident immigrants over the past twenty years, and the multiplication of political actors involved in immigration policy?

There is, first, the element of unintended consequences, whether of immigration policies themselves or of other policies that have an impact on immigration. For instance, the 1965 U.S. Immigration Act had consequences neither intended nor foreseen by its framers (given its emphasis on family reunion, there was a general expectation that the act would bring in more of those nationalities already present in the country—that is, Europeans).[14] Another example is related to the internationalization of production and foreign aid, both of which have often turned out to have unexpected impacts on immigration.[15] Similar unintended consequences have been associated with military aid and subsequent refugee flows, such as those from El Salvador in the 1980s.[16] Although immigration policy rarely has been an explicit component of U.S. foreign policy making, foreign policy has had a significant effect on immigration beyond the well-known fact of refugee flows from Indochina.[17]

Domestic U.S. policies also can contribute to emigration from countries overseas. There is the case of sugar price supports in the early 1980s, when U.S. taxpayers spent $3 billion annually to support the price of sugar for U.S. producers. This kept Caribbean Basin countries out of the competition and resulted in a loss of 400,000 jobs in the region from 1982 to 1988 (the Dominican Republic, for example, lost three-quarters of its sugar export quota in less than a decade). It is quite possible that this encouraged large flows of emigrants to the United States from that region in the 1980s.

A second element in the decline of state control over immigration rests on a kind of "zero-sum" argument. Recent history shows that if a government closes one entry category, another will rise in numbers. A variant on this dynamic is that if a government has, for instance, a liberal policy on asylum, public opinion may turn against all asylum-seekers and close the country totally; this in turn is likely to promote an increase in irregular entries.[18]

There is a third element in the reduction of state autonomy in controlling immigration. Large-scale international migrations are embedded in complex economic, social, and ethnic networks. Immigration flows are highly conditioned and structured. States may insist on treating immigration as the aggregate outcome of individual actions, distinct and autonomous from other geopolitical and transnational processes, but they cannot escape the consequences of those larger dynamics.

The analysis of constraints on the state's capacity to regulate immigration is not meant to heighten the sense that there is a crisis of control.[19] Rather, only by attending to these issues can we extend the immigration policy question beyond the familiar range of the border and the individual as the sites for regulatory enforcement. Such an analysis reinforces the idea that international migrations result in part from conditions produced by economic and political internationalization in both sending and receiving areas. While a state may have the power to write the text of its immigration policy, it is dealing with a complex, deeply embedded, and transnational process that it can regulate only partly through immigration policy as conventionally understood.

While the state continues to play the most important role in immigration policy making and implementation, the state itself has been transformed by the growth of a global economic system and other transnational processes. These have brought yet another set of conditions to bear on the state's regulatory role, including its role in the area of immigration. All the highly developed countries (and many developing countries as well) have participated in the development of a global economic system and in furthering a consensus around the pursuit of this objective. This participation has transformed the state itself, affected the power of different agencies within it, and furthered the internationalization of the interstate system. It is thus no longer sufficient to examine the role of the state in migration policy design and implementation; it is necessary also to examine the transformation of the state and what it entails for the regulation of migration flows and settlement. It is important to take into account these transformations of the state and the interstate system precisely because the state is a major actor in immigration policy and regulation.

Beyond Sovereignty: Economic Globalization and the Reconfigured State

The limits on state autonomy arising from the emerging consensus in favor of free trade, deregulation of domestic financial markets, and open borders for the circulation of capital and information are quite different from those in the immigration arena. Yet in altering the nature of sovereignty they may well have a long-term impact on the state's capacity to regulate immigration.

Globalization and deregulation have reduced the role of the state in the governance of economic processes.[20] But the state remains the ultimate guarantor of the rights of capital, whether national or foreign.[21] Firms operating transnationally want to ensure that the state continues to carry out its traditional functions in this realm of the national economy. In acting as guarantor of property rights, the state embodies a technical administrative capacity that cannot be replicated at this time by any other institutional arrangement; furthermore, this capacity is backed by military power. But in developed countries this traditional pursuit has been realigned, with power shifting from those governmental agencies most closely tied to domestic social forces (as was the case in the United States during the Pax Americana) and toward those closest to the transnational process of consensus formation.[22]

There also has been a shifting or displacement of once-public functions to non- and quasi-governmental institutions.[23] This is well illustrated by comparing earlier arrangements under the Pax Americana with today's World Trade Organization (WTO). In the United States, such a displacement is perhaps most sharply evident in the growing weight of the central bank in setting national economic policy. Decisions of the Federal Reserve, a body that prides itself on its autonomy from the government, are sharply influenced by the financial markets, which are increasingly internationalized.[24]

More generally, economic internationalization can have different types of consequences for the interstate system.[25] Under the Pax Americana, leading economic sectors—especially manufacturing and raw materials extraction—were subject to international trade regimes that strengthened the interstate system. Individual states adjusted their national economic policies to further this type of international economic system, often under the hegemonic influence of the United States. (Even in this period, certain sectors did not fit comfortably into what was largely a trade-dominated interstate regime; the Euromarkets and offshore tax havens of the 1960s are outcomes of this awkward fit.)

The evolution of international finance and the corporate services sector in the past two decades suggests that economic globalization has taken place partly outside the interstate system.[26] The ascendance of international finance has produced regulatory voids that lie beyond the capacities not only of states, but also of the institutions of the interstate system.[27] Existing systems of governance and accountability for transnational economic activities and entities leave much ungoverned when it comes to these industries.

The deregulation of key operations and markets in the financial industry can be seen as a compromise between nation-based legal regimes and the consensus among a growing number of states in favor of furthering the world economy.[28] The issue is not simply that the global economy extends beyond the national realm. It also has to do with the formation and legitimation of transnational legal regimes that operate in national territories. In some of the major developed countries, national legal fields are becoming more internationalized, while transnational legal regimes are becoming more important and beginning to penetrate previously closed national fields.[29]

There are other instances of formerly government functions of economic governance shifting to non- or quasi-governmental entities. Two of the most important of these in the private sector today are international commercial arbitration and the variety of institutions that fulfill rating and advisory functions. Over the past twenty years, international commercial arbitration has been transformed and institutionalized as the leading contractual method for the resolution of transnational commercial disputes. In a major study, Yves Dezalay and Bryant Garth conclude that international commercial arbitration provides a delocalized and decentralized market for the administration of international commercial disputes, which avoids national courts as venues for settlement.[30]

Similarly, debt security and bond rating agencies that have come to play an increasingly important role in the global economy as mechanisms of "governance without government."[31] They have leverage because of their distinct gatekeeping functions with regard to investment funds sought by corporations and governments and in this regard can be seen as a significant force in the operation and expansion of the global economy. As with business law, the U.S. agencies have expanded their influence overseas.[32] Timothy Sinclair notes that in the early 1980s Moody's Investors Service and Standard & Poor's had no analysts outside the United States; by 1993 they each had about one hundred in Europe, Japan, and Australia.

Among the main points to extract from this examination are, first, the changed articulation of the public functions of the state with major economic sectors;[33] and, second, the shifting of what were once governmental functions to non- or quasi-governmental entities. There are two distinct issues here. One is the formation of new legal regimes that negotiate between national sovereignty and the transnational practices of corporate economic actors. The second is the particular content of this new regime—one that strengthens certain types of economic actors and weakens others. Accordingly, we can posit two distinct issues regarding governance. The first centers on the effort to create viable privatized systems of coordination/ order among the powerful economic actors now operating globally, such as international commercial arbitration and credit rating agencies. A second governance issue focuses not on creating order at the top, but on equity and distribution. This issue must be addressed in the context of a globally integrated economic system with immense inequalities in the profit-making capacities of firms and the earnings capacities of households. It is in this second context that the question of immigration is partly ensconced, and it is here that the challenge of innovation in immigration policy lies.[34]

Implications for Immigration Policy

How much does current immigration policy in advanced receiving economies need to take these transformations into account? There is some consensus that there is a growing gap between the intent of immigration policy and its reality in the major developed receiving countries.[35] One possibility is that the ineffectiveness of current migration policy is due partly to its neglect of these transformations; that is, policy in this area continues to be characterized by its formal isolation from other major processes, as if it were possible to handle migration as a bounded, closed event.

We can see today in all highly developed countries a drive to create border-free economic spaces confronting a quest for renewed border control to keep immigrants and refugees out. The juxtaposition of these two dynamics provides one of the principal contexts in which efforts to regulate immigration assume their distinct meaning.

Current immigration policy in developed countries is increasingly at odds with other major policy frameworks in the international system and with the growth of global economic integration. There are, it seems, two major regimes, one governing the flow of capital and information; the other, immigration. Both of these regimes are international, and both enjoy widespread consensus among states.

The coexistence of different regimes for capital and immigrants has not been recognized as an issue in the United States. The case of the EU is different. In their effort to create a single internal market, European states are discovering the difficulties, if not the impossibility, of maintaining two such diverse regimes. The discussion, design, and implementation of policy aimed at forming a European Union has made clear that immigration policy must take into account the facts of rapid economic internationalization. The EU shows us with great clarity the moment when states need to confront this contradiction in their design of formal policy frameworks. The other major regional systems in the world are far from that moment and may never reach it. Yet they contain less formalized versions of the juxtaposition between border-free economies and border controls. The North American Free Trade Agreement (NAFTA) is one such example, as are various other initiatives for greater economic integration in the Western Hemisphere discussed below.

Making Immigration Policy Today: De Facto Transnationalism

There are strategic sites where it becomes clear that the existence of two very different regimes for the circulation of capital and the circulation of immigrants poses problems that cannot be solved through the old rules of the game, and where the facts of transnationalization impinge on the state's decisions regarding immigration. One example is the need to create special regimes for the movement of service workers within both the

General Agreement on Tariffs and Trade (GATT) and NAFTA as part of the further internationalization of trade and investment in services.[36]

These regimes represent a version of temporary labor migration, but one overseen by entities that are autonomous from the government. This points to an institutional reshuffling of some of the components of sovereign power over entry. Moreover, it can be seen as an extension of the general set of processes whereby state sovereignty is being partly decentered onto non- or quasi-governmental entities involved in the governance of the global economy.

NAFTA's chapters on services, financial services, telecommunications, and business contain considerable detail covering the operations of people in countries of which they are not citizens. For instance, Chapter Twelve, entitled "Cross-Border Trade in Services," includes among its five types of measures those covering "the presence in its territory of a service provider of another Party" under Article 1201, with provisions for both firms and individual workers. Under that same article are clear affirmations that nothing in the agreement on cross-border trade in services imposes any obligation regarding a non-national seeking access to the employment market of the other country or any right with respect to employment.[37] Similarly, Chapter Thirteen, "Telecommunications," and Chapter Fourteen, "Financial Services," contain specific provisions for service providers, including detailed regulations applying to workers.

The NAFTA regime for the circulation of service workers and businesspeople has been uncoupled from any notion of migration but in fact represents a form of temporary labor migration. For both NAFTA and the GATT, the regime for labor mobility falls under the oversight of entities that are quite autonomous from governments.[38] In some ways this is yet another instance of the privatization of that which is profitable and manageable. Like the cross-border legal and regulatory regimes for international business described in the preceding section (such as international commercial arbitration and credit rating agencies), NAFTA represents the privatization of certain components of immigration policy—specifically, the high value-added (that is, persons with high levels of education, capital, or both) and manageability (those working in leading sectors of the economy who are, hence, visible migrants and subject to effective regulation). In its most extreme version—one I do not concur with—governments can be seen as stuck with the "difficult" and "low value-added" components of immigration (low-wage workers, refugees, dependents) and potentially controversial "brain-drain" flows. These developments may change what and who is considered under the category of "immigrant," with attendant policy implications.

The development of provisions for workers and businesspeople also signals the difficulty of *not* dealing with the circulation of people in the implementation of free trade and investment frameworks. This is the case not only for NAFTA, GATT, and the EU, but for other regional groupings in Latin America, which have sharply increased their attention to the international circulation of people. MERCOSUR, the Andean Group, and the Central American Common Market all have launched initiatives in recent years on international labor migration among their member countries. These regional blocs were founded (or revitalized) in a context of globalization, deregulation, and privatization. It is the increased circulation of capital, goods, and information made possible by such regional groupings that has brought to the fore the question of the circulation of people.

MERCOSUR, created in 1991, represents a new generation of regional agreements. The founding treaty was signed by the presidents of Argentina, Brazil, Paraguay, and Uruguay only in 1991, although it actually absorbed earlier cross-border agreements in the region that had been dormant for years. The group acquired legal status in international law with the 1994 Ouro Preto Protocol, which put into effect a customs union among member countries. Not long after MERCOSUR's founding, migration and labor officials of member countries set up two working groups, one of which included a commission on migration control and border-control simplification. Additional committees and working groups are concerned with general border, social, and labor questions. Labor migration is on several agendas and is the subject of various agreements.[39]

The Andean Pact is a much older arrangement that has recently been reactivated. An agreement on labor migration dates from the early stages of the pact: the 1973 Simón Bolívar Agreement on Social and Labor Integration resulted in an operational agreement, the 1977 Andean Labor Migration Statement. Parallel administrative agencies were created in each country's ministry of labor to implement and enforce migration principles. But these principles, along with the general agreement on the Andean common market itself, became inactive. It was not until the 1989 signing of an "Andean Strategy" by the presidents of the member countries that the Andean Group reemerged. The outlook of the group on migration and other issues has shifted since its earlier period, reflecting the sharp changes in the overall global and regional context.[40]

The Organization of Central American States was created in 1951, followed by the Central American Common Market in the 1960s. It was not until 1991 that a Central American Migration Organization (OCAM) was set up. OCAM has been very active over the past few years, but the issues it faces are radically different from those confronting the two regional blocs discussed above: Central America's devastating civil wars have created large refugee flows across the region, and the cessation of the worst military conflicts has brought with it complicated flows of returning refugees. While refugee issues dominate, the 1990s also have seen a strong interest in regional economic integration and a framework for the circulation of persons linked to it.[41]

In the case of the United States and its major immigration source country, Mexico, it appears that the signing of NAFTA also has had the effect of activating a series of new initiatives regarding migration—a sort of de facto bilateralism that represents a radically new phase in the handling of migration between these two countries. It is worth treating this development in some detail.

U.S.-Mexican Relations: Toward De Facto Bilateralism?

As elsewhere in Latin America, we are seeing in the U.S.-Mexican relationship a reactivation of older instruments and a flurry of new activity around the question of international migration. To provide better coordination between the two countries, a U.S.-Mexico Consultative Mechanism was established in the 1970s, leading to the formation of the U.S.-Mexico Binational Commission in 1981 to serve as a forum for meetings between cabinet-level officials from both countries. This was conceived as a flexible mechanism that would meet once or twice a year. One of the earliest working groups formed under its aegis was the Border Relations Action group, set up in 1981.

The key change over the past two years lies in the frequency, focus, and actual work taking place in the meetings of the U.S.-Mexican working groups. NAFTA has strengthened the contacts and collaboration of these groups. Particularly active is the working group on Migration and Consular Affairs, which has become an effective means of resolving serious border problems of mutual interest.[42] This group is charged with ensuring the safe operation of borders and eliminating violence affecting migrants both in transit and in border communities. The group also has reaffirmed its commitment to protecting the human and civil rights of all Mexican migrants in the United States, regardless of their legal status. Members of the working group from both countries seem convinced that this is a new and unprecedented phase of collaboration and communication. It also marks the first time the Mexican government has become so deeply involved in international migration issues.

Disagreements between the two delegations are discussed openly. These have become sharper since the passing of the 1996 immigration law in the United States. Notably, the Mexican delegation is concerned about growing anti-immigrant measures in the United States, and U.S. efforts to expand and strengthen border fences at various locations, emphasizing the threat to border communities and to Mexican efforts to improve border security in the most troubled locations. Notwithstanding these serious disagreements, and perhaps precisely because of them, both delegations are convinced of the importance of continuing the collaboration and communication that have developed since 1995.

A key meeting of the working group on Migration and Consular Affairs was held in Zacatecas, Mexico, in February 1995, before the new 1996 immigration law was passed, when the group's potential was great.[43] One outcome was an agreement that the Mexican government would create groups to combat violence in border locations. Activities of the human rights organization BETA have expanded, while a Citizens Advisory Panel on the U.S. side is undertaking a review of procedures for dealing with reports of abuse at the border. The Zacatecas meeting also led to an effort to facilitate documented migration and the return of undocumented migrants in full compliance with human rights codes. Both sides are developing criteria, procedures, and legal conditions consistent with international practices for the safe and orderly repatriation of undocumented Mexican migrants to ports-of-entry within Mexico, without intermediate stops, and with full respect for their human rights.

Both delegations recognized the central importance of information about migration and therefore supported the ongoing Binational Study on Migration. The expectation is that the efforts of this expert panel will facilitate the development of new and constructive long-term policies to deal with bilateral migration flows.

Unofficial indications of a move toward de facto bilateralism include the enormous expansion and strong government support over the last decade of the Colegio de la Frontera Norte, with headquarters outside Tijuana but units all along the border. The goal of this university is to develop a body of research and a cadre of professionals who understand the border as a distinct region. A second example is the formation in 1995 of the U.S.-Mexico Consultative Group, sponsored by the Carnegie Endowment for International Peace in Washington. This group seeks to facilitate cooperation on U.S.-Mexican migration and attendant labor issues by engaging senior policy-makers and nongovernmental experts from the two countries in an ongoing off-the-record dialogue.

Human Rights and Immigration

Beyond the new conditions brought about by economic internationalization, immigration policy and practice are also affected increasingly by the new international human rights regime.[44]

Unlike political, social, and civil rights, which are predicated on the distinction between national and alien, human rights are not dependent on nationality. While rooted in the founding documents of nation-states, human rights are today a force that can undermine the exclusive authority of the state over its nationals and thereby contribute to transforming the interstate system and international legal order.[45] Membership in territorially exclusive nation-states ceases to be the only ground for the realization of rights. All residents, whether citizens or not, can claim their human rights.[46] Human rights impinge on the principle of nation-based citizenship and the boundaries of the nation by eroding the legitimacy of the state if it fails to respect international human rights codes.[47] Legitimacy no longer attaches automatically to invocations of national self-determination—a significant shift.[48]

The growing influence of human rights law is particularly evident in Europe. These judicial notions began to be applied in the United States in the 1980s, but it still lags behind.[49] American definitions of nationhood have led courts in some cases to address the matter of undocumented immigrants within American constitutionalism by applying the idea that persons enjoy inalienable and natural rights without reference to territorial confines. It was not until the mid-1970s and early 1980s that domestic courts began to consider human rights codes as normative instruments in their own right. The rapid growth of undocumented immigration and the shrinking state capacity to control the flow led courts to pay greater attention to the international human rights regime, which allows them to rule on basic protections for individuals not formally included in the national territory and legal system, notably undocumented aliens and unauthorized refugees.[50]

The growing accountability of states to international human rights codes and institutions, together with the fact that individuals and nonstate actors can make claims on states in terms of those codes, signals a development that goes beyond the expansion of human rights within the framework of nation-states. It contributes to redefining states' bases of legitimacy under the rule of law and the notion of nationality. Under human rights regimes, states increasingly must take account of persons *qua* persons, rather than *qua* citizens. The individual is now an object of law and a site for rights whether he or she is a citizen or an alien.[51]

In accumulating social and civic rights and even some political rights in countries of residence, immigrants have diluted the meaning of citizenship and the specialness of the claims citizens can make on the state. When it comes to social services (such as education, health insurance, welfare, and unemployment benefits), citizenship status is of minor importance in Western Europe. What matters is residence and legal alien status. Most of these countries will pay retirement benefits even if recipients no longer reside there, while some countries (Sweden and the Netherlands) have granted local voting rights. Aliens are guaranteed full civil rights either constitutionally or by statute. The United States maintains sharper differences between citizens' rights and those of legal immigrants, and these have been strengthened by the 1996 immigration law. Lawsuits contesting this infringement of the rights of legal immigrants are likely.

Even unauthorized immigrants can make some of the claims mentioned above. Peter Schuck and Rogers Smith have noted that new "social contracts" are being negotiated in the United States every day between undocumented aliens and U.S. society—contracts that cannot be nullified through claims about nationality and sovereignty.[52] Courts have had to accept the fact of undocumented aliens and extend to these aliens some form of legal recognition and guarantees of basic rights. Various decisions have conferred important benefits of citizenship on undocumented aliens, clearly undermining older notions of sovereignty.

Conclusion

The developments described above point to a de facto transnationalizing of immigration policy and practice. First, wherever the formation of transnational economic spaces has gone the farthest and been most formalized, it has become clear that existing frameworks for immigration policy are problematic. In the long run it is probably not viable to have very different regimes for the circulation of capital and the circulation of people. Awareness of this fact is most evident in the legislative work necessary for the formation of the EU. But it is also apparent in NAFTA and the major Latin American trading blocs, all of which have had to address the circulation of people as an integral part of cross-border trade and investment.

Second, we see government functions beginning to be displaced onto non- or quasi-governmental institutions. Not only are new transnational legal and regulatory regimes being created in the context of economic globalization, but special regimes are being created for the circulation of service workers and businesspeople within both GATT and NAFTA. Although these regimes have been separated from any notion of migration, they represent a version of temporary labor migration. And they exist in good part under the oversight of entities that are quite autonomous from governments.

Third, the legitimation process for states under the rule of law calls for respect and enforcement of international human rights codes regardless of nationality and legal status. While enforcement is precarious, it nonetheless signals a major shift in the legitimation process. This is perhaps most evident in the strategic role that the judiciary has assumed in the highly developed countries when it comes to the rights of immigrants, refugees, and asylum-seekers.

All these developments have the effect, first, of reducing the autonomy of the state in immigration policy making and, second, of multiplying the sectors within the state that are addressing immigration policy, thereby expanding the opportunity for intrastate conflicts. The simple assertion that the state is in charge of immigration policy is less and less helpful. The state has been transformed by its participation in the global economy, but of course it never was a homogeneous actor; rather, it is constituted through multiple agencies and social forces. Indeed, it can be said that although the state has central control over immigration policy, the work of exercising that claimed power often begins with a limited contest between the state and interested social forces.[53] These interest groups include such diverse entities as agribusiness, manufacturing, humanitarian groups, labor unions, ethnic organizations, and supporters of zero population growth. We must add to this the fact that the hierarchies of power and influence within the state are being reconfigured by economic globalization.[54]

Immigration policy is being made and implemented today under conditions that range from the pressures of economic globalization and its implications for the role of the state to international agreements on human rights. The institutional setting for immigration policy varies as well, ranging from national states and local entities to supranational organizations.

Why does this transformation of the state and the interstate system matter for immigration? The shift of governance functions away from the state to nonstate entities affects the state's capacity to control its borders. New private and public systems of governance are being created that conflict with the state's capacity to regulate immigration in the same old ways, and that conflict may increase. Further, the transformation of the state itself through its role in implementing global processes may contribute to the emergence of new constraints, options, and vested interests. Finally, the ascendance of agencies linked to furthering globalization and the decline of those linked to domestic equity is likely eventually to have an effect on the immigration agenda.

Part Two

The Reconfigured United States

Chapter 5

The Burden of Interdependence:
Demographic, Economic, and Social Prospects for
Latinos in the Reconfigured U.S. Economy

Jorge Chapa

In *The Burden of Support,* my co-authors and I examined the projected population sizes and age distributions of Anglos, African-Americans, Asians, and U.S.-born and immigrant Latinos.[1] We noted that the Latino population would grow very rapidly under most assumptions; even in the event of no future international in-migration, the number of Latinos would rise. An important corollary of this growth is that the proportion of Latinos in the younger age groups will be even higher. The other minority populations studied also were projected to increase faster than the population as a whole and to have relatively young age distributions. In marked contrast, the Anglo population was projected to become a smaller proportion of the total population and to be concentrated increasingly in the older groups.

Several implications follow from this age-race shift. In many large metropolitan areas, Latinos already constitute a majority of the youth, and in the coming years will make up a growing proportion of the work force. Since Latinos' earnings are much lower than average, this has the immediate economic implication of decreasing the national level of per capita earnings. This decrease will be particularly noticeable as Anglo baby boomers reach retirement age. The passage of this large group from prime earners to retirees will place a tremendous demand on Social Security and Medicare at the same time that earnings will be decreasing nationally. All these developments suggest a potential for dissension between young Latinos and aging Anglos.

The demographic shifts outlined above will take place within a context of increased global interdependence. A major component of the economic landscape will be the consequences of internationalized trade on the employment and earnings of U.S. Latinos. Since the mid-1970s, real wages of Americans with low levels of education have decreased. Some argue that this decrease is due in large part to the increasing internationalization of the U.S. economy. The post-NAFTA prospect is for more, or much more, of the same. Most Latinos fall into the low-education category; a relatively small proportion are well educated and likely to benefit from ongoing economic changes. To understand the impact of globalized trade on these populations, three topics must be addressed:

1. Immigration is one of the demographic consequences of an increasingly globalized economy, and the principal connection between international trade and U.S. population composition. In the long run, international trade measures such as NAFTA probably will result in vastly improved economic conditions in Mexico. However, in the time required to enact these changes, millions of Mexicans will lose their livelihood. This may well result in increased pressure to migrate to the United States, regardless of current efforts to reform immigration policy.

2. Latinos' earnings and employment prospects will be affected by the internationalized U.S. economy. Latinos have had substantially lower unemployment rates than African-Americans since 1973, when such statistics were first collected. In the past few years, Latino unemployment rates have been increasing when compared with Anglos and African-Americans. In January 1995, for the first time ever, Latinos and African-Americans had equally high rates of unemployment.

3. The reconfigured U.S. economy will have a special impact on the social prospects for U.S. Latinos. Several analysts have claimed that William Julius Wilson's description of the underclass does not apply to Latinos because strong family and community support networks help people through hard times.[2] This may have been true in the past, but increased migration and decreased economic opportunities will weaken that safety net, a trend illustrated in the city of San Antonio.

Immigration

Immigration has been at the forefront of the nations attention in recent years. Most popular sentiment has been negative, as reflected in the work of the U.S. Commission on Immigration Reform and the passage of California's Proposition 187. Nevertheless, economic integration will boost Latino, and especially Mexican, immigration to the United States. Under NAFTA, U.S. exports will undermine broad sectors of the Mexican economy, dislocate millions of workers and their dependents, and increase the motivation for emigration. Agriculture is the sector where the demographic impact of these developments will likely be the greatest. Even while disagreeing with this widely accepted prediction, Wayne Cornelius and Philip Martin admit that migration pressures in Mexico will increase sharply and probably lead to higher migration, although they argue that the effect will not be as large or long-lasting as many suppose.[3]

Other analysts are more explicit, claiming that in the short run NAFTA will increase migration from Mexico to the United States over current levels, while in the longer run migration will be less than it would be without NAFTA.[4] I have no disagreement with this position. Of course, it is impossible to know precisely how many Mexicans will emigrate to the United States over the next decade, but it is a safe bet that they will number in the millions.

Economic integration will contribute to increased migration not just because of hardship at home, but because of the new opportunities provided by free trade to entrepreneurs, sales representatives, consultants, and so on. The size of this migration will be demographically negligible compared with the traditional migrant stream, but it could be socially and politically significant. The result will be an identifiable group of middle-class and upper-middle-class Mexican and Latino immigrants whose education and employment will make it relatively easy for them to speak out and be heard. Unsophisticated media and an unsophisticated U.S. public will take the opinions of this group as representative of the immigrant population as a whole. In fact, however, the "free traders'" social and economic backgrounds make it very likely that their interests will diverge from those of most Latino immigrants.

Apart from NAFTA, the simple fact that current immigration rates are high and expected to remain so means that immigration will be a significant factor in shaping the future composition of Latino communities in the United States. Under the current regime the Census Bureau reports the net admission to the United States of about 800,000 immigrants each year. This figure represents a 33 percent increase over the immigration numbers for the 1980s, and forms the basis for Census Bureau projections of the future population.[5]

These arguments were formulated before the devaluation of the Mexican peso and the devastation of the Mexican economy in late 1994 and 1995. That crisis put an end to any remaining doubts about the coming increase in immigration. Newspaper headlines tell the story:

- "Plunge of the Peso and Hard Times to Follow May Spur Surge of Mexican immigration to U.S.," *Wall Street Journal*, January 6, 1995
- "Mexican Shock Waves," *Financial Times*, January 31, 1995
- "Border Patrol Records Increase in Number of Arrests in Valley," *Austin American Statesman*, March 21, 1995
- "Mexicans Boxcar Journeys Alarm U.S. Border Officials," *New York Times*, June 11, 1995

A second consequence of the peso devaluation was higher unemployment among U.S. Latinos, with the impact particularly noticeable along the U.S.–Mexican border. Again, this story can be seen in the headlines:

- "Pesos Fall Sends Jobs, Not Goods, to Mexico," *Austin American Statesman*, March 31, 1995
- "Pesos Drop Hurts South Texas Business," *Austin American Statesman*, April 15, 1995
- "Pesos Silver Lining: Mexico Nets Huge Surplus with U.S., but Theres a Price to Good News: 700,000 [Mexican] Jobs Lost," *Los Angeles Times*, April 20, 1995
- "NAFTAs Effect So Far: Jobs, Trade Headed South," *Austin American Statesman*, July 20, 1995

Some argue that the peso crisis was exacerbated by the Mexican government's decision to delay a necessary downward adjustment of the pesos value for political reasons, followed by the decision to devalue rapidly and without warning.[6] Thus, the specific consequences of the devaluation could arguably be tied to these human actions rather than to some inherent aspect of increased economic interdependence between Mexico and the United States. For the purposes of this chapter, however, this distinction is not important. The specific events surrounding the peso devaluation and the ratification of NAFTA accelerated long-term trends that were already under way. There is ample reason to believe that immigration to the United States would continue at a high level and that Latinos in the United States would face economic difficulties even if the devaluation had been managed in the best manner possible.

My research on recent but pre-NAFTA immigration trends helps clarify the picture of immigration.[7] The "push" factors that NAFTA is likely to increase have grown stronger in the past decade. Recent Mexican immigrants are less educated than earlier immigrants and seem to be migrating at a later age. The migrants' age, like the growing use of the phrase "economic refugee," probably reflects the increasingly troubled state of the Mexican economy and its importance as a factor stimulating migration. Their decreasing educational level suggests that migration to the United States is a social process now open to a wider range of Mexicans.

Several of my previous studies showed that Mexican-Americans are not attaining educational, economic, or occupational parity with Anglos, even when third-generation Mexican-Americans are compared with third-generation Anglos.[8] The educational levels of a substantial portion of third-generation Mexican-Americans show no indication of converging with Anglo levels, while their earnings and occupational status have decreased in comparison. In related research, I have shown that many Mexican-Americans are maintaining a separate social structure and culture. Dropping out of high school is associated with all three are as described above: educational, economic, and occupational attainment. In addition, the dropouts' economic characteristics parallel those described by William Julius Wilson as criteria for inclusion in the underclass.

One key concern in the immigration debate focuses on the future incorporation or lack of incorporation of the children of immigrants. Gender-, generation-, and cohort-specific examination shows that third-generation Mexican-Americans have lower levels of educational attainment than the second generation. Among Mexican-Americans, U.S.-born generations have much lower attainment levels than U.S.-born non-Hispanic whites. Both institutional barriers and discrimination may explain this apparent ceiling for Mexican-Americans as a whole. The disaggregation of the Mexican-American population into class groups indicates that economic and social incorporation is possible for those Mexican-Americans who do well in school. The large proportion who do not do well in school have lower degrees of social and economic incorporation.

In the same earlier work I have shown that instead of following the European pattern of assimilation, the Mexican-American pattern has many similarities with the one Wilson describes for African-Americans: a well-educated middle class largely integrated into the society and economy, coexisting with a relatively uneducated, economically superfluous, and self-perpetuating underclass. Further, I have shown that there are significant differences in the level of sociostructural assimilation between Chicanos who are attaining parity with Anglos and those who are not. In the picture that emerges from my interpretation of the data, a Chicano middle class is assimilating economically and sociostructurally, while a lower class that is not achieving socioeconomic parity retains a social structure distinct from the Anglo mainstream.

It was only in comparison with the economic situation of African-Americans that the Chicano situation looked positive in the past. Unlike African-Americans, who are split, Wilson argues, into a middle class and an underclass, Chicanos can be divided into an assimilating middle class and a large lower class that is socially separate from the larger society. Whereas the underclass is outside the regular economy and occupational structure, the Chicano lower class can be characterized as having had a firm grip on the bottom rung of the occupational ladder. If, however, current economic and political trends continue to diminish the quality of opportunities available to Chicanos with low educational levels and lower-class jobs, they may lose this grip and also become members of the underclass. The increasing trend toward international economic integration will likely result in an even more precarious economic situation for all low-skilled (that is, low-educational-level) workers. Latinos, of course, are disproportionally represented in this group.

Joan Moore, Carlos Vélez, and others have argued that the underclass concept does not apply to Latinos. This may have been true in the past,

but the factors that will shape the life chances of Latinos in the future—
increasing immigration, decreasing employment opportunities and wages
for workers with low skills and low education levels—are reasons for
pessimism. A look at how Latinos will fare in an internationalized U.S.
economy supports this negative outlook.

Latinos in the Internationalized U.S. Economy

It is difficult to distinguish a long-term trend from random variation in
recurrent measures. One hot summer is not necessarily evidence of global
warming. Similarly, one month's unemployment statistics do not allow us
to claim that a specific threshold has been reached. Nonetheless, one
cannot ignore the potential significance of the fact that in January 1995
the Latino unemployment rate equaled the African-American for the first
time ever. In the past, almost all monthly measures of unemployment for
African-Americans had found it to be about twice the Anglo rate. The
Latino unemployment rate would typically lie between these two extremes. In recent years, however, Latino unemployment rates have been
increasing in comparison to other groups. In January 1995 the Anglo rate
was 4.9 percent, while the rate for both African-Americans and Latinos
was 10.2 percent.[9] Until now, it could accurately be said that many Latinos were poor because they worked in low-wage jobs. If this pattern and
level of unemployment are sustained over a number of years, Latinos, like
many African-Americans, will be poor because they do not have jobs.

Once all the data are available, it will be clear that these high rates of
Latino unemployment are due to both short-term and long-term factors.
Workers with low skills and educational levels have faced decreasing wages
and diminishing opportunities for employment since the mid-1970s. The
future employment prospects for such workers are even more bleak than in
the recent past.[10] In addition, the continued rapid increase in the number
of young Latinos, especially those at the age of labor force entry, means
that Latino youth could face an especially high rate of unemployment.
These factors must be put into the context of continued, massive educational failure for Latino children across the nation. Finally, the fact that
many low-paying jobs do not yield a living wage can act as a disincentive
for those considering entry to the labor force.

Long-Term Factors: The Restructuring of the U.S. Economy

Everyone agrees that the U.S. economy has undergone major changes, but
the reasons continue to be debated. The essence of recent economic change
in the United States is that wages have stopped growing and even, for many
workers, decreased. Correspondingly, income inequality has risen. Frank

Table 5.1. Male Median Income by Race

	1970	1980	1990
Anglo	$21,160	$21,830	$22,070
African-American	$12,800	$13,130	$12,970
Hispanic	$18,440	$15,120	$13,500

The table shows median income for all males 15 and older, in constant 1989 U.S. dollars.

Source: Roderick J. Harrison and Claudette E. Bennett, "Racial and Ethnic Diversity," in Reynolds Farley, ed., *State of the Union: America in the 1990s,* vol 2: *Social Trends* (New York: Russell Sage Foundation, 1995), pp. 204–5.

Levy's periodization of post–World War II American economic history helps put these changes in perspective:

- The first quarter-century (1947–1973) saw rapid earnings growth and moderating income inequality.
- From 1974 through 1979, earnings growth slowed to the point of stagnation (although living standards continued to rise), while income inequality grew slightly.
- From 1980 through 1989, average earnings continued to stagnate, but income inequality increased sharply . . . and the majority of changes worked against the less-educated workers.
- From 1990 through at least 1993, the economy passed through an extended recession in which job losses and wage decline now reached white collar workers, particularly older, college-educated men.[11]

This historical context has shaped the assumptions of most adults now living and working in the United States. The failure of the economy to meet widely held expectations of continual growth is also the source of seemingly ubiquitous public discontent. Most workers today simply are not enjoying the high rates of economic growth that they experienced or saw their parents experience during the boom years between the end of World War II and 1973.

Latinos, for a number of reasons, did not enjoy fully the fruits of the postwar boom and, like all workers with low levels of education, now find themselves increasingly marginalized, with unemployment up and wages down. The information in Table 5.1 presents a striking indication of how much Latino earning power has decreased since 1970.

Table 5.2 shows the dramatic recent decrease in earnings and employment for high school dropouts. A similar analysis by Johanne Boisjoly and Greg J. Duncan also found that Latino workers had very high job displacement rates between 1987 and 1992, substantially higher than the

Table 5.2. Changes in Wages and Employment by Education
Level, 1989-92

Education Level	Change in Real Hourly Earnings	Employment Share 1989	Employment Share 1992
High school dropout	-15.9%	18.2%	14.3%
High school graduate	-6.4%	31.1%	34.2%
B.A. or higher degree	-6.9%	20.9%	23.4%

Source: David A. Brauer and Susan Hickok, "Explaining the Growing Inequality Across Skill Levels," *Federal Reserve Bank of New York Economic Policy Review* 1 (January 1995): 65.

rates for African-Americans or Anglos. They write, "The reasons for the higher Hispanic rate include a more youthful demographic composition, a much lower level of education, and a much higher rate of employment in occupations vulnerable to layoffs."[12] When viewing Table 5.2, it is important to keep in mind that Latinos have, by far, the largest proportion of adults with less than a high school education.[13]

Possible causes of this economic deterioration include increased international trade, technological change, widespread computerization, industrial decline, increased immigration, increased variance in the quality of education, skill restructuring, and the decreasing consequence of unions, labor laws, and other wage-setting institutions.[14] The literature makes it clear that is no one factor explains all of the economic changes in all of the sectors over the postexpansion period. It also is clear that whether they are cause or consequence, all these factors are implicated in the increased internationalization of the U.S. economy and the decreased opportunities for Latinos with low levels of education.

Short-Term Factors:
Proposition 187 and the Peso Devaluation

Two events that had a large and sudden impact on Latino unemployment were Proposition 187 and the peso devaluation. Although Proposition 187 was targeted against undocumented immigrants, its blunderbuss impact is likely to hit citizens and documented residents as well. "Many Latino workers are held back by outmoded skills, job inexperience and weaker educational credentials," Robert Hershey notes. "But these days they are also finding themselves increasingly subject to intense suspicion, resentment and, in many cases, outright discrimination." He quotes Juan Vargas, deputy mayor of San Diego: "There's no doubt that discrimination has increased against Latinos. Proposition 187 has created almost a crisis in the Latino community. It has employers panicked."[15] These comments suggest the negative impact that Proposition 187 may have on Latino employment in California. Since California is home to about 30 percent of the Latinos in the United States, it might well be felt on a national scale.

The peso devaluation also had an immediate, localized effect on Latino unemployment, one that could conceivably be reflected in national statistics. With the formalization of NAFTA and an overvalued peso, Mexico went on a sustained shopping spree in the United States and particularly in Texas border cities. The peso devaluation halted the spree overnight. Because the population and labor force in many of these cities is predominantly Latino, any regional dropoff in economic activity may lead to increased Latino unemployment locally and nationally.

Social Prospects for U.S. Latinos: The Case of San Antonio

In some areas the trends that will shape the future for Latinos already can be seen. The major developments affecting Latinos' life chances are short-term population growth, followed by a decrease in immigration; low earnings and high unemployment; and continued low levels of educational attainment.

Let us imagine that ultimately (say, in ten or twenty years) NAFTA and other policies succeed in lowering in-migration. If the same policies also succeed in undermining current employment in low-wage industries, then many cities of the future may look like San Antonio today—a city with few manufacturing jobs and a large Latino population composed predominantly of U.S.-born rather than immigrant Latinos. San Antonio offers an opportunity to see what the Latino population may be like after a generation in the United States.[16]

Social and Economic Profile

As a southwestern city originally settled by Mexicans, San Antonio maintains its distinctly Mexican roots. The city encompasses most of Bexar County and accounts for nearly 80 percent of the county's population. In 1990 Latinos made up a plurality (49.7 percent) of the county population and a majority (52 percent) of the city population. Persons of Mexican origin make up over 90 percent of the identified Hispanic population in Bexar County.

San Antonio is the largest city in the United States where people of Spanish origin constitute over 50 percent of the population. Historically, it has been an important site for gauging the economic, social, and political well-being of Mexican-Americans in Texas. During the 1980s, Bexar

County's total population grew nearly 20 percent, from 988,800 to 1.2 million. The Latino growth rate was about the same.

Unfortunately, San Antonio also has a much higher poverty rate (19.5 percent) than the U.S. average (13.1 percent). This poverty is often attributed to the area's poorly diversified economic base, weak manufacturing sector, and low wage scale. In addition, San Antonio has had a long history of discrimination against its Mexican-American population. Although Mexican-Americans and Latinos constitute about half of the population, they represent more than 70 percent of those living in poverty.

San Antonio continues to play a central cultural and economic role for the Mexican-American population in the Southwest. In 1990 about 1.8 million Mexican-Americans were living in South Texas. The size and growth of the Mexican population in this region—which includes the Lower Rio Grande Valley, the smaller towns and cities along the border, and San Antonio itself—constitute an important aspect of the national Mexican-American experience. The incidence and persistence of poverty in the region is disproportionately high in the population of Mexican origin.

Educational and Employment

There are marked differences in the educational attainment of Anglos, Chicanos, and Mexicanos in the San Antonio metropolitan region. While approximately 80 percent of the non-Hispanic adults in the area had completed high school, only about 55 percent of Hispanic males and females had done so. In addition, the proportion of college graduates in 1990 was far lower among Hispanics (7 percent) than for the city as a whole (about 20 percent).

In contrast to many other major cities with high concentrations of Latinos, San Antonio never developed strong manufacturing industries in either durable or nondurable goods. In 1990 less than 10 percent of the San Antonio civilian work force held jobs in manufacturing. An examination of census documents shows that manufacturing jobs were scarce as far back as 1940, although employment opportunities grew rapidly in producer services (financial services, insurance, real estate), social services (especially health services), and entertainment/tourism. Each of these sectors offers bifurcated employment opportunities characterized by either high-wage/high-skill or low-wage/low-skill jobs. Many San Antonio residents, especially those with little education and skills, are faced with the prospect of part-time, seasonal, or low-wage employment. The result is that a large proportion of the population and a disproportionately high percentage of the Latino population are mired in poverty.

The low economic status of most of San Antonios Latinos is connected to the globalized economy, as the following story illustrates. From

1985 to 1990, Levi Strauss & Co. closed ten manufacturing plants located in San Antonio. The last and largest closing, in February 1990, displaced more than a thousand garment workers, almost all of whom were Latinas and Latinos. The *San Antonio Light* summarized the situation as follows: "Levi Strauss & Co. said it had no choice but to close its San Antonio plant and move the jobs to Costa Rica and the Dominican Republic. The lure of Third World workers performing the same tasks at half the cost is proving irresistible to the garment industry. Levi simply joined an inexorable trend." Ironically, by moving the plant to Costa Rica, Levi Strauss found not only cheaper wages, but also a better-educated work force. The newspaper reported that "25 percent of San Antonians are at least marginally illiterate; in Costa Rica, only 7 percent can't read and write."[17] The basic elements of this story are repeated in countless decisions by employers. Many Latino workers in San Antonio and across the United States have few, if any, skills that distinguish them from their cousins south of the border. Indeed, factors in addition to low wages (like education) may attract corporations to foreign locations.

Latino Poverty and Underclass Characteristics

The Social Science Research Council (SSRC) recently reported on the occurrence of five characteristics associated with the underclass:

- Low education: Householder (HH) did not complete high school
- Single parenthood: HH is single, divorced, or separated and family includes a person under age 18
- Poor work history: HH worked less than 26 weeks or usually worked less than 20 hours per week
- Public assistance recipiency: At least one member of the household received public assistance
- Poverty: Family income was below poverty level[18]

The SSRC publication estimated in 1990 that there were 20,637 Latino households in San Antonio with all five of these characteristics—a 60 percent increase since 1980. The city of Los Angeles, with a Latino population more than three times that of San Antonio, had only 24,067 Latino households with all five characteristics—an increase of about 35 percent since 1980.

The thrust of the evidence presented above is that many Latino families in San Antonio are barely able to keep their heads above water. Again, San Antonio Latinos are largely U.S.-born and live in a city facing major economic challenges (such as the closing of military bases). Their precarious economic position can be seen in the high proportion of Latinos with a full set of underclass characteristics.[19]

Conclusion

The future seems certain to include broad cutbacks in government spending and decreasing opportunities for low-skilled workers. Circumstances suggest that the worst-case scenario my colleagues and I identified in *The Burden of Support* is very likely to occur as immigration continues without an improvement in current economic circumstances. Any useful policy discussion must address the question of how low-wage, low-skilled workers can earn a decent living. Today, many Latinos are poor because they work in low-wage jobs. In the future, they may not be able to find jobs at all.

Two other considerations provide even greater grounds for pessimism. An ugly anti-immigrant mood is widespread in the United States. Anti-immigrant actions hurt all Latinos, documented and undocumented, U.S.- and foreign-born alike. At the same time, the 1994 congressional election seemed to repudiate government programs designed to help the poor. Californias Proposition 187 is the most notorious of these developments; others include changes in immigration policy currently being discussed, the University of California regents' decision to end affirmative action programs, and many of the "welfare reform" proposals of the Republican Congress. All these recent political initiatives threaten Latinos. Positive policy interventions seem unlikely in the near future.

Chapter 6

From Estrangement to Affinity:
Dilemmas of Identity Among Hispanic Children

Patricia Fernández-Kelly

The progression from migration to ethnicity is gradual. In most cases, the transition is short lived—a stepping stone in the journey toward assimilation. In others, the passage toward incorporation is never accomplished, and the children and grandchildren of immigrants slowly acquire a minority status. It takes time for migrants to learn to perceive themselves as members of ethnic groups. When crossing international borders, individuals tend to identify on the basis of nationality; in areas of destination, however, they are perceived as constituents of unfamiliar, often disdained, categories. Mexicans, Nicaraguans, and Cubans find their national differences obliterated by their common designation as "Hispanics," a term coined by the U.S. Bureau of the Census in 1980. Mexicans are subject to yet other labels: "*cholo*," "Chicano," "Mexican-American," or "Latino"—all words with particular histories, undertones, and ramifications.

Embracing or resisting ethnic nomenclatures reflects how people view themselves and believe they are viewed by others. The acceptance of terms used to denote impoverished or despised groups can impose a heavy toll upon immigrant children. In contrast, identities based on national origin, immigrant status, or religious conviction seem to act as protective shields and a brake against downward mobility. Choices about identity are thus part and parcel of interactions that result in adjustment, contestation, and resistance. Moreover, group identity can be manipulated as circumstances demand. Recently arrived Mexicans may reject "Chicano" as a term fit for outcasts, while their children will wear the same label as a badge of honor. Cubans fervently assert their national origin and repudiate "Hispanic" as a stigmatizing tag. Nicaraguans, on the other hand, are likely to adopt the very same term as a way of escaping negative stereotypes associated with their national origin. Even more surprisingly, individuals hopscotch among ethnic designations as they confront new or familiar environments. There is nothing static about ethnic identity.

Immigrants repeatedly engage in purposeful acts to signify their intended character and the way in which they differ from other groups. When defining themselves, immigrants refer to the image of the urban underclass to delineate their own place in the new society. Recent writings have reexamined the relationship between the black migration from the rural South and the subsequent emergence of persistent poverty in American cities,[1] but most people have only a faint memory of that connection. Immigrants do not perceive inner-city blacks as the disaffected children and grandchildren of older migrants but as the very antithesis of their own condition. Whereas new arrivals view themselves as industrious, individualistic, and self-reliant, they see poor blacks as lazy, dependent, and troublesome. Social distress is thus seen as the consequence of values and behaviors inimical to those that immigrants expect to deploy in their own pursuit of success.

Across generations, the picture shifts. Many immigrant children do not think of black and Latino youngsters living in tough neighborhoods as a vantage point for self-differentiation. Some do precisely the opposite, seeing such youths as the architects of a new adversarial culture of success. Through interactions with them in schools, parks, and other public spaces, immigrants learn a distinct way of being American. This makes for high drama. Whether immigrant children shun or embrace the purported culture of the ghetto will have a measurable impact upon their potential for economic and social advancement. In the hazardous geometry of race, class, and ethnicity, outcomes vary in unforeseen ways.

In this chapter I explore some of the ways in which Hispanic families and their children view themselves and their place in American society. Group identities bolster or limit options in education and the labor market. Shaped by the interplay between definitions preceding migration and definitions imposed in areas of destination, a group's identity depends on physical and social context. It is toponomical in character—essentialist arguments based on culture must give way to socially situated explanations.

My discussion is divided into three parts. In the first I sketch a theoretical framework that assigns priority to interpersonal networks and social capital as the underpinning of group identity, and economic activity as well. Immigrants able to draw upon the knowledge and economic assets of earlier migrants will share an experience very different from the experience of immigrants lacking a connection to opportunities and high-quality resources.

In the second section I provide a profile of Hispanic families and their children followed, in the third section, by a comparative discussion of collective identities. My analysis centers on three groups and two locations: Cubans and Nicaraguans in South Florida and Mexicans in Southern California. The data on which this comparison is based come from two complementary sources: a national survey of children of immigrants between the ages of twelve and seventeen, conducted between 1992 and 1996, and a series of ethnographic case studies carried out in the latter part of 1993, 1994, and 1996 with approximately two hundred families of immigrant children (a small subset of the original sample). By combining the strengths of quantitative and qualitative analysis, I draw a profile of diverging adaptations and emerging identities.

Immigrant Assimilation and Ethnic Identity

Identity and self-definition are issues of central importance in psychological analysis. The child development literature, for example, identifies self-worth as a measurable attribute that correlates positively with academic achievement and high aspirations.[2] Sociological inquiry has established similar connections with regard to various aspects of labor market performance and satisfaction in personal life and employment. Less well understood is the relationship between group identity and socioeconomic performance.

The elaboration and effects of group identity raise elusive theoretical and methodological questions. How, for instance, can one isolate group effects from individual endowment, or separate the influence of ethnic identity from that of social class? Are Cuban children more successful in school because of their membership in a particular national group or their comparatively affluent status? Do Mexican and Nicaraguan children reject educational achievement because they are Mexican or Nicaraguan, or because their aspirations have been leveled by poverty, exploitation, and neglect?

Three broad themes guide the following discussion. First, group identity results from the interplay between self-definitions that precede migration and definitions imposed in areas of destination. Second, a permanent minority status emerges from processes leading to stagnant or downward social mobility. Finally, group identity materializes, like the tip of an iceberg, atop a foundation constituted by the interaction among social capital, the types of resources available to the members of a particular group, and the attributes of interpersonal networks.

One way to conceptualize group identity is by focusing on the life cycle. Individuals are born into a series of nested collectivities whose boundaries are indeterminate and often overlapping. As time advances, the awareness of membership in the immediate kin network, the extended family, and the peer group is augmented by a sense of belonging to other categories—for example, a religious denomination, a social club, or a political organization. Whether consciously or not, individuals use group membership not only to achieve feelings of security but also to gain access to material and intangible resources, including information. An internalized sense of group membership, of "we-ness," also serves to control behavior and exclude outsiders.[3]

Although national identities are of comparatively recent vintage—

most European and Latin American states emerged only within the past two centuries—they have played a definitive role in the lives of migrants. Once consolidated, states imposed a new logic on the potential for mobility. As state-centered definitions of membership and exclusion were forged, international demarcations defined rights and obligations for both citizens and foreigners. When crossing borders in search of opportunities, individuals had no recourse other than to define themselves in terms of nationality. In the United States, the contentious relationship between generations of immigrants—some established, some struggling to gain acceptance—began to define national identity in the mid-nineteenth century.

That process became a cornerstone of nascent sociological research. Pioneers in the study of migration coined the term "assimilation" to denote a transition entailing immigrants' abandonment of foreign or hyphenated self-definitions to become fully American.[4] The expectation was that assimilation would bring about social and economic advancement. Optimistic accounts (symbolized by the image of the melting pot) coexisted with the early expansion of the Fordist economy, when millions of jobs were generated, almost a third in manufacturing, most of which required little or no previous skill. The economic growth that promoted higher wages and mass consumption during the early stages of American capitalism made plausible the idea of a middle America on the rise. Those still struggling on the river banks were expected to join the broadening stream of economic progress.

Of course there were deviations from that sanguine forecast, notably among African-Americans, Mexicans, and Puerto Ricans. The industrial growth of the North fueled a demand for labor that, at the time of World War I, began to be filled by black migrants from the rural South where cotton agriculture was declining. African-Americans appeared in Chicago, New York, Boston, Philadelphia, and other cities under conditions that Robert Park regarded as optimal for assimilation.[5] Yet the process did not bring about the anticipated outcome: for several generations, blacks have been disproportionately represented among the poor and politically disenfranchised.[6] Neither did the mass migration of Puerto Ricans into cities like New York during the 1940s and 1950s lead to successful assimilation. Mexicans, who have carried on the longest sustained migration to the United States, have experienced striking social and economic stagnation as well. While successful groups shed self-definitions based on ethnicity, it is among those for whom prosperity remained elusive that ethnic identities emerged. In the United States ethnicity is, therefore, an effect of thwarted assimilation—the product of incorporation into the lower rungs of American society, or what Alejandro Portes calls "segmented assimilation."[7]

In the 1960s and 1970s, the civil rights movement focused attention on the persistent exclusion of ethnic minorities, mainly African-Americans, from the mainstream of American society. New waves of immigrants from Asia, Latin America, and the Caribbean provoked a renewed public debate. The virtues of assimilation began to be challenged by neo-Marxist structural approaches. Research on immigrant enclaves and middleman minorities turned the original conception of assimilation on its head by describing alternative, and often more effective, modes of incorporation. Self-employment, business formation, and the maintenance of shared cultural understandings outside the American mainstream were shown to enhance and accelerate economic mobility, shielding recent arrivals from the leveling effects of competition in the lower strata of the labor market.

Structural perspectives acknowledged the importance of personal endowments but assigned equal priority to social arrangements that facilitate or impede economic advancement. Work on internal colonialism, ethnic enclaves, and middleman minorities privileged labor market inclusion and exclusion patterns, as well as their effect on social mobility.[8] Persistent inequalities were traced to the social and physical location of immigrant groups and racial and ethnic minorities within the larger society.

In this context, a consensus emerged that the outcome of migration, including the shedding or adoption of ethnic identities, depends on the interaction of three forces: the internal composition of the groups to which immigrants belong, especially in terms of class stratification; their degree of concentration in specific locations; and their mode of reception and incorporation into specific labor market niches.

As the economic base began in the 1960s to shift from manufacturing to services, many cities deteriorated. Paradoxically, some also began to attract professionals linked to lucrative sectors of the new economy, such as international banking and finance, communications, and software design. The presence of a new technocratic class in urban centers invigorated the demand for labor-intensive products and services—ranging from domestic help to restaurants to customized furniture and apparel—creating interstices for the employment of new waves of immigrants, many of them undocumented, from Asia, Latin America, and the Caribbean.

More so than in the past, the fate of immigrants today depends on their particular mode of assimilation into various segments of society. That, in turn, is related to their membership in specific interpersonal networks and their ability to use group identity to gain access to material, social, and political resources.

Writings in the field of economic sociology have reasserted the connection between social factors and economic action. This insight affords avenues to understanding the differentiated outcomes of assimilation. Once an immigrant community emerges in a particular location, it achieves a degree of autonomy from the pressures of the market that serves to reduce the cost and risks of migration and allows for the movement of new immigrants in relatively bounded economic spaces.[9] The concentration of immigrants of similar national origin in specific sites depends to some extent on the nature of labor demand but also on the preexistence of social networks with a common experience, national background, and language.

The importance of social networks as a source of situated knowledge is exemplified by the functioning of the economic enclave. In assembling a remarkable business conglomerate in Miami, Cubans relied on personal contacts within and outside their own group. They avoided discrimination from mainstream financial institutions by obtaining loans to capitalize their firms from banks whose owners and employees were Latin American and, therefore, Spanish-speaking. Beyond their strong feeling of membership in the same community, Cubans benefited from their inclusion in a network characterized by high levels of diversity in terms of social standing. The presence of a critical mass of professionals and entrepreneurs enabled many working-class Cubans to find employment in places characterized by national and cultural affinity. This accelerated their social, economic, and political advancement.

Mexicans have had a different experience. Most of them are of humble origins, and a significant proportion cross the border illegally. Like other new arrivals, they have met a good measure of hostility. Even more important is the absence of government policies facilitating their settlement and the lack of access to high-quality interpersonal resources. The absence of a significant mass of professionals and entrepreneurs among Mexican immigrants has meant that the majority find work in the most exploitative and least protected areas of the labor market. Their confinement in neighborhoods characterized by residential segregation, ineffective schools, and, increasingly, social dismemberment has arrested their social mobility.

The two cases also illustrate ways in which group membership can translate into differential access to vital assets through the deployment of social capital. Social capital has been defined as a process through which individuals use their membership in particular groups to gain access to valuable resources, including information, jobs, and status. In contrast to human capital, it does not presuppose formal education or skills acquired through organized instruction, but originates in shared feelings of social belonging, trust, and reciprocity. The workings of social capital are manifest in such phenomena as workers of a common nationality clustering in the same company, drawn by word of mouth, the flow of valuable commodities without a need for contractual agreements among members of an immigrant community, and cooperative arrangements among immigrant families to reduce survival costs.[10]

As important as social capital is the quality of the resources that can be tapped. Interpersonal networks are distinguished as much by their ability to generate a sense of cohesiveness as by their ability to parlay that cohesiveness into access to good schools or jobs. What distinguishes impoverished from wealthy groups is not a different capacity to use social capital but a varying ability to reach assets of high quality. Similarly, what immigrant children learn about becoming American hinges on what they see around them and the types of contacts they are able to establish. Living quarters, local businesses, places of leisure and entertainment, and, most decisively, schools have a powerful impact on their self-image and their place in American society.[11]

Cuban, Mexican, and Nicaraguan Children: A Profile

Before addressing particular forms of ethnic identity, let us outline the characteristics of Cuban, Mexican, and Nicaraguan immigrants in the United States.[12] Table 6.1 condenses information about school performance, parents' human capital, and children's aspirations among Cubans, Nicaraguans and Mexicans. Cuban children in private schools display high grade point averages and the highest standardized test scores. Mexicans and Nicaraguans lag behind. The performance of Cuban students in private schools dramatically exceeds that of Cubans in public institutions, illustrating the critical effect of social class even within that highly integrated community.

The figures for Mexican children are consistent with their characterization as a highly homogeneous working-class group, as are data on parents' educational achievement, socioeconomic status, and occupational aspirations. Mexicans are the only group with a large proportion of members who expect never to achieve a college education.

The data on Nicaraguans are especially interesting. Although youngsters express high aspirations and display adequate test scores, other indicators suggest that they are experiencing downward mobility. Large numbers of Nicaraguans now living in Miami came from middle-class, urban environments. In moving to the United States during the 1980s, after the ascent of the Sandinista regime, most considered themselves exiles and expected to follow in the Cubans' footsteps. U.S. authorities did not view them as exiles, and many Nicaraguans became deportable aliens struggling for survival in poor Miami neighborhoods. For their children, this experience has translated into elevated high school dropout rates.

Table 6.2 provides information about the friendship networks within the three groups. Regardless of national origin, most children associate with members of their own group, and a large number of their friends are foreign-born. Within that context, Cubans have the highest degree of contact with members of their own group and the lowest proportion of friendships with outsiders. Oddly, Nicaraguans report a higher degree of

Table 6.1. School Performance, Parental Human Capital, and Children's Aspirations

	School Performance				Parental Human Capital					Child's Aspirations			
	GPA[a]	Std Math Test[b]	Std Reading Test[b]	English Index Score[c]	% Father College	% Mother College	Father Occup SEI[d]	Mother Occup SEI[d]	Occupational Aspirations[e]	% Less Than College	% College	% Graduate School
Cuban, private School (N=183)	2.6	80	69	15.3	55	42	50.4	47.3	65.4	3	32	67
Cuban, public School (N=1,044)	2.2	56	45	15.4	24	18	37.5	36.9	62.9	18	37	46
Nicaraguan (N=344)	2.3	55	38	14.8	45	31	39.2	30.5	62.7	21	34	45
Mexican (N=757)	2.2	32	27	13.9	9	5	26.3	24.9	58.3	39	32	29

All column differences between national origin groups significant at the .001 level.

[a] Grade Point Average as reported by school district.

[b] Stanford Achievement Test, 8th edition, percentile score.

[c] Self-rated proficiency in reading, writing, speaking, and understanding English.

[d] Duncan socioeconomic index score, based respectively on father's/mother's current occupation.

[e] Treiman occupational prestige index score for child's desired occupation.

Table 6.2. Friendship Networks

	Number of close friends from abroad			Percentage with friends who are[a]		
	None %	Some %	Many/ Most %	Cuban %	Nicara- guan %	Mexi- can %
Cuban, private school (N=183)	1.1	5.5	93.4	*98.9*	7.3	na
Cuban, public school (N=1044)	2.5	23.2	74.2	*93.8*	29.0	na
Nicaraguan (N=344)	5.1	18.8	76.2	78.1	*79.4*	na
Mexican (N=757)	6.6	44.6	48.8	na	na	*82.9*

All column differences between national-origin groups are significant at the .001 level.

[a] Percentage of those who report having close friends from abroad (i.e., excludes those with none). Numbers in italic represent the right-to-left axis of conationals.

interaction with Cubans than Cubans report with respect to Nicaraguans. This discrepancy is explained by two tendencies: that of Cubans to see themselves as a closed community and that of Nicaraguans to be more permeable to other groups in their environment. Moreover, the relationship is marked by status differences: often Cubans are reluctant to admit they know Nicaraguans, a trend mirrored by Nicaraguans' generalized feelings that Cubans discriminate against them. Overall, Cubans display the lowest degree of porousness of the three groups.

Most revealing is the information summarized in Table 6.3 on perceptions of discrimination and self-identification. Cuban youngsters report the least discrimination—an understandable perception when, as Table 6.2 indicates, the overwhelming majority of their contacts are with members of their own group. Nevertheless, Cuban children in public schools experience higher levels of discrimination from both blacks and whites than those in private schools. In contrast to private institutions, public schools expose children to many ethnic and national groups and are, therefore, less able to shield them from friction, conflict, and the imposition of negative stereotypes.

Nicaraguans see Cubans as a significant source of discrimination. This may be related to a panethnic effect in Miami, where the Hispanic community is diversified internally in terms of national origin, with Cubans occupying a preeminent position and easily identifiable as a source of hostility, particularly toward other Hispanics. On the other hand, the case of Mexicans in San Diego shows that membership in a large coethnic community does not shield children from discrimination. That too may be due to localized factors: Mexicans have become convenient scapegoats for an economic downturn in the early 1990s that followed deep cuts in

Table 6.3. Perceptions of Discrimination

	Percent Who Experience Discrimination	Perceived Source of Discrimination[a]			Percent Residing in U.S. 5–9 years	Percent Born in U.S.
		Anglos	Blacks	Cubans		
Cuban, private school (N=183)	31.7	46.4	28.6	1.8	3.3	91.3
Cuban, public school (N=1044)	39.1	31.6	28.9	3.7	10.1	67.6
Nicaraguan (N=344)	50.6	27.8	22.2	25.0	57.8	7.6
Mexican (N=757)	64.3	42.2	34.4	na	28.4	60.2

All column differences between national origin groups are significant at the .001 level

[a] These figures report the percentage of those who are discriminated against who attribute the bias to each group.

Table 6.4. Socioeconomic Status of National Origin Groups

	Low SEI (%)[a]	Middle SEI (%)[a]	High SEI (%)[a]	% Attend Maj. Black School[b]	% Attend Maj. Latin School[b]	% Attend Maj. Anglo School[b]	% Attend Central City School[c]	% Attend >2/3 Poor School[d]	% Attend 1/3-2/3 Poor School[d]	% Attend <1/3 Poor School[d]
Cuban, private school (N=183)	7.7	49.2	43.1	0	100	0	0	0	0	100
Cuban, public school (N=1044)	25.8	60.1	14.1	2.1	84.2	3.9	26.1	31.1	28.8	40.0
Nicaraguan (N=344)	23.8	65.8	10.4	7.3	79.4	1.5	27.6	39.4	16.3	44.3
Mexican (N=757)	66.9	30.4	2.7	.4	17.7	.4	57.7	51.3	38.0	10.7

All column differences between national origin groups are significant at the .001 level.

[a] Based on score on composite index using father's and mother's occupations, education, and home ownership. The categories correspond to working-class (e.g., busboys, janitors, laborers), middle-class (small business owners, teachers), and upper-middle-class (lawyers, architects, executives).

[b] "Majority" in these three columns means more than 60 percent of students. Note that we cannot distinguish within the Latin group between immigrants and U.S.-born students.

[c] Geographically located within the central city area of Miami and San Diego.

[d] "Poor" here is measured by the proxy variable of the percentage of the student body eligible for federally funded free or subsidized lunch.

military spending. These economic trends contributed to a climate of animosity against Mexican immigrants in California epitomized by the successful campaign for Proposition 187.

Table 6.4 presents selected characteristics of the schools attended by Hispanic children in the sample. The patterns revealed are consistent with the descriptions above. Taken as a whole, Cuban families show a higher degree of class heterogeneity as reflected in the proportions of children receiving free or subsidized lunches, a proxy measure for poverty. Mexican children are located in schools that mirror their position at the lower end of the class hierarchy. Table 6.4 underscores the extent to which schools function as segregative forces, sorting out children in terms of social and physical location.

The Dilemmas of Ethnic Identity

Ethnographic chronicles like the ones that inform this section underscore the vital role of collective identities in the process of assimilation. Even under auspicious conditions, migration is a jarring experience that pushes individuals and groups to acquire new knowledge as they negotiate survival and adjustment. Immigrants learn how they fit within the larger society through the contacts they establish in their new environment. Whether youngsters sink or soar depends on how they see themselves, their families, and their communities. The immigrant condition forces children and their parents to contemplate themselves even as they are being surveyed by others.

It is evening in Little Havana as the Angulo family prepares for dinner in their shabby apartment. (Pseudonyms are used for all the families described here.) Originally from Managua, Nicaragua, Mr. Angulo holds a degree in chemistry and for a time was the manager of a sizable firm in his home country. His wife comes from a family with connections to the military. They arrived in Miami in 1985 when their son, Ariel, was eight and their daughter, Cristina, only two years old. Both think of themselves as exiles but are not recognized as such by the U.S. government. Earnestly, Mr. Angulo explains:

> We came with high hopes escaping the Sandinistas, thinking this was the land of opportunity . . . ready to work and make progress but we were stopped in our tracks. We haven't been able to legalize our situation. Every so often, we get these notices saying we'll be thrown out of the country; it is nerve-wracking. As a result, we haven't been able to move ahead. Look around; this is the only place we've been able to rent since we came [to Miami] . . . I work for an hourly wage without benefits, although I perform the duties of a professional for a pharmaceutical company. They

know they can abuse my condition because I can't go anywhere, no one will hire me!

Mrs. Angulo works as a clerk for a Cuban-owned clinic. She worries that Ariel, who is approaching college age, will not be eligible for financial assistance. She does not expect him to go beyond high school, although she and her husband place a premium on education and have typical middle-class aspirations. As it is, Ariel cannot even apply for a legal summer job because of his undocumented status. He attends a troubled school where he mingles primarily with other Central Americans and African-Americans. Conflict is rampant and academic standards are low. He complains that other students ridicule Nicaraguans. Ariel feels that his parents are too demanding; they do not understand the pressures at school or give him credit for his effort. Even more distressing is the fact that he cannot speak either English or Spanish fluently. Almost seventeen, he shares with his mother a dim view of the future.

Ariel's experience is in stark contrast with that of fifteen-year-old Fernando Gómez, whose family migrated to Miami in 1980 as part of the Mariel boatlift. Originally from Oriente (Manzanillo), Cuba, Fernando's father was employed as a heavy equipment operator and then as a clerk a metallurgical firm prior to his migration to the United States. Since his arrival, he has worked as a mechanic for Dade County. His wife, who was a teacher in Cuba, now provides care for the elderly. Although they hold working-class jobs, the couple's tastes evince higher aspirations. Their home is part of a Cuban-owned residential development that features pathways bordered by russet tiles and lush vegetation, pale exteriors, wrought-iron gates, and roofs of a generic Iberian appearance. The family's living room is embellished with new furnishings.

Proudly, Mr. Gómez states that he has never experienced discrimination; he explains that he is not the kind of man who would ever feel inferior to anyone. He expects Fernando, an even better student than his older brother, to go far. There is no doubt that he will finish college, perhaps work toward an advanced degree. Although Fernando wants to become a police officer like his brother, Mr. Gómez dismisses that idea as a passing whim; he would like his son to work with computers because "that is where the future of the world is."

More than three thousand miles away in San Diego, Carlos Mendoza's home stands next to a boarded-up crack house. Prior to the police raid that shut it down, the Mendoza family had covered their own windows with planks to avoid witnessing what went on across the alley. The neighborhood is an assortment of vacant lots, abandoned buildings, and small homes protected by fences and dogs. Fourteen years ago, the family entered the United States illegally in the trunk of a car. Their goal was to earn enough money to buy a house in their home town in Michoacán, and although they succeeded—and purchased the house in San Diego as well—they laughingly note that somehow they never made it back to Mexico. The family has now achieved legal status under the amnesty program promoted by the 1986 Immigration Reform and Control Act.

For the past ten years, Mr. Mendoza has worked as a busboy in a fancy restaurant that caters to tourists, a position he secured through a Mexican friend. He is a hard-working and modest man who wants his son, Carlos, to study so that he can get a good job, and "be better than me, not for my sake but for his sake and that of his own family." Mrs. Mendoza irons clothes at a Chinese-owned laundry and complains bitterly that her employers are prejudiced toward her and other Mexicans.

Carlos is doing well in school; he was the only boy at Cabrillo Junior High to be elected to the honor society last year. He wants to become an engineer and go back to Mexico. Life in San Diego has been hard on him; the gold chain his parents gave him as a gift was ripped from his neck by neighborhood toughs; his bicycle remains locked up inside the house, for to ride it would be to lose it to the same local bullies. His younger sister, Amelia, is not doing as well in school and dresses like a *chola* (female gang member), although she insists it is only a matter of style. Her parents worry but feel helpless.

The three cases sketched above provide a glimpse into widely dissimilar experiences, but the variations are not arbitrary; they represent the experiences of the groups to which the families belong. Nicaraguans expected to achieve refugee status in the United States but in most cases those hopes were unrealized. Bereft of supports in the receiving environment, these new immigrants are undergoing a rapid process of downward mobility despite the fact that many have middle-class backgrounds. Those of humbler provenance are unable to advance. Especially disturbing is the predicament of children who, confined to immigrant neighborhoods but having spent most of their lives in the United States, can speak neither English nor Spanish with ease. Unable to regularize their immigrant status and facing acute economic need, these youngsters are choosing low-paying jobs over education. With an increasing number of high school dropouts and out-of-wedlock pregnancies, Nicaraguan youngsters appear to be repeating aspects of the African-American experience.[13]

Cubans, in contrast, represent a rare case of accelerated immigrant success. The first large cohorts of Cubans arrived in Miami during the 1960s, prompting the customary response of more established populations: departure to the suburbs. In the beginning, Cubans too were perceived as an undesirable minority. Nevertheless, in comparison with other arrivals they were a highly stratified group that included professionals as well as business entrepreneurs. As a result, many were able to escape the pressures of the labor market through self-employment.[14] This advantage, along with a shared opposition to the Castro regime and assistance from the U.S. government, allowed Cubans to form a cohesive community. Through preexisting social networks, Cubans were able to reconstitute the society they had known in their own country, including a private school system for those who could afford it.

In 1980, the Mariel boatlift jolted Miami with new waves of mostly working-class Cuban immigrants, many of whom were of Afro-Caribbean descent. They too were received with some hostility, and even older Cubans felt ambivalence. Nevertheless, continued support from the U.S. government and the preexisting ethnic enclave allowed the newcomers to adjust rapidly. At present, Mariel refugees exhibit demographic and employment profiles similar to those of other Cubans.

Mexicans represent the longest unbroken migration of major proportions to the United States. Partly as a result of the presence of a significant number of undocumented aliens among them, and partly because of the geographical proximity to their country of origin, many Mexicans do not see moving to the United States as a long-term decision; instead, they consider themselves sojourners guided by an economic motive whose real homes remain south of the border. Such expectations diminish Mexicans' involvement in entrepreneurship and business formation.[15] They also have had an impact upon children's prospects. With little differentiation in terms of social class, Mexicans do not have the power to resist the embattled conditions in their neighborhoods. The preceding section and the short ethnographic accounts above suggest regularities in the relationships among class structure, social capital, and the types of resources available to the members of an immigrant community. Collective identity emerges as both cause and effect from this triangular interaction. Although material circumstances lead to the formation of distinctive identities, these are not a mechanical product; rather, they are autonomous processes that can reinforce or alter behavioral outcomes. Such a generalization helps explain identity trends defining particular groups, but, perhaps more importantly, it also allows for an understanding of the exceptions to those trends. It is in the deviations that individual agency is manifested.

For example, I have described the correlation between strong national identity and rapid socioeconomic mobility among Cuban children. In contrast, the adoption of ethnic and panethnic labels seems to be associated with stagnant or declining mobility among Mexicans and Nicaraguans. Nevertheless, there are departures from the general tendency in all three cases. What explains those variations is the ability of families and youngsters to deploy alternative self-definitions. Cuban children in public schools who identify as Hispanics are more likely to feel discriminated against; they also have lower standardized test scores and lower grade point averages. Conversely, Nicaraguan youngsters who deflect negative stereotypes about their national origin by emphasizing other criteria, such as religious conviction or their immigrant condition, are more likely to overcome the leveling forces that shape the broader group experience. Among Nicaraguans the label "Hispanic" carries a connotation diametrically opposed to the one it has among Cubans, serving to defuse negative national stereotypes by symbolically linking upwardly mobile Nicaraguans to other successful Spanish-speaking groups, most notably—and paradoxically—Cubans. The capacity to choose among alternative identities and use them to gain control of circumstances is a distinctive mark of human agency.

The shape that group identity takes is mediated by pivotal experiences in the life of immigrants. The ethnographic accounts below show that schools, the capacity of parents to retain authority, and perceptions about opportunity determine to a great extent the self-image of immigrant youngsters. At school, children mingle with groups differentiated by their own self-perceptions and the perceptions of external observers. Especially when they equate success with localized power attained through conflict and physical force—as in the case of youth gangs—those groups can exert a strong downward pull upon immigrant children. The paths that lead youngsters toward specific clusters are complex. However, one of the most effective antidotes to downward mobility is a sense of membership in a group with an undamaged collective identity. The Méndez children illustrate that proposition.

But for the fact that they are illegal aliens from Nicaragua, sixteen-year-old Omar Méndez and his younger sister Fátima could not be more attuned to the American dream. They have lived in Miami since they were five and three years old, respectively. They are superb students full of verve and ambition. They attend a school where discipline is strict and teachers can communicate with parents in Spanish. Most decisively, they see themselves as immigrants, an identity that protects them from incorporation into more popular but less motivated groups in school. In Fátima's words: "We're immigrants! We can't afford to just sit around and blow it like others who've been in this country longer and take everything for granted." To maintain her independence, she withdraws from her peers and endures being called a "nerd." She does not mind because her center of gravity lies within her family.

The factors that account for strength in a particular context can lead to failure in a different setting. At seventeen, Camilo Figuera, whose parents are working-class Cubans living in Hialeah, is barely enrolled in high school. He has nothing but disdain for academic achievement. His parents hope he will mature, but he doubts it: "America, America, what is America? The country where the mighty dollar reigns. Sure you can become a professional this or that, but life is short and I want to make the most of it; live fast, live good. That's why I like the rappers, you know, they're not afraid of nothing." Camilo sports long hair, an earring, and baggy jeans. He thinks most Cubans are prigs.

The influence of commercial media and the desires nurtured by the market economy compete with parents' efforts to steer their children in the right direction. María Ceballos, a Cuban mother, despairs about her daughter's interest in material trinkets and her low level of academic motivation: "At Melanie's age," she says, "I was very determined; maybe because I was born in a different country, I wanted to prove that I was as good as real Americans. My daughter was born here and [therefore] she doesn't have the same push."

Similar perceptions are held by Carmen Angulo, Ariel's mother: "[Youngsters] don't go to school to study but to model the latest fashions. They demand shoes that cost [a lot] even when parents can't afford them. It's all competition. If a kid brings a beeper to school, everybody wants one."

Migrants, as noted above, must acquire new knowledge in order to adjust and survive. Because the most important lessons are learned within the family and with friends and contacts established in everyday environments, the knowledge acquired by various immigrant groups varies significantly, as do the ways in which they negotiate life's contingencies. This is critical for the understanding of immigrant children's options. Parents' ability to prevail upon the young depends on the credibility they command on the basis of their own trajectory, the quality and quantity of the resources with which they back up behavioral demands, and the extent to which they can serve as channels and interpreters of information originating elsewhere, such as in the media and at school. Parents lacking credibility, impoverished parents, and parents who are uninformed have difficulty controlling their children's behavior.

Other than finding a job and a place to live, the paramount challenge faced by immigrant parents is how to retain control over their adolescent children in the new environment. Although they speak highly of the United States as a place of opportunity and freedom, immigrants believe that the character of elementary and secondary education is inferior here and the sense of community much diminished in comparison to their countries of origin. In addition, an emphasis on material acquisition competes, often successfully, with their attempts to instill discipline and educational ambition in their offspring. When immigrants belong to social networks characterized by low levels of internal differentiation, and when they confront inhospitable modes of reception their authority over their children is weakened further. According to thirty-nine-year-old Carmen Rivas from Masaya, Nicaragua: "If people . . . study, they can become anything they want, anything! But there is too much freedom in the United States. My son was bumming around with a bunch of friends, like in a gang, you know. He . . . ended up in jail. But why should that surprise me? The quality of education is very poor, and there are all kinds of discipline problems in schools."

Even more telling is the case of fifty-year-old Aura Maldonado, a divorced Nicaraguan who has lived in the United States since 1976. Although she does not speak English, she has always worked in garment factories where everyone else speaks Spanish. She makes a heavy mortgage payment of $900 a month for a rundown home in Little Havana. Her living room is cluttered with bundles of fabric that she receives from a garment contractor. Her grandson, recently arrived from Masaya, is already sewing T-shirts in the covered porch.

Mrs. Maldonado, who says she believes in education as the road to success, worries most about her daughter, Julliette, who is planning to marry at seventeen. There is little hope she will ever finish high school. Unknown to her mother is the fact that Julliette is already three months pregnant. All but one of Mrs. Maldonado's five children have problems ranging from incarceration for attempted theft to out-of-wedlock motherhood. Despite her search for better alternatives, she feels like a failure. Julliette has similar feelings. She admits that marriage is her chance "to get away." She has worked long shifts at a fast food restaurant, where she earns $4.25 an hour, since she was sixteen and resents the fact that her mother expects her to use all her earnings to help support the family. In Spanish she explains: "I don't mind giving something because I see the need, but I can't understand why she wants all my money. . . . That means I have to work longer hours to get some money for myself and, so, what does she mean when she says I should stay in school? The truth is she wants me to work and bring more money home."

The contrast between the perceptions of mother and daughter is striking. Mrs. Maldonado believes that she has always encouraged her daughter to study and achieve, but her credibility is undermined by the discrepancy between normative values and the requirements of a precarious economic situation. Julliette's sense of identity and her sense of possibility are framed by that mixed message.

Her decision to have a baby is related to a belief that, having worked to support her family since she was sixteen and having known her boyfriend for even longer, it is time for her to be recognized as an adult. Such ideas are common among impoverished adolescents, as reflected, most dramatically, in the experience of African-American girls in urban ghettos. Believing, often correctly, that schools in their neighborhoods will not provide them with skills that can be parlayed into good jobs, many youngsters turn to their bodies in search of feelings of empowerment. Making a substantial contribution to the support of a family and having a child lead, almost inevitably, to the abandonment of educational aspirations among adolescents of both sexes.

In the case of Nicaraguans and Mexicans, an undocumented status further debilitates parents' authority and children's commitment to school. Even youngsters with high ambitions have felt tempted to go to work to assist their families. Such is the case for fifteen-year-old Omar Lacayo, who applied for legal residency in order to qualify for a summer job and save for college. His application was denied. Although he is an excellent student who would like to become a psychologist, Omar thinks about dropping out of school "a lot, because . . . I feel guilty that my parents have to struggle so much; if I got a job [even an illegal one], I could help them. For us Nicaraguans in the United States, education is but a dream."

In part because of their irregular status, many Nicaraguan and Mexican families end up living in areas where resources are costly but of reduced quality. Aura Maldonado is paying an exorbitant mortgage for a dilapidated home, while working-class Cubans pay less for more attractive properties in modern residential developments. This contrast signals the importance of social and physical locations as factors that delimit options. In migrating, individuals rely on relatives, friends, or acquaintances already concentrated in points of destination; they gravitate toward populations with whom they share common traits. Although these areas may have disadvantages, immigrants tend to remain there because they can gain access to a home without providing references or a security deposit. Lack of English fluency or an undocumented status further isolates many new arrivals, who end up paying more in the long run for services, food, and shelter.

English proficiency, legal residency, and a home in a good neighborhood neutralize the effect of preponderant trends even among the most vulnerable groups. Harold Tijerino and his family are Nicaraguan, but they enjoy legal status. They live in Miami's Coral Park, a middle-class neighborhood. Harold's father has a bachelor's degree from the University of Managua and works in the import–export department of a cruise company. The Tijerinos share a three-bedroom home with other relatives, with whom they pool earnings. They make a smaller mortgage payment than Aura Maldonado for a property of superior quality. Mr. Tijerino is very satisfied with his son's school; he has not had any problems controlling his children and expects Harold to complete college. His perceptions are on a par with those of Cubans living in similar circumstances.

In answering questions about who they are, immigrants resort to antitheses, defining other groups in terms opposed to the ones they use to define themselves. Others are generally symbolized by the casualties of earlier migrations, especially inner-city blacks. Typically, immigrants see blacks as the victims of their own individual and collective liabilities. Martín López, a Mexican father, explains: "Blacks in this country . . . don't want to work; [they] feel very American; they know government has to support every child they breed. [As immigrants] we can't afford to slacken the pace; we have to work hard."

For working-class Cubans, the problem of identity is equally complex, but for different reasons. As members of a successful group, many resent being melded into the broader Hispanic classification. Such is the case with Doris Delsol, an assertive divorcee who lives on welfare because of a disabling affliction. Although her daughter, Elizabeth, experienced some early setbacks in grade school, Mrs. Delsol doggedly sought to uplift her. "We Cubans are not used to failure," she explained. She does not like being called Hispanic: "We all speak [Spanish] but there are differences. [Cubans] always had self-respect, a sense of cleanliness and duty towards children, a work ethic. Miami used to be a clean city until the Nicaraguans came and covered everything with graffiti." As for American blacks, Mrs. Delsol thinks they are adversarial to all kinds of people, disruptive, prone to ruin their homes, and lazy. In her view, both Nicaraguans and blacks evince attitudes opposite to those of Cubans.

Ironically, many Nicaraguans think of themselves as Hispanics precisely because they hold perceptions similar to those voiced by Mrs. Delsol and experience a strong dissociative push away from their own national group. Sixteen-year-old Elsie Rivas avoids discrimination by shifting between a Hispanic and a Nicaraguan self-definition at school and at the supermarket where she works. She does not like the way Nicaraguans speak: "They are vulgar, ignorant. . . . When I am with my Cuban friends I can speak to them normally, but some Nicaraguans make me feel ashamed and I am tempted to deny my nationality; they make all of us look bad because of the way they express themselves, with all the bad words and the cussing." Like the majority of immigrant children, Elsie's younger sister, Alicia, does not care for those distinctions. She feels Nicaraguan-American:"My parents came from Nicaragua and I like the food, but I am really American, more American than those born in this country; here is where I grew up and here is where I am going to stay."

Mexicans are particularly sensitive to the stigma accumulated over several generations. In addition to an assortment of degrading terms used by the larger society, Mexicans in the United States have coined designations such as "*cholo*," "Chicano," and "Mexican-American." How individuals define themselves depends on the context. Miguel Hernández, an illegal Mexican alien who has been in San Diego since 1980, explains that he and his wife define themselves "depending on "who we are talking to. If we are talking to American people and they don't know the difference, we say 'Latinos'; that's easier for them and we avoid hassles." Miguel consciously avoids being labeled a "Chicano" because "it's a slang word for lower-class types who don't know who they are; they don't want to be Mexicans, but they don't want to just be American; they don't even speak English but they don't know Spanish either [and they] fight for and about everything."

Their son, Alberto, sees the world differently:

> No matter how you cut it, we're Chicano with a history of exploitation and abuse in this country. *Teníamos una historia distinta* [we had a different history] in Mexico *pero* [but] here *las cosas no son iguales* [things are not the same]. You can say that we're too defensive, that we're walking around with a chip on our shoulder, but maybe it's just that we know who we are: Chicanos who want to recover *el respeto perdido* [the lost respect].

As the excerpts above suggest, the perceptions of immigrants and their children about themselves and other groups are not always accurate. However, what matters is that, as social constructions, those perceptions are an integral part of a process of segmented assimilation that eventually will yield what Robert Bellah calls communities of memory.[16] In their journey, the immigrant children of today are already forging tomorrow's ethnic identities. Contact, friction, negotiation, and their eventual incorporation into distinct sectors of the larger society will depend, in the final analysis, upon the insertion of immigrant children into various niches of the restructured economy. Collective self-definitions will improve or worsen depending upon the structure of opportunity.

Conclusion

In exploring some of the underpinnings of ethnic identity among Mexicans, Cubans, and Nicaraguans, I have argued that group self-definition is part and parcel of a process of segmented assimilation. Although objective factors such as class structure, social capital, and resources define the experience of immigrant communities, the identities immigrants forge serve to reinforce or change that character.

Like other groups, immigrants define themselves in comparison to other groups and through repeated interaction with them in actual and symbolic fields. The opportunity structure interacts with individuals' and groups' perceptions of themselves and others. A hopeful self-image is, paradoxically, often bolstered by negative definitions of other migrant groups whose children and grandchildren have experienced arrested mobility.

Damaged or buoyant group identities do not emerge in a vacuum; they are mediated by such mechanisms as schools, parents' ability to shield their children from the leveling pressures exerted by institutions, and the

broader market economy. How youngsters define themselves often depends on whether their parents have waged successful battles in resisting
those pressures.

Above all, I stress the fluid nature of group identity. Terms like
"Hispanic" can either impose or deflect stigma, depending on circumstances. For recently arrived Mexicans, "Chicano" has a distinctly negative connotation, but for new generations of Mexicans growing up poor
in the United States, the same term can salvage honor by allusion to an
ennobling history. In the reflux of hope and despair, defensiveness and
compliance, resistance and accommodation, group identity emerges both
as the imprint of structural factors impervious to individual control and
as the manifestation of human agency fighting against those structures.

Chapter 7

The Economic Development of *El Barrio*

Edwin Meléndez

Few themes have attracted as much intellectual interest during the past two decades as the global economy. The initial research impetus came largely from a need to understand changing trade, production, and investment patterns in international markets and the repercussions of these changes for national economies. The oil shortage of the early 1970s marked a turning point for macroeconomic dynamics in the United States and other industrialized and developing countries. Subsequently, much attention was given to the dismantling of welfare states and privatization, increased inequality, and migration flows. As many authors in this volume observe, these changes had tremendous consequences for the Latino population in the United States. Latino communities, in turn, have become active participants in subsequent processes of economic development. Recent national policy debates have centered on topics such as the North American Free Trade Agreement (NAFTA), immigration and welfare reform, persistent poverty and income inequality, and the growing disparities between cities and suburban areas. Understanding conditions facing Latino populations is central to the formulation and implementation of public policies in these areas.

Surprisingly little attention has been paid to the effects on ethnic communities of the restructuring of national economies and the globalization of production and labor markets. For Latinos, this discussion is informed by a somewhat disparate literature encompassing the adaptation and assimilation of immigrant populations and the role that social networks play for Latino organizations; persistent poverty and the increasing isolation of the poor; and the prominent role that certain large cities have played in the development of the global economy. While it is not possible to summarize such a diverse body of work in this chapter, it is important to emphasize that *el barrio* is a key conceptual category.

In this chapter, *el barrio* refers to an urban neighborhood or group of neighborhoods in which Latinos are the predominant population. The fabric of these communities is made up of ethnic networks, businesses, churches, civic organizations, and other social institutions.[1] An examination of the literature suggests several lessons that are particularly relevant here. First, the heterogeneity of the Latino population in terms of coun-try of origin and history of incorporation into U.S. society produces a diversity of experiences regarding barrio formation and economic devel-opment. I will focus on the experience of Mexicans, Cubans, and Puerto Ricans as a way of illustrating these contrasting patterns. Second, the institutional adaptation of Latinos has been influenced largely by their own agency. In this regard, numerous examples of "best practice" suggest that neighborhood groups can be effective in influencing Latinos' eco-nomic adaptation and success. And, finally, ethnicity can play a key role in our understanding of community economic development and in the de-sign of successful community strategies and public policy.

What are the implications of these general lessons about the Latino experience in economic development for the formulation of public policy? My objective here is to present an alternative, community-based strategy for promoting the economic development of *el barrio*. I argue that the economic development of poverty-stricken areas depends on identifying community assets, building their capacity, and strengthening the links from this web of organizations and individuals to the mainstream econ-omy. The relevant group of organizations and actors includes the small business sector and those who link residents to employment, create hous-ing, or engage in other capacity-building and networking activities in the community. These groups have generated numerous successful strategies, and I give examples of best practice to illustrate how community action and public policy can effectively address specific problems in community economic development.

Community economic development, in this context, refers to the pro-cess whereby local actors stimulate and promote spatially based economic activity. Obviously, this is a broad definition that includes a vast array of activities from job creation to physical infrastructure development. Here I focus on such key areas as community development corporations (CDCs), small business development, and employment and training. Within these areas, numerous organizations and programs can serve as models for the design of successful community strategies and public policy intended to foster the development of economically distressed neighborhoods. The ex-amples presented here are representative of well-designed popular responses to the broader problems of economic restructuring and the decline of the economic base of neighborhoods.[2]

We know from research and direct experience that the poor and others who live in the inner city have developed organizations and social networks that allow them to cope with daily problems and survive harsh economic times. These networks provide information and contacts related to employment as well as services otherwise unavailable to the poor. Frequently, these networks are built along racial and ethnic lines. Latinos, in particular, have developed their own set of institutions and mechanisms of solidarity. Understanding the ethnic basis of solidarity is essential to unraveling the economic problems of the inner city.

In the following sections, I first provide a conceptual framework for the formulation of policy and community strategies. I argue that a community development strategy for Latino barrios should begin by identifying the assets that constitute the neighborhood's social capital. Attracting external resources and building economic capacity at the neighborhood level can only occur within this context. Then I use the social capital framework to assess community strategies in the areas of small business development, CDCs, and employment and training. Best-practice cases illustrate the application of the social capital framework to the development of an economic revitalization agenda for the barrio.

In the final section I draw some conclusions. Perhaps the most important is that the formulation of successful policy strategies (that is, state responses to the problems of the inner city) must begin with a clear view of the indigenous resources and the economic priorities developed by neighborhood residents themselves. If this proposition is accepted, the now-contentious process of policy formulation and program development becomes strikingly simple, a matter of supporting the economic development agenda of the residents and organizations in the barrio.

Social Capital, Community Organizations, and Economic Development

Latino communities throughout the United States have developed a broad array of strategies and resources to cope with the effects of globalization, increased inequality, and poverty. A vast literature documents immigrant communities' neighborhood-based networks providing support for families, job information, and other resources.[3] Small businesses in the community supply consumer services and credit to the poor, and many merchants provide leadership.[4] Similarly, economic development corporations, service-providing agencies, and other nonprofit organizations attract government and private resources to the area and provide an important institutional base for the community. What these institutions and processes have in common is that they connect people to jobs and financing, attract government services to the area, and provide access for residents to resources and opportunities outside their neighborhood. Where outsiders see disorganization and disconnection, residents and community leaders recognize valuable social assets and access to social resources for economic survival.

The most important lessons from our research on poverty are that it is largely the result of structural factors, such as joblessness associated with economic restructuring, and is perpetuated by the lack of connections between growing sectors of the economy and residents and businesses in areas with a high concentration of the poor.[5] Because of the social isolation of poor communities, neighborhood networks work better for some things, such as providing support among families,[6] than for others, such as connecting residents to business opportunities or well-paying jobs.[7] Small businesses in the community lack the financial resources and market opportunities to grow beyond small-scale operations and achieve long-term stability; they can provide only limited jobs to community residents. Similarly, funding and political considerations limit the role community-based organizations (CBOs) and CDCs can play in revitalizing urban economies. Despite such limitations, migrant networks, small businesses, CDCs, and CBOs constitute the foundation for revitalizing the barrios. These assets serve as catalysts for institutional development within neighborhoods and make the fundamental connections to external organizations and resources.

Recognizing the key role that community institutions play in mediating the impact of globalization, poverty, and increased inequality has this important implication: the economic revitalization of areas with a high concentration of the poor requires strengthening and developing the neighborhood institutions that mediate residents' access to jobs, services, and financial resources. Community strategies and public policy should promote the development of community intermediaries as an endogenous process—one that takes place within the barrio and is influenced by those most affected by urban economic transformations. In this context, community economic development is the process whereby individuals and organizations develop the web of social relations that gives them access to economic resources, connecting residents to employment in regional labor markets, mobilizing public resources and services, and attracting investment and other financial resources to the neighborhood or local area economy. The key issue thus becomes how to develop strategies that connect low-income neighborhood residents to good jobs, promote the commercial revitalization and industrial development of the area, and strengthen the capacity of community-based organizations and other intermediaries promoting economic development and providing social services to residents.

Like Robert Putnam, I believe that "building social capital," or strengthening community organizations located in and serving residents of the barrio, is the guiding principle for the formulation of specific community economic development strategies and public policies that respond to and strengthen such strategies.[8] Putnam defines "social capital" as all those features of social organization, such as networks, norms, and trust, which facilitate coordination and cooperation among residents in a community for their mutual benefit. Social capital enhances the benefits of investments in physical and human capital. Space has a lot to do with the development of relations among individuals and groups, particularly in low-income areas, where location overdetermines access to school, employment opportunities, and other formal and informal support systems. For social networks to be effective, they must complement an existing endowment of capital and labor resources and provide access to a larger set of opportunities.[9] In fact, a neighborhood's endowment of social capital markedly differentiates the quality of life and social organization of areas with a high concentration of poverty, often referred to as underclass areas, from those in low-poverty areas.[10]

A clear idea of community priorities is also essential. The recommendations of Latino policy centers and the activities embraced by Latino community organizations all point to employment and training, small business and industry, housing, and community services and planning as the main elements of an economic development strategy for the barrios.[11] In each of these areas, the test for public policy is whether or not the resulting programs and services enhance the economic opportunities of residents and organizations in a targeted area. This judgment requires the community to identify good programs and organizations, learn about best practices, and replicate effective programs.

Once the community economic development agenda is determined, several players become instrumental in its implementation. To begin with, residents play a critical role. Effectiveness usually depends not only on the soundness of the chosen strategy, but also on the commitment and enthusiasm of participants. Small business support programs require the involvement of local entrepreneurs, employment training depends on the efforts of unemployed workers, and so on. Elected and appointed Latino officials (and non-Latino officials with a large Latino electoral base) are also important players in barrio economic development. Politicians' careers are built on promoting their constituents' access to state and private resources. Given diminishing state and city resources and increasing competition for program funding, the incorporation and participation of political leaders in the community's economic agenda is necessary to attract external resources. Advocacy groups, service providers, religious organizations, CDCs, and other community organizations and leaders have the responsibility to develop, implement, or support economic development programs. These are the actors who organize and mobilize the community around a common understanding of needs and ways to satisfy them. Equally important in promoting linkages to the mainstream economy are small businesses and professional and technical workers in the private sector.

Identifying the range of actors engaged in community economic development may seem beside the point to those engaged in the practical aspects of policy and program development. But it is imperative, since the need for broad representation is often ignored or forgotten when local coalitions on economic development are being established. Each of these actors has a primary economic activity that largely determines its social interactions and associations. The challenge to those engaged in economic development is to overcome the barriers of daily routine and develop links with practitioners outside their primary activities. These links generally are established within categories (such as small business, housing, employment, and training) or within a particular neighborhood. Just as important are the links built with economic institutions outside the barrio. Bennett Harrison credits these kinds of networks with the greatest success in promoting employment and business opportunities for community residents.[12]

The conceptual basis for community mobilization responds to the relationships, both internal and external, that community residents are able to establish. Latino communities share a history of migration, cultural solidarity, common language, class situation, and residential spaces. In this context, ethnicity becomes the basis for political mobilization and economic empowerment.[13] For Latinos, *el barrio* represents not only the spatial dimension of ethnic identity but also the shared social reality of marginal work and poverty, lack of access to public resources and services, and racial prejudice. While there are differences between Mexican and Puerto Rican barrios, discrimination and the impact of public policies such as the Immigration Reform and Control Act (IRCA), English-only campaigns, and Proposition 187 create the foundation for a panethnic identity and solidarity unique to Latinos in the United States.

Ethnic identity forms the basis not only for the political mobilization of the community but also for its economic empowerment. As noted above, one of the keys to the economic development of *el barrio* is strengthening community organizations and programs, the foundation of the community's social capital. These organizations have been built upon the solidarity networks developed by Mexicans, Puerto Ricans, Cubans, and other Latinos as they migrated to the United States.[14] For Puerto Rican barrios in Massachusetts, economic success depends not only on the community's institutional makeup but also on these organizations' ability to establish links to employers, develop political coalitions, and initiate relations with other external forces.[15] The objectives of developing a community base and seeking closer external relations need not be contradictory; they are, in fact, related. A strong community base permits coalition building with other ethnic and racial groups. Conversely, coalitions without a strong ethnic base may produce an economic development agenda that is not fully responsive to Latino concerns and diverts resources from neighborhood institutional development.

If poverty is associated with social isolation and disconnection from economic sectors experiencing growth or providing better-paid and more stable jobs, then the economic development of *el barrio* depends on breaking social isolation and forging connections to employers, financial institutions, and other resources in the private and public sectors outside the community.[16] Fortunately, agents for economic change already exist in our communities. These are individuals and organizations that have for many years worked to develop programs, build institutional capacity, nurture leadership, and promote connections to government agencies and the private sector. We have a wealth of organizations and programs from which we can learn valuable lessons, allowing us to promote the adoption of best practices and the replication of programs that work.

The Ethnic Enclave

The study of economic development in Latino communities offers an opportunity to examine how race and ethnicity can contribute to more effective community strategies and public policy. Since poverty in urban centers is highly concentrated in areas populated by ethnic and racial minorities, ethnic and racial solidarity can have an important impact on economic development. Ethnic and racial identity, solidarity, and mobilization are key determinants of social and neighborhood organization, often serving as a form of social capital.[17] New strategies that provide mechanisms linking expanding industries and businesses to the job and business readiness of ethnic and racial minorities may help close the gap between economic growth and equity without resorting to race-specific policies. Now that race-conscious policies are out of fashion, the enhancement of such business linkages can play an important redistributive role.

In many ways, the Latino experience in economic development and public policy illustrates the dichotomy between business-oriented programs and programs directed at poverty alleviation. Indeed, most of the academic literature on this topic focuses on the enclave economy and the adaptation of Cuban immigrants. Less documentation exists for housing access, the formation and impact of CDCs, links between skills development programs and expanding industrial sectors, or other relevant policy areas. The Cuban enclave of Miami is a well-documented example of an ethnic economy. Like the Chinese restaurant and garment businesses of New York City and the Korean import and distribution businesses of Los Angeles, the Cuban ethnic-enclave economy demonstrates how ethnic solidarity is translated into opportunities for economic advancement.[18]

Alejandro Portes and colleagues have defined the ethnic enclave as an economic formation "characterized by the spatial concentration of immigrants who organize a variety of enterprises to serve their own ethnic market and the general population."[19] This type of economy has two critical and interrelated characteristics. First, the ethnic enclave has a large number of interconnected small or medium-sized businesses that provide employment opportunities to a growing and continuous flow of immigrants. Between 1967 and 1976, for example, Cuban-owned businesses in Miami grew from fewer than one thousand to more than eight thousand,[20] concentrated in the textile, leather, furniture, cigar, construction, and finance industries. Cubans owned 40 percent of construction firms, 30 percent of local banks, and most restaurants, supermarkets, clinics, and other service businesses in the city of Miami.[21]

A high density of businesses owned by individuals with the same ethnicity in a particular industry and region offers "economies of agglomeration." Business contacts and information, access to capital, and sharing of other resources give the ethnic entrepreneur an advantage over native competitors in the area. And, as Roger Waldinger has pointed out, the benefits of ethnic solidarity embedded in business networks and associations are reaped whether businesses are heavily concentrated in one area (as in the Cuban or Chinese cases) or spread out (as in the Korean case).[22] Thus, from an economic development policy perspective, ethnic economies could be regarded as a special case for business and industry support programs.

A second characteristic of the ethnic enclave is the continuous influx of immigrants who work and purchase ethnic goods in the area.[23] Jobs in ethnic-owned businesses offer unique employment opportunities for immigrants with limited English skills and restricted access to the social networks that would facilitate their adaptation to a new social environment. Indeed, immigrants in this protected labor market may actually have better earnings and employment outcomes than immigrants with similar characteristics working outside the enclave economy. Although immigrants must work long hours for many years before they can seek employment outside ethnic-owned businesses or start their own businesses, many immigrants eventually are able to do so. They start their own businesses or adapt their skills and education to new labor market requirements and eventually move to better employment outside the enclave.

The success of Cuban-owned businesses in Miami is explained by the interaction of several factors. Obviously, immigrants' social networks and ethnic solidarity played a critical role. According to Alejandro Portes and Alex Stepick, access to start-up capital through "character loans" was common among Cuban entrepreneurs.[24] But the Federal Cuban Refugee Program also provided tremendous assistance to Cuban immigrants in the form of business and student loans, retraining for new professional and educational opportunities, and welfare and housing assistance. Silvia Pedraza-Bailey estimates that the U.S. government spent nearly $1 billion assisting Cubans over a short period.[25] The high educational and entrepreneurial level of the first waves of political refugees from Cuba was another factor.

Despite the hardship of employment in the secondary labor market, the enclave economy offered Cubans the opportunity for upward social mobility and political advancement. Today, Miami is largely a Cuban city. To a certain degree, Anglos have changed their negative view of Cuban immigrants and have come to accept their cultural and economic contributions. But Miami is also a global city where many immigrants from Latin America settle. The city thus has become the commercial gateway to Latin American countries.

There is nothing comparable to the Cuban experience among Mexicans and Puerto Ricans (the two largest Latino groups in the United States) or among other recent immigrant groups from Latin America. Although there are many Mexican-owned businesses in the Southwest[26] and Puerto Rican-owned businesses in New York, Chicago, and other northeastern cities, Mexicans and Puerto Ricans do not have a geographically concentrated business or self-employed class like that of the Cubans in Miami. Frank Fratoe studied business participation rates among ethnic groups, finding a national average of 48.9 per thousand. The lowest rates were found among Mexicans (18.6), Dominicans (14.6), and Puerto Ricans (10.6).[27] On the other hand, Mexicans and Puerto Ricans participate more prominently than other Latino groups in antipoverty programs and have developed a broad institutional base of CDCs and CBOs that conduct a variety of housing, job training, and educational programs.

Few studies document and explain these differences. The many studies of other ethnic groups suggest that groups with more class and ethnic resources tend to outperform groups with fewer resources.[28] Cubans have a higher share of professionals and managers and higher educational levels and access to capital than other groups.[29] However, the experience of the African-American community suggests that other factors might also be at work. Roger Waldinger and Howard Aldrich attribute the underdevelopment of black-owned businesses to the lack of a business tradition or protected market, a fragmented social structure, and discrimination.[30] These are all important factors to consider when explaining differences in business formation among ethnic and racial groups.

The evidence on public programs to assist minority-owned businesses points to the rigidity of the above-mentioned barriers. Most state and city set-aside programs are unsuccessful because minority-owned businesses remain undercapitalized and unable to compete in the open market. Equal opportunity loans, perhaps the most important minority business assistance program, have historically high rates of delinquency.[31] Public policy regarding small business assistance for disadvantaged urban communities seems to face a critical dilemma: if public assistance focuses on the most disadvantaged, high rates of default and failure should be expected; if assistance is directed to more established firms, it has less of an impact on targeted populations.

Clearly, conventional small business development programs are insufficient to promote economic development in distressed minority communities. The development of the Cuban enclave economy in Miami was made feasible by a combination of factors (including a geopolitical context that rationalized support for Cuban immigrants) that are unlikely to be replicated. Small businesses alone are unlikely to produce the volume of employment and capital necessary for sustained economic development in distressed urban communities. Nonetheless, the enclave economy is a valuable demonstration of the importance of ethnic solidarity for economic development, particularly as it pertains to disadvantaged populations.

Although markedly different from the Cuban enclave experience, the Mexican and Puerto Rican experiences in small business and neighborhood revitalization illustrate the potential of best-practice programs to overcome the public policy dilemma posed by traditional business assistance programs in minority communities. What these strategies have in common are the dual objectives of building effective capacity within Latino organizations, based upon ethnic identity and solidarity, and deploying this organizational capacity to link neighborhood residents to the larger economy. These two objectives are clearly interrelated: the development of ethnic leadership ultimately facilitates access to jobs and financial and other resources.

Small Business Development

Ever since President Nixon introduced the idea of "black" capitalism as a solution to the problems of the inner city, many progressive policy-makers have seen small business development as a dubious strategy. They contend that small businesses create few jobs at the community level and have only a limited impact on earnings and income. Regardless of the merits of this, it is inappropriate to evaluate the impact of small businesses exclusively in terms of job generation and income. Small businesses have many important spillover effects in neighborhoods, such as direct services and credit to the poor.[32] They also provide a social space where people connect to each other and find information about job and business opportunities. Small business owners often provide leadership in obtaining services from city hall and police headquarters. Ultimately, small businesses are among the few stable economic activities in the barrio.[33] If nothing else, they provide ethnic amenities and maintain the Latino character of the neighborhood.

The term "small businesses" covers a diverse set of economic organizations, each with a different role in the community and a different impact on the local economy. The self-employed are at one end of the spectrum. The typical self-employed person is a small merchant or professional who may or may not employ others. Examples range from the recent immigrant selling *pupusas* (a pancake-like Salvadorean dish) on a street corner to the most successful business consultant, and earnings are similarly varied. Many start-up businesses fall into the self-employment category; more often than not, these are workers who have not secured long-term employment in the formal economy. In many ways, this category is similar to that of the microenterprise.

"Microenterprise" assumes the employment of at least a few workers, but for the majority of microenterprises in the informal economy, the workers are family members. In barrios, many of those operating microenterprises had previous experience in Latin America and have simply transposed the same business practices to their new home. Most self-employed people and microentrepreneurs serve a primarily Latino clientele and are largely confined to the barrio.

Bodegueros (mom-and-pop grocery stores) and other retail establishments share many characteristics with the self-employed and microentrepreneurs, but they are forced to comply with more state and city regulations. Typically, they use a rudimentary accounting system to pay for supplies and keep track of expenses. Storefront operations sometimes employ local residents and are concerned about the services provided to the commercial strip by the local government, particularly sanitation and police surveillance. Large restaurant, bakery, and supermarket owners usually occupy positions of leadership because of the size of their operations and their visibility in the community. In contrast to most other small businesses, these merchants are anchored in the community, both spatially and in terms of their consumer base.

Small businesses that are certified to conduct business with the state or compete in the marketplace for contracts are at the upper end of the small business spectrum. Here, too, one finds great variation among firms in terms of size, working capital, capacity, bonding, and insurance capability. Latino firms in this category are numerous in large cities where Latinos have been present for several generations, particularly where an enclave economy has developed. In areas where Latinos have arrived in the past decade, only a few firms have become important players in the local economy.

Each of these small business sectors has very different technical and financial assistance needs, and each can play a specific role in the economic development of the barrio. The most salient characteristic of Latino small businesses in urban areas is their isolation from the mainstream economy. Only in a few places like Miami, Los Angeles, and New York can one talk about relatively large Latino businesses that employ more than a hundred workers. For all practical purposes, when discussing small business policies and the development of programs, we are talking about capital and equity formation in Latino neighborhoods and the development of an entrepreneurial class whose economic ties are located within the barrio. These small business owners are an important element of the potential community leadership.

Given the diversity of needs implicit in the above categorization, what kinds of organizations and programs can best serve Latino businesses? The Regional Alliance for Small Contractors in New York and New Jersey, a multiethnic organization created by the Port Authority of New York, is extremely effective in promoting linkages of minority-owned businesses to corporate America.[34] Latinos make up only 23 percent of the small businesses within the alliance, although the overwhelming majority of its members are enterprises owned by minorities or women. Whether minority-based or not, social networks among the participants play a critical role in the success of the program. The alliance has grown from twelve to sixty-two corporate partners since its inception in 1989, and currently serves more than nine hundred firms. It provides a variety of technical, educational, and financial services, with the objective of building the capacity of the small firms that participate.

The alliance benefits the small contractor by facilitating access to regular subcontracting for large construction projects and benefits the major construction companies by providing access to a reliable pool of subcontractors. The program is based on mutually beneficial business transactions and not on set-asides, although it directly benefits the targeted ethnic business community. The main objective is to improve the quality of subcontractors available for major development projects and connect small businesses to mainstream economic actors. Technical assistance to participating businesses, which builds capacity in the Latino community, is provided without the public perception that the alliance is a poverty-alleviation program. Ultimately, the alliance provides a unique mechanism to link Latino entrepreneurs to the key actors in the construction industry and the regional economy as a whole.

In addition to small businesses in the private sector, there are income-generating small businesses operated by worker cooperatives and non-profit organizations. These relatively recent job creation initiatives stem from frustration with funding sources and the limited access of community residents to jobs. Community enterprises are intended both to create jobs and to provide capital formation in the neighborhood. They are hybrids incorporating aspects of the private sector (selling goods and services and accumulating capital) and the community (collective ownership and some reliance on volunteer work).

A recent study conducted in Puerto Rico illustrates the potential of these community-owned businesses, which are found across the United

States.[35] A furniture factory in the town of Coamo and a juice-processing plant in San Lorenzo are two good examples of community enterprises. Formally, their legal structure is that of a nonprofit corporation. In actuality, they operate like private firms selling their products in the marketplace. In both cases, the projects were initiated to create employment for local residents. The furniture factory, Bellas Artes Metalarte, began as a training program for unemployed youth run by the local parish. Today, it is the largest furniture manufacturer in Puerto Rico, employing about eighty workers. The juice-processing plant, Organización de Agricultores del Barrio Espino, created a pulp-processing plant to serve the needs of passion fruit producers when the only processing plant on the island closed down. Eventually, the group built a modern plant that employs about twenty workers and serves close to seventy local farmers.

In studying these organizations, we found a new type of social entrepreneur—one possessing a rare combination of business know-how and social consciousness. These are people who could (and in some cases did) succeed in the private sector or in their own businesses, but chose instead to participate in social projects. Social entrepreneurs are rare. Typically, community leaders have a great deal of enthusiasm but are short on business skills, while entrepreneurs with business know-how have no particular interest in social causes. In any case, the expertise of these socially conscious business leaders was instrumental in establishing the community enterprise and developing a market strategy. It is not coincidental that these projects, like most successful income-generating projects in Latin America, are established in competitive markets and in industries that satisfy basic needs. Usually competitive market conditions imply relatively easy access to markets and economies of scale, thereby avoiding price or other barriers that impede entry into the market. However, social entrepreneurs' most important contribution is to use their business experience to forge a vision of what is possible through community action.

The most interesting characteristics of such community enterprises are directly related to the central theme of this chapter: that community enterprises mobilize community residents and workers and promote networks that cross traditional boundaries. In Spanish, the word *autogestión* implies some notion of collectivity and self-help, a collective effort to build economic empowerment. *Autogestión* was instrumental in the success of these community enterprises. Volunteer work by residents and technical personnel substituted for operating capital in the initial stages of the business. For barrios with low capital formation, this is a particularly relevant finding. *Autogestión* also can be instrumental in attracting resources to the barrio. Foundations and government officials like to be associated with projects that are regarded highly in the community, just as brand name products benefit from association with sports or entertainment celebrities with a positive public image. Having a base in the community facilitates the development of networks and the ability to gain financial support beyond the boundaries of the barrio. The most successful projects are able to move across boundaries and build networks based on the success achieved in organizing community resources.

These examples of successful community-based small business development strategies are instructive in several ways. First, it is apparent that no one program can serve the diverse needs of the small business community. The Regional Alliance is an intermediary organization that facilitates access to subcontracting for large construction firms and development organizations. Businesses must have attained a certain capacity in order to benefit from the program. The program helps entrepreneurs build that capacity and matches them to business opportunities. The community-owned businesses identified job creation as the most important community objective, and their main goal was to provide jobs for residents of a given area or serve the needs of local farmers. In each case, the program was developed to respond to local needs and targeted a particular segment of the small business community. Another important lesson is that these projects are based on a perceived common interest and market-based business transactions. The Regional Alliance is successful because large companies find it beneficial to subcontract with minority-owned businesses. The projects in Puerto Rico were helped by foundation and public subsidies but survived because they put a competitive product on the market.

The Latino experience in economic development also indicates that many organizations play an important role in the revitalization of barrio economies. Las Américas supermarket (located in Upham's Corner, one of Boston's poorest areas) has been highlighted by the local media.[36] In less than a year, the supermarket returned from the brink of failure to employ more than fifty workers. Technical assistance provided to the owners permitted the turnaround, but ongoing commercial revitalization efforts preceded the supermarket purchase and served to stabilize the commercial strip, attracting new customers to the area. Certainly, the opening and expansion of the supermarket helped in that process, but the supermarket itself would not have been successful without a broader community effort to revive the Upham's Corner commercial district. Local business and community leaders, by controlling crime and traffic, made the area attractive for customers. The effort was successful because of the broad participation of CDCs and other nonprofit organizations, banks, and city officials, among others. This example illustrates the holistic nature of neighborhood change that allows private ventures to prosper.[37]

Las Américas supermarket also exemplifies the linkage of the U.S.

Latino community to Latin America. Like other Latino-owned small businesses along the same commercial strip, Las Américas engages actively in business transactions with Puerto Rico, the Dominican Republic, Mexico, El Salvador, and other countries. Its operations serve as an anchor for music distributors, restaurants, and furniture stores. Commercial transactions, along with remittances, provide an important connection between the economic development of *el barrio* and that of Latin America.

Minority-owned small businesses in the inner city are neither the only nor the primary engine of growth in these communities, but they are an important part of the solution to the problems of economic development. Community strategies to support the small business sector in our barrios must take into consideration the wide range of its characteristics and needs. Programs that are grounded in local communities and have direct contact with small business seem to work better in providing support services and in linking the store owner or self-employed person to mainstream financial institutions and other types of assistance and resources. However, centralized citywide alliances with large corporations and authorities do more for larger firms able to bid for contracts outside the neighborhood. Finally, community-owned, income-generating projects seem to be gaining momentum. Like other small businesses, the community enterprise will also require specific strategies and services.

CDCs and Community Revitalization

In contrast to small business development, where the Latino experience has been fragmented, the Mexican and Puerto Rican populations have been active in housing and community revitalization, and best-practice examples abound. As in the African-American community, many of the CDCs active in these areas were founded in the late 1960s or 1970s as part of the Model Cities Program. Because Latinos are generally less segregated from the rest of the population than blacks and experienced rapid population growth during the 1980s due to immigration, they tend to live in ethnically mixed neighborhoods.

Ross Gittell and Margaret Wilder describe two successful CDCs operating in predominantly Latino communities. Both cases illustrate how ethnic identity and solidarity can be translated into effective multiethnic alliances for economic development and institutionalization of community participation.[38] Mission Housing Development is a CDC that evolved from a Mexican-led, multiethnic coalition formed to block urban renewal plans for the Mission neighborhood of San Francisco. Since its inception in 1971 through the Model Cities Program, it has developed more than three hundred new housing units and rehabilitated more than a thousand existing units. Caritas Management Corporation, a for-profit subsidiary, owns over four hundred and fifty units and oversees more than a thousand units for the CDCs and other private and nonprofit organizations in the area. Its housing programs provide integrated social services to residents and are part of a neighborhood collaboration that provides housing for individuals who are homeless, disabled, HIV-infected, and alcoholic, as well as other needy and hard-to-serve populations. Perhaps as important as its direct service to neighborhood residents, Mission Housing Development engages in a host of economic and neighborhood planning activities, ranging from child care, tenant organizing, and educational programs to the development of "Centro del Pueblo"—a combined residential and commercial facility that houses many of the area's nonprofit organizations.

The Coalition for a Better Acre (CBA) was founded in 1982 as a community response to an economic revitalization plan for Lowell, Massachusetts, that focused on downtown and high-tech industrial development to the exclusion of low-income neighborhoods. The Acre neighborhood historically has served as an entry port for French Canadians, Irish, and other immigrants. More recently, the neighborhood has become predominantly Puerto Rican, with an increasing Asian immigrant population. CBA programs have focused on affordable housing and community development, including small business assistance, revolving loan funds, and training for mothers receiving federal welfare assistance. CBA also supports youth programs and other social services. Known in Lowell for its political activism, CBA has helped change the composition of the city council, influenced key government appointments in the area, and supported the election of state-level representatives.

The East Los Angeles Community Union (TELACU), the largest Latino CDC in the country, was founded in 1968 by Mexican activists to promote socioeconomic development in the distressed East Los Angeles area. TELACU has owned and developed seventeen affordable housing projects comprising more than twelve hundred units valued at over $80 million. This alone would make it one of the largest CDCs in the country, but its activities go well beyond housing to include the development of industrial and commercial space, banking, construction, and many other businesses. For instance, TELACU founded an industrial park in 1977 to redevelop a vacant forty-eight-acre tire plant formerly owned by B.F. Goodrich. Since then, the facility, which consists of 9,000 square feet of industrial space, has served dozens of businesses. It currently houses twenty-seven businesses, most of which are minority-owned. TELACU's commercial buildings rent space to more than fifty firms that employ over two thousand workers. In addition to these housing and business activities, TELACU provides a wide range of educational and social services to the community.

Like other Latino CDCs, Los Sures was established in 1972 to promote the social and economic development of the south side of Williamsburg, one of the poorest Puerto Rican communities in New York City. Although originally focused on housing (successfully developing more than two thousand units over the years), Los Sures has engaged in numerous economic development projects and provided a wide variety of social services to the community. In addition to these traditional CDC activities, Los Sures is involved in community-planning and coalition-building activities. Most notably, it works with the United Jewish Organizations to improve relations between the Hasidic Jewish community and Latino residents in Williamsburg, two communities with a history of contentious and sometimes violent confrontation. Participants believe that collaborative efforts in economic development and job creation are the best strategy to improve interethnic relations. The first project involves rehabilitating a six-story building in the Hasidic neighborhood that will eventually be occupied by both Latino and Jewish tenants.

Like most successful CDCs, Mission Housing Development, CBA, TELACU, and Los Sures are truly representative of community interests and are governed and staffed by local leadership and long-time residents. Funding for their operations comes from many city, county, state, and federal agencies, as well as charitable foundations and private corporations. Long-term partnerships and networking are an intrinsic part of their operations. The key to the success of these intermediary organizations, whether they focus on small business assistance or housing and real estate development, has been the articulation of a dual mission of community leadership and institutional development and the effective use of external relations to attract resources to the neighborhood. Like Coastal Enterprises (Maine), Bethel New Life (Chicago), New Community Corporation (Newark), and many other successful CDCs around the country, these Latino CDCs represent a new type of community institution. The new breed of CDCs understand long-range trends in regional economic development and focus their community revitalization strategies on taking advantage of such opportunities. Ethnic identity and solidarity, in this context, are translated into effective grassroots civic participation.[39]

Employment and Training

Employment and training is one of the most difficult areas in which to implement successful community strategies and redirect public policy. The significant structural changes experienced by the U.S. economy and the consequences for labor markets and the workplace have rendered the institutional context for employment policy inadequate and, in many instances, obsolete. Since the mid-1970s, heightened competition in global markets has induced major changes in large corporations. In response to new competitive pressures, Gastón Institute researchers found, employers have cut labor costs and achieved greater work force flexibility. In many cases, employers have induced the erosion of internal labor markets and promoted the greater use of contingent employment arrangements.[40]

Recent studies document that Latinos experience job displacement relatively more than other workers, their unionization rate and work opportunities have declined, and their seasonal and part-time employment has risen; the spatial rearrangement of jobs has been particularly harmful to Latinos in the Northeast. All these factors disconnect workers from long-term employment relations. The situation is aggravated by the concentration of Latinos in occupations where vocational skills may be difficult to transfer to other occupations.

Discrimination in the workplace constitutes a major barrier to the recruitment, hiring, and promotion of Latinos. It is particularly prevalent for urban jobs that do not require a college degree and are not widely advertised. Once Latinos are interviewed, they often are steered to a limited number of positions. Those who do penetrate the corporate world lack culturally sensitive mentors. Such mentors could help Latinos to overcome the stereotype of the poor and uneducated worker who lacks potential as a leader and manager, and to capitalize on their positive cultural traits.

Many see lack of English language fluency and skills as the primary impediment to Latino economic advancement. However, I believe that structural changes in the labor market and discrimination in the workplace have become greater impediments over the years.[41] Many studies suggest that employment and training programs are largely ineffective in enhancing skills and winning long-term employment.[42] Successful employment and training programs exist, however, and some are discussed below.

The most effective programs seem to involve collaborations or networks of several community organizations in one region that focus on adult education and placement. Cities that have the most successful in employment and training programs have developed umbrella organizations that bring together not only community groups but also state and local agencies, employers, community colleges, and others involved in vocational skills training for disadvantaged populations. Pittsburgh's Northside Partnership and Cleveland's Wire Net are examples of successful partnerships at the city level.[43]

The Center for Employment and Training (CET), which originated in San José, California, is the only program that has been shown to produce long-term earnings and employment gains for disadvantaged

participants. The CET model integrates vocational and basic skills education, including English as a Second Language (ESL) training. The CET
philosophy holds that gains in education and skills are related to work and
employment. Students are not screened for skills or language proficiency
upon entering the program, and they graduate when they find a job. All
occupational skills programs are developed in cooperation with employers. This vocational skills training model seems to work well for high
school dropouts, young mothers receiving public assistance, dislocated
workers, former criminal offenders, and others considered hard to serve
by traditional programs. Linked to the farm workers' movement when it
started more than twenty-five years ago, CET now has dozens of offices
throughout California and the Southwest and is expanding along the East
Coast, from Florida to Connecticut, and to Chicago.[44]

Quality Employment through Skills Training, or Project QUEST, is
one of the most successful training programs in the nation.[45] Among other
honors, it has received the American Government Award from Harvard
University and the Ford Foundation. Launched in 1993, Project QUEST
was founded by two influential advocacy organizations in the San Antonio
area. Communities Organized in Public Service (COPS) serves primarily
the poor in the south and west sections of town. The Metro Alliance serves
the central city and San Antonio's east and north sides. The two organizations first joined forces to mobilize the community in response to the
closing of a Levi Strauss factory that employed over two thousand people.
These organizations are part of a much broader network of community
organizations linked by the Industrial Areas Foundation, which serves as a
funding and technical assistance intermediary for training and community
planning.

Project QUEST executes a comprehensive vision of connecting residents in targeted areas to regional employment opportunities in growing
businesses and industries. The building block of the program is the implementation of an employment development plan for each participant.
Trainees attend a weekly counseling meeting organized by occupational
group and receive a host of complementary support services. The program ensures that trainees have access to social services such as individual
and joint counseling, educational financial assistance, and so forth. Like
CET, Project QUEST places a strong emphasis on mediating relations
with employers and facilitating trainees' access to jobs. Currently, Project
QUEST and CET are being replicated at the regional and national levels,
respectively.

Project QUEST and CET are designed to respond to different community needs and to target distinct segments of the labor market. While CET
focuses on workers who lack relevant job skills and experience and aims at
entry-level positions in growing industries, Project QUEST requires a high

school equivalency diploma and seeks to link participants to jobs that require more specialized education and skills. These organizations illustrate the need to design training programs with a clearly defined market niche in mind. They also exemplify the critical role of access to external resources, community ownership and participation, and the development of institutional capacity in program success.

All of the most successful employment and training programs have in common a close connection with employers and strong relations with program participants. Indeed, in a review of successful community-based training programs, Bennett Harrison concluded: "For community-based groups, the single most important key to gaining access to quality employment training services is not to expand their individual organizational capacities to do [employment training], so much as it is the ability to find their way into existing or evolving networks whose members share information, resources, and access."[46] One can argue that it is precisely the ability to develop solidarity among community organizations and to project that energy to the external world that generates the ability to connect people to jobs. Skills enhancement is necessary, but without systematic connections to employers, it is very difficult to promote the employment of disadvantaged workers.

A word of caution is necessary. The focus on linking the activities of several community organizations assumes that such organizations exist in the community and have the necessary experience of providing vocational training and basic education. Latino barrios vary widely in this regard, depending on the maturity of the community, the history of community organizing and advocacy, and other factors. In the area of employment and training, Latinos currently have a great need to expand capacity by developing new programs and strengthening existing ones. The challenge is to build this capacity while simultaneously making connections to other employment and training organizations, employers, and state agencies.

Skills enhancement and connections to employers constitute only part of the solution to the problem of access to jobs. The economic advancement of Latinos in labor markets and within work organizations requires several complementary strategies. Establishing caucuses, or informal and formal networks, within large corporations, government agencies, and professional organizations is one workplace strategy to promote Latino advancement. No study to date documents the number of such caucuses or their benefits, but journalistic and anecdotal data suggest that, like African-Americans and members of other ethnic communities, Latinos are quite active in workplace organizations. These groups promote workplace multiculturalism, serve as a recruiting mechanism, provide informal mentoring, and induce advancement within corporations and government agencies. In some areas these caucuses interact through professional networks, but their activism has been restricted to the least controversial issues. Continuous interaction between those who develop community-based networks and associations of Latino professionals is crucial for both the community and the caucuses.

An economic empowerment strategy for the Latino community also requires a connection to the traditional labor policy agenda. Progressive policy change is increasingly unlikely at the federal level in areas such as the minimum wage, universal health care, unemployment insurance, labor relations, and equal employment opportunity. It is at least possible at the state level. A higher minimum wage was enacted in Texas with no negative effect on employment, and New York and California have mandatory data disclosure and posting of job openings in public sector employment. Latino workers, in particular, would benefit from legislation creating and expanding funding for programs serving displaced workers, minimum-standard benefits for part-time and seasonal workers, protective health standards for agricultural workers, and immigrant naturalization programs.

In short, an employment strategy for Latinos must begin by building community organizations that offer integrated language, skills, and cultural programs. These organizations must have strong connections among themselves and with employers. On the basis of a strong community movement, coalitions can be developed with players who mediate employment relations in the regional economy (such as government boards, trade associations, foundations, and community colleges). A necessary complement to a strategy of building capacity and networking is to pursue the organization of Latinos in the workplace. A more active collective effort may help break the relatively short employment cycle for Latinos and bring about higher payoffs for job-specific skills and experience. Latino caucuses, nonetheless, should eventually become more active on broader workplace issues. The elements of the proposed employment and training strategy are similar to the ones guiding programs for small business development and other economic areas.

Conclusion

Economic empowerment is a concept that has eluded clear definition. I have examined several areas typically associated with community economic development and provided examples of best practice in these areas. The essential elements of the proposed strategy to revitalize the inner city are attracting resources to the barrio and connecting neighborhood institutions and individuals to the main economy. In this context, economic empowerment refers to how residents in a neighborhood participate and succeed in developing programs and processes that connect workers to good jobs, small businesses to capital and market opportunities, and community organizations to private and public funding resources. The social capital of the barrio is developed to the extent that individuals and organizations enhance external relations and formalize mechanisms to gain access to social resources. These two aspects of the economic development process are interrelated: building capacity in neighborhood-based organizations is necessary to mobilize community resources around an economic development program, while the effectiveness and success of community organizations and leaders depends heavily on the successful articulation to institutions and resources in the larger regional economy.

The Latino experience illustrates how ethnic identity, reinforced by the continuous flow of migrants from Latin America, and the mobilization of resources based on cultural ties and solidarity provide the foundation for the revitalization of the inner city. The best-practice cases highlighted above indicate that Latino community-based organizations can provide effective links to resources outside the barrio. These cases show that effective strategies depend on both the mobilization of leadership and other resources internal to the community and their articulation to those mainstream economic institutions that ultimately provide access to jobs and financial resources for residents and business. In this context, the development of intermediary organizations that match workers to job opportunities or small businesses to financial and technical assistance resources facilitates and, in many cases, is a prerequisite for the successful development of poor areas. Another important lesson from the Latino experience is that a combination of strategies is more likely to succeed than any single program. Neighborhood revitalization depends precisely on the synergy and impact of multiple efforts.

The lessons from the Latino experience can be understood in a broader context of inner-city revitalization. Obviously, minority-owned small businesses have an important role to play in the economic revitalization of the inner city. And, by implication, it is important to recognize the role that racial and ethnic identity and solidarity play in the economic survival of inner-city businesses. Undoubtedly, programs assisting minority-owned businesses are more effective when linked to expanding sectors of the economy, as are Cuban-owned businesses in Miami or construction-related businesses affiliated with the Regional Alliance in New York City. Well-targeted sectoral strategies also have helped CDCs like Mission Housing and employment training programs like CET.

Finally, it is important to recognize the unique circumstances under which the development of ethnic-enclave economies is viable. Cities like Miami, San Antonio, Los Angeles, and New York City, where there are unusually high concentrations of Latino businesses, are the exception. In most areas, the contribution of small business to job creation, the provision of (affordable) housing, or organizing community resources to promote economic development is minimal. Under those circumstances, other community institutions become important components of an economic development strategy. Employment and training programs facilitate access to jobs, CDCs promote commercial revitalization and build affordable housing, and so on. Rather than regarding community nonprofit organizations as redundant, public policy must recognize social and community service organizations as partners in business development.

Part Three

The Politics and Identity of Diaspora

▩▩▩▩▩▩▩▩▩▩▩▩▩▩▩▩▩▩▩▩▩▩▩▩▩▩▩▩▩▩▩▩▩▩▩▩▩

Chapter 8

1995—*Terreno Peligroso*/Danger Zone: Cultural Relations Between Chicanos and Mexicans at the End of the Century

Guillermo Gómez-Peña
Translated by Clifton Ross

In February 1995, the first stage of a binational performance project called "Terreno Peligroso/Danger Zone" was completed. For an entire month—two weeks in Los Angeles and two in Mexico City—eleven experimental artists whose work challenges stereotypical or official notions of identity, nationality, language, sexuality, and the creative process worked together daily. Representing Mexico were Lorena Wolffer, Felipe Ehrenberg, Eugenia Vargas, César Martínez, and Elvira Santamaría; from California were Elia Arce, Rubén Martínez, Nao Bustamante, Luis Alfaro, Roberto Sifuentes, and myself. Chosen by the curators and producers, Josefina Ramírez and Lorena Wolffer, this group was as eclectic and diverse as our two cultures (Chicano and Mexican). The performances were presented at the University of California (UCLA) and in the Ex-Teresa Alternative Art Space (Mexico City).

Our performance work covered a wide spectrum, from the most intimate ritual actions to the most confrontational activist performance; it included *tableaux vivants,* avant-cabaret, spoken word poetry, apocalyptic rituals, and street "interventions." Our goals (at least those we consciously expressed) were to create art together (border art is collaborative by nature); to open the Pandora's box of North/South relations and unleash the border demons; to destroy taboos; and to replace simplistic views of cultural otherness with more complex visions. Here are some of the problems the artists confronted during this binational encounter.

At the close of 1993, many artists of Latin American origin who were living in the United States ingenuously believed that NAFTA, or the *"Tratado de Libre Comer-se"*[1]—despite its grave omissions in the areas of ecology, human and labor rights, culture, and education—would, at least indirectly, create the conditions for a rapprochement between Chicanos and Mexicans. That idea backfired. Instead, ferocious nationalist movements arose in response to the globalization of the economy and culture.

Xenophobic proposals reminiscent of Nazi Germany—such as Operation Gatekeeper and California's chilling Proposition 187—were brandished to confront the increasing and inevitable mexicanization of the United States. We watched, perplexed, as the sudden opening of markets coincided with the militarization of the border and the construction of a huge metal wall to separate several border cities. Capital, hollow dreams, and assembly plants easily crossed from one side to the other, but human beings—along with critical art and ideas—were denied passage. It seemed that culturally, as well as economically, the *maquiladora* model had been perfected: Mexicans would provide the raw material and do the arduous, badly paid work; Anglos would run the show; and Chicanos would be left out of the picture.

We are like tiny, insignificant spectators at a great end-of-the-century wrestling match: the Invisible Octopus of Pseudo-internationalization versus the Hydra of Neo-nationalism. In Round One, the neoliberal formula of a continent unified by free trade, tourism, and digital high technology confronts indigenous, campesino, environmental, and human rights movements. *Coitus interruptus.* The Mexican peso plummets, foreign capital flees, and the Marlboro dreams of neoliberal elites vanish in a cloud of sulfurous smoke. *Cambio.*

The crises are also becoming globalized. In the topography of the end-of-the-century crisis, Bosnia is strangely connected to Los Angeles (L.A.- Herzegovina), just as Chiapas is connected to the Basque country and to Northern Ireland. Mexicans in California confront a dilemma similar to that faced by Palestinians and black South Africans, and the young people of Mexico City (members of Generation MeX) manifest the same existential and psychological illnesses that plague New Yorkers or Berliners.

The paradoxes multiply *locar*hythmically. In the era of computers, faxes, virtual reality, World Beat, and "total television" (à la CNN), it has become increasingly difficult for us to communicate across the borders of culture and language. The smaller and more concentrated the world becomes, the more foreign and incomprehensible it seems to us. We are now exposed to many languages, but we lack the keys to translate them. We have access to incredible amounts of information, but we don't have the codes to decipher it. The seductive virtual universe, with its unlimited options and multidirectional promises, confounds our ability to order information and to act in the world with ethical and political clarity.

If anything could be said to define "postmodernity," it is the steady increase in symptoms of border culture, the endless syncretisms with a complete lack of synchronicity, misencounters and misunderstandings: "I am, as long as you (as the representative of racial, linguistic or cultural otherness) no longer are"; "I cross, therefore you exist (or vice versa)"; "Fuck you, therefore I am" (and others better left unsaid). Contemporary art—at its most critical, irreverent and experimental—is an involuntary chronicle of the ontological and epistemological confusion that is affecting all of us equally.

Chicano rap, Mexican alternative rock, independent cinema, and performance art converge on these key points: the brave acceptance of our trans-borderized and de-nationalized condition; the *ars poetica* of vertigo; the metaphysics of fragmentation; and the total collapse of linear logic, dramatic time, and narrative aesthetics. (This book is hopefully an example of this.)

The myths that once grounded our identity have become bankrupt. Sixties-era pan-Latinamericanism, *la mexicanidad* (unique, monumental, undying), and *Chicanismo* (with thorns and a capital *C*) have all been eclipsed by processes of cultural borderization and social fragmentation. Like it or not, we are now de-nationalized, de-Mexicanized, trans-Chicanized, and pseudo-internationalized. And worse, in fear of falling into a new century we refuse to assume this new identity, roaming around instead in a Bermuda Triangle. We live in economic uncertainty, terrorized by the holocaust of AIDS, divided (better yet, trapped) by multiple borders, disconnected from ourselves and others by strange mass cultures and new technologies that appeal to our most mediocre desires for instant transformation and psychological expansion.

In this bizarre landscape, politics becomes pop culture, and technology turns into folklore. Mass culture, popular culture, and folklore are no longer distinguishable from one another: it seems that our only true community is television. Perhaps our only real nation is also television. Mexico is and continues to be "one" by virtue of television; without television perhaps it would cease to be. Televisa is Mexico's macro-Ministry of Communications, Culture, and Binational Tourism, all in one. In the United States of the 90s, the most famous Mexicans are TV personalities such as Gloria Trevi, Paco Stanley, "Verónica," and Raúl Velasco. Sadly, Mexican immigrants maintain their main connection with that marvelous, imaginary country called Mexico via soap operas. If we are familiar with "El Sup" (Subcomandante Marcos) and Superbarrio, it is because they are skillful manipulators of the symbolic (and performative) politics of the media. In this context, we "untelevisable" performance artists are asking ourselves what role will be left for us to perform in the immediate future. Maybe our only options will be to make conceptual commercials for MTV or appear in artsy rock videos. For the moment, I'm having a hard time imagining more dignified alternatives.

North Americans (in the U.S.) used to define their identity in direct opposition to the "Soviet threat." With the end of the Cold War, the

United States fell into an unprecedented identity crisis. Today its place in the world is uncertain and its (fictitious) enemies are multiplying left and right. On the eclectic list of recent anti-American "others" one finds fundamentalist Muslims, Japanese businessmen, Latin American drug lords, black rap musicians, and, more recently, "illegal aliens" in both senses of the word: cultural Martians invading "our" institutions, and seditious laborers who are "stealing jobs from *real* Americans."

This identity crisis translates into an immense nostalgia for an (imaginary) era in which people of color didn't exist, or at least when we were invisible and silent. The political expression of this nostalgia is chilling: "Let's take our country back." The far right, people like Pete Wilson, Newt Gingrich, Jesse Helms, and Pat Buchanan, along with many Democrats, are in agreement on the following: this country must be saved from chaos and collapse into third-worldization; "illegal" immigrants must be deported; the poor should be put in jail (three strikes, you're out); welfare, affirmative action, and bilingual education programs must be dismantled; and the cultural funding infrastructure which has been infiltrated by "liberals with leftist tendencies" (the National Endowments for the Arts and the Humanities, and the Corporation for Public Broadcasting) must be decimated. In the euphemistic Contract with America, ethnic "minorities," independent artists and intellectuals, the homeless, the elderly, children, and especially immigrants from the South are all under close watch.

In Mexico, ever since the implementation of NAFTA, the border no longer functions as the great barrier of contention against which official Mexican identity is defined. This has created its own large-scale identity crisis. Without the continuous harassment from Washington's Power Rangers, the *yupitecas* and the *mariachis* have had no alternative but to go off to a cantina and drown themselves in the depths of lost love and neo-*Porfirista*[2] nostalgia. The social explosion in Chiapas has complicated things further and has literally torn the country in two. *Salinista* Mexico preferred to think of itself as *posmoderno* and international, desiring at all costs to look outward and northward, but the unfolding internal political crisis has forced the country's gaze inward to confront its racism against indigenous peoples and its abysmal contradictions.

Although the roots of our crises are of a very different nature, both Califas (California) and Tenochtitlán (Mexico City) are living through unprecedented identity crises. And, for the first time in the twentieth century, there is a growing consciousness on both sides of the border that the crises and dangers that we are undergoing are similar. This mutual recognition could be the basis for new, more profound cultural relations between Chicanos and Mexicans: if we recognize that we're all equally screwed, perhaps at the same time we are equally capable of greater compassion and mutual understanding.

At present, the only thing that unites those who left Mexico and those who stayed is our inability to understand and accept our inevitable differences. We detect the existence of these invisible borders, but we are unable to articulate them, much less cross them with tact. This phenomenon is clearly evident in the area of cultural relations between Mexicans and Chicanos. It is here that the contradictions abound, that the wound opens and bleeds, and that the poisoned subtext of mutual (and largely fictional) resentments rises to the surface.

We, the post-Mexican and Chicano artists from "over there/the other side" look to the South with a certain ingenuousness, a distorting nostalgia and admiration, always dreaming of our possible return. Meanwhile, the Mexicans who remain south of the border look at us with a combination of desire and repudiation, fear and condescension. The mirrors are always breaking. While we on the California coast—where the West literally ends—look toward the Pacific, those in Mexico City look attentively toward Europe and New York; and they—in spiritual and artistic bankruptcy—are carefully watching both Chicanos and Mexicans, searching for novelty, inspiration, and exoticism to decorate the blank walls of their nihilist crisis.

The missed encounters continue. In the United States, Latino artists work in the flammable context of the multicultural wars and identity politics. We define ourselves as a culture of resistance, and in our eagerness to "resist the dominant culture" we frequently lose all sense of a continental perspective and end up assuming ethnocentric and separatist positions. Meanwhile, the Mexican artistic communities—with some exceptions—are undergoing a stage of nonreflective extroversion and rejection of textually political or politicized art, which they associate with "minor" art and with official Mexican cultural discourse. Although they are the protagonists and witnesses of their country's most serious crisis in modern history (perhaps comparable to that of Eastern Europe), many Mexican experimental artists have chosen not to "textually" use *la crisis* as subject matter in their work. Right now, they are more inclined to create a personal, intimate art of an existential or neoconceptual style.

When Mexican artists "go North," they do so with the intention of breaking into the commercial gallery circuit. They are prejudiced by the solemnity and virtual failure of official cultural exchange projects, and to them Chicano art appears didactic, reiterative, and poorly executed. Our themes—racism, immigration, the obsessive deconstruction of identities, and the subversion of media stereotypes of Mexicans—seem distant and irrelevant to their purely "Mexican" reality. They seem not to fully grasp the magnitude of their own crisis and refuse (not entirely without reason) to be seen as a "minority." The Chicanos, hypersensitive to this fragile relationship, feel rejected by the Mexicans, and the gap between the two cultures grows wider.

The long and convoluted history of cultural exchange between Chicanos and Mexicans can be translated as a chronicle of missed encounters. For fifteen years Chicanos have tried, without success, to "return" through the great door and to reconcile themselves with their Mexican relatives. With few exceptions, the reception has been openly hostile or, at best, paternalistic. Despite the numerous and fashionable projects of binational interchange facilitated (or inspired) by NAFTA, Mexico's predominant vision of Chicano art is still antiquated. In 1995, most Mexicans still believe that all Chicano artists make barrio murals, write protest poetry, and erect neon altars to Frida Kahlo and the Virgin of Guadalupe; that they all speak like Edward Olmos in *American Me* and dance to Tex-Mex music; that they all drive low-riders. They ignore the actual diversity and complexity of our communities, and remain unaware of the influence of the Central American, Caribbean, and Asian communities that have moved into the Chicano neighborhoods. The influence of gay and lesbian communities of color, challenging the excessive dose of testosterone from which Chicano culture has suffered for the last two decades, is also completely overlooked. The processes which have brought us to more fluid and interactive models of a Chicano/Latino multi-identity are still unheard of in Mexico City, and two generations of young artists who have publicly questioned conventional, static notions of *Chicanismo* remain outside the realm of most Mexicans' consciousness.

In 1995, *la mexicanidad* and the Latino/Chicano experience are becoming completely superimposed. The two hundred thousand Mexicans who cross the border every month bring us fresh and constant reminders of our past (for Mexican-Americans, the continual migratory flow functions as a sort of collective memory). And the opposite phenomenon also happens: the mythic North (which represents the future) also returns to the South, searching for its lost past. Many of the Mexicans who come to "the other side" become "Chicanized" and return to Mexico—either on their own or by force of the immigration authorities. In the act of returning they contribute to the silent process of Chicanization with Mexico is currently undergoing.

This dual dynamic, as expressed in popular culture, functions as a sort of X-ray of the social psyche: the "northern" sounds of rap and *quebradita* (a fusion of north Mexican *banda* and techno-pop) can already be heard from Yucatán to Chihuahua; while the songs of Mexican bands such as Los

Caifanes, La Lupita, Maldita Vecindad, and Los Tigres del Norte are being hummed from San Diego to New York. Selena, the "queen of Tex-Mex" (RIP), is venerated in both countries. The sounds of *"tecno-banda"* and *quebradita* (no one can deny that these are immigrant sounds) re-Mexican-ize Chicano music. The *"cholos"* and the *"salvatruchos"* (young Salvadorans in L.A.) are wearing Stetson hats and cowboy boots, while Aztec punk-rockers in Mexico City, Guadalajara, and Tijuana are expropriating Chicano iconography and fashion, and talking in Spanglish *que no?*

Mexican identity (or, better, the many Mexican identities) can no longer be explained without the experience of "the other side," and vice versa. As a sociocultural phenomenon, Los Angeles simply cannot be understood without taking Mexico City into account, its southernmost neighborhood. Between both cities runs the greatest migratory axis on the planet, and the conceptual freeway with the greatest number of accidents.

As transnationalized artists, our challenge is to recompose the fragmented chronicle of this strange end-of-the-century phenomenon. And so, the performance begins . . .

Chapter 9

Visions of Dominicanness in the United States

Silvio Torres-Saillant

What is the Dominican perspective on the Latino community and the global society? The inclusion of a Dominican voice in this volume says a great deal about the rise of Dominican immigrants as an important branch of the Latino population in the United States. It also acknowledges that tackling the difficult challenges currently facing our community requires a plurality of voices. The adoption by the United States of economic and political measures prompted by the imperatives of globalization can be expected to shake the relationship of Latinos to the mainstream society. But an equally important concern is the extent to which the logic of the global society will make it possible for Latinos to see ourselves as a diverse yet unifiable human formation—a community capable of speaking with a complex but single voice.

One ultimate consequence of the relaxation of national borders implicit in the North American Free Trade Agreement (NAFTA) and other such treaties may be a weakening of our claim, as a U.S. minority, to entitlement and services on the basis of our contribution to the larger society and our having "paid our dues" in the course of a painful immigrant experience. Even within a national group, competition for resources in the quest for survival may create trauma. Imagine a scenario in which—borders having been made flexible by some regional accord—Dominicans may come to the United States straight from the home country and gain easy access to the social and economic spaces that U.S. Dominicans have struggled for through the years. One can only speculate on the consequences, for Dominicans in the United States as well as those in the Dominican Republic.

Latinos and Diasporic Identity

Latinos in the United States are a composite of diverse historical realities, national experiences, and collective existential traumas. Before emigration from the native land, which for each distinct group corresponded to different sociohistorical and geopolitical events, one did not see oneself as Latino or Hispanic but as Puerto Rican, Cuban, Colombian, or Dominican, to name only a few of the Latino groups that are most visible in my current base of operation, New York. As members of a diaspora, however, we have become unified in significant ways. We share the experience of being uprooted by large socioeconomic forces from our original homelands. We come from societies with a history of unequal association with the United States, a country that has influenced and sometimes even dictated political behavior in Latin America. The image of "backyard," often invoked by U.S. policy-makers to identify Latin America's geographical proximity to the United States, entails a qualitative view that construes the region not as a partner but as a subordinate.

By the third decade of the twentieth century, a good many Latin American nations already had ascertained, through the incursion of U.S. armed forces into their territory, the concrete inequality of their relationship with their North American neighbor. They had also become acquainted with the views that often informed these military invasions. For instance, Senator Albert J. Beveridge of Indiana, speaking before the U.S. Senate in 1901, had declared: "God has made us the master organizers of the world to establish systems where chaos reigns. . . . He has made us adept in government that we may administer government among savages and senile people."[1] Similarly, President Theodore Roosevelt is known to have publicly decried the Cubans', Dominicans', Haitians', and Nicaraguans' conduct of their political lives. The famous "corollary to the Monroe Doctrine" in Roosevelt's annual message to Congress in 1904 hints at the U.S. sense of moral and political superiority vis-à-vis the peoples of Latin America. "Chronic wrongdoing or an impotence which results in a general loosening of the ties of civilized society, may in America, as elsewhere, ultimately require intervention by some civilized nation, and in the Western Hemisphere the adherence of the United States to the Monroe Doctrine may force the United States, however reluctantly, in flagrant cases of such wrongdoing or impotence, to the exercise of an international police power."[2]

The popular view of the Spanish-speaking inhabitants of the hemisphere that prevailed in the United States during the first half of the century is reflected in a poll conducted in 1940 by the Office of Public Opinion Research. The questionnaire gave respondents nineteen adjectives with which to describe Latins. "Dark-skinned" came first, chosen by 80 percent of the respondents, followed by "quick-tempered," "emotional," "religious," "backward," "lazy," "ignorant," and "suspicious," chosen by 40 to 50 percent of those who answered. At the very bottom, chosen by a mere 5 percent, came "efficient," preceded by the adjectives "progressive," "generous," "brave," "honest," "intelligent," and "shrewd," none of which obtained a ranking higher than 16 percent.[3] The perceptions suggested by this list of adjectives helped shape the reception accorded to Latin Americans upon their arrival in the United States.

Coming, as we do, from subaltern societies, it is no wonder that we occupy not the center but the margins of U.S. society. This marginalization has been intensified because, except for Mexicans and Puerto Ricans, most of us immigrated at a time when the country's economy was less expansive than during earlier waves of immigration. The arrival in the United States of Dominicans, Cubans, Colombians, and Central Americans coincided with the virtual transformation of economic life in former industrial centers such as New York, where the service sector has become the primary area of employment. Instead of fostering integration, this arrangement has produced a widening gap between recent Latino immigrants and the mainstream of productive economic life. New York exhibits what scholars have called a "dual city" model,[4] where recent Spanish-speaking immigrants almost invariably occupy the less prosperous side of the divide, with clear implications for our sense of identity. Our political, economic, and cultural marginality relegates us to a condition of "otherness" with respect to the dominant social structure.

The awareness of this otherness leads us to assert our commonality with those who share our condition, particularly when we can claim linguistic, ethnic, and historical links among our various national groups. The experience of diasporic uprooting and the sense of living outside the dominant realm of the receiving society penetrate the core of our Latino identity. For, even though Mexicans, Puerto Ricans, and Dominicans became ethnic communities in the United States through profoundly different processes, we are bound by political imperatives to see ourselves as one. Ironically, Simón Bolívar's desideratum of a unified Latin American nation and the ideal upheld by Eugenio María de Hostos of an Antillean federation find in us a strange kind of fulfillment. We have come to articulate a collective identity, not in our native homelands, as Bolívar and Hostos had dreamed, but within the insecure space of the diaspora. The feeling that ours is a contested terrain, that we do not inherit our social space but must carve it out for ourselves in the face of adversity, leads us to lift the banner of our oneness despite differences in the circumstances under which each of our distinct groups came to the United States. The language of unity functions as an instrument of survival.

Dominicans in the Latin American Diaspora

The encompassing Latino identity described above, however, does not satisfy the need for each of our national groups to articulate its own sense of itself as offspring of a particular historical experience. It is within this frame that I would like to discuss some of the issues now faced by the Dominican portion of the Latino community. After three decades of massive migration to the United States, Dominicans are passing through a stage where it is necessary for the community to define itself collectively. Dominicans in the United States have lost the privilege of individuality — that is, the ability of a person of Dominican descent to commit a crime or perform an act of charity and be judged individually, rather than as an instance of the collective behavior of his or her national group. Therefore, many Dominicans, especially academics and others with the potential to influence public discourse, have begun the quest for definition. Recently a group of Dominican scholars and educators agreed to create a Dominican Studies Association, with one of their clearest goals being to ensure that the image of Dominicans in American society is crafted by knowledgeable and sensitive Dominican spokespersons.

A central purpose of this enterprise is to ensure that the Dominican community affects the prism through which Dominicans are seen. The Bildner Center for Hemispheric Studies at the Graduate School of the City University of New York, for instance, has for the last few years conducted a program of seminars on Dominican issues. The organizers are non-Dominicans, and the speakers invariably have been scholars brought from the Dominican Republic or from parts of the United States that do not have a recognizable Dominican immigrant community. The sole Dominican scholar listed by the Bildner Center as collaborating with their Dominican project is one who, perhaps not incidentally, lived and worked for many years in Mexico and cannot claim strong ties to any of the New York Dominican enclaves. This selectivity has worried New York Dominican scholars, many of whom are committed to the idea that the study of the Dominican experience must encompass not only the production of knowledge but also a research agenda aimed at securing the spiritual and material survival of the Dominican community in the United States. Any venture into Dominican studies that does not exhibit a recognizable vision of the future of the Dominican community is cause for concern.

Which and whose perceptions are privileged when examining things Dominican? Dominicans in the diaspora have serious reasons for wanting a say the answer. For example, in the best-selling *Out of the Barrio*, Linda Chavez magnifies the prosperity of Dominicans in New York to strengthen her case about the inadequacy of Puerto Ricans: "The vibrant commercial areas, even the manner in which the people moved on the street, attested to the vitality of neighborhoods. By contrast, the streets of the South Bronx were filled with men and women whose bearing suggested they had no place to go," Chavez writes, contrasting the neighborhoods of Dominicans and other Latinos with those of Puerto Ricans.[5] To diminish the effects of racism on the labor participation of Puerto Ricans, she claims that "other Hispanic groups who share Puerto Ricans' mixed racial background, most notably Dominicans, face the same labor market conditions and yet manage to find jobs and retain a far higher degree of labor market attachment. This is so even among women who are single heads of households."[6] Dominican scholars from the diaspora would take issue with her representation of Dominicans, since, apart from its questionable factual basis (no statistics are provided), it pits us against Puerto Ricans, our most crucial ally in the struggle for survival.

Similarly, when scholars configure the socioeconomic profile of Dominicans in the United States, their work has political implications. The literature on Dominican migration already shows divergent views on the condition of the community, with striking differences corresponding to the particular emphases of individual scholars.[7] One can also point to a body of knowledge that has denormalized Dominicans, describing the members of the community in terms characteristic of zoological observation.[8] Defamatory portrayals of Dominicans in the press have serious detrimental effects on the community. These negative images effect the community's lobbying power and bring about a loss of influence with political institutions. Our community may fail to obtain a hearing from government agencies or the corporate sector when the demand for inclusion is satisfied by importing a Dominican presence from a space other than immigrant enclaves in the United States.

Already, corporate lawyers from the Dominican Republic, in alliance with their American partners, have reached important institutions in the United States. The Santo Domingo-based Dominican-American Assistance Fund has for the last several years celebrated what it calls Dominican Week in Washington, Miami, and various cities in New Jersey and New York. The venture, which has enlisted the support of former New York governor Mario Cuomo, Congressman Charles Rangel, and State Department officials, is made up of prominent individuals committed to attracting U.S. investors to the Dominican Republic. Can their agenda coexist with the interests and needs of the Dominican community in the host country, or will a time come when the members of the Dominican diaspora are forced to compete with compatriots based in the homeland for attention from business and government?

These concerns suggest that the definition of Dominican identity is problematic. The question of identity is compounded by history—the identity of Dominicans as a community in North America is developing in the context of prevalent and longstanding perceptions that took root before Dominicans established an immigrant settlement here. Societal perceptions of immigrant groups normally correspond to shifts in the relationship between the host and the sending countries. In placing this discussion within the framework of community formation and interdependence for

Latinos in the United States, it is useful to keep in mind that every immigrant group inherits historical baggage from earlier stages of the relationship between home and host country.

The "prehistory" of Dominican migration to the United States may shed some light on the process by which an immigrant community's self-definition (which necessitates a measure of political empowerment) comes into being on the battleground of an existing discourse and as a corrective challenge to perceptions deemed oppressive to the community. The Dominican community's articulation of its identity encounters the images of Dominicanness found in American public discourse, and the resulting dynamic not only adds a measure of complexity to the community's drive to control its own destiny but also colors the interaction of Dominican immigrants with other Latino communities as well as with Dominicans in the native land.

Global Order and National Identity

In the second decade of the present century, with the Dominican Republic under direct rule by an American military government, the historian Otto Schoenrich saw in the Dominican case "a striking illustration of the rule that large bodies attract nearby smaller or weaker bodies whether in the world of physics or in international politics."[9] For him the U.S. armed forces' occupation of the Dominican land came as no surprise: once Puerto Rico and Cuba were occupied, "the attraction exerted on Santo Domingo was powerfully increased"; from then on "the Dominican Republic was in fact a protectorate of the United States, though neither American nor Dominican statesmen would have admitted it."[10] Schoenrich gave his book the telling title *Santo Domingo: A Country with a Future*; the "future" he imagined for the country was inextricably linked to the future of the United States. He predicted that the United States would continue to shape the life of the smaller nation "with greater strength than ever, despite all that may be said or done, on either side, to oppose it," since the historical dynamics involved transcended the will of politicians or citizens: "Conditions in Santo Domingo, in the United States, and in the world at-large are the causes of this force of attraction, for which the government of neither country is responsible."[11]

Schoenrich was speaking about the imperatives of the global economic order as it manifested itself around 1918, when his book was published. At the time, of course, it was not called the global economy. The young Fidel Castro invoked the founder of Cuban nationhood: "Martí pointed to the danger hanging over America and called it by its name: imperialism."[12] For Latinos in the United States, the most pertinent difference between the present and the former versions of the global economic order is the emergence in the core countries of immigrant communities from peripheral nation-states that have assumed a diasporic identity, asserting themselves as voices of otherness. In carving an existential and political space for themselves, in asserting their right to name themselves, U.S. Dominicans, consciously or unconsciously, contend with the images bequeathed by commentators from a former era in U.S.–Dominican relations. They must come to terms with a prior body of narratives fashioned by the likes of Schoenrich long before the massive exodus of Dominicans. For the most part, that discourse has its roots in a long history of unequal relations between the United States and the Dominican Republic.

Schoenrich believed fervently that the Dominicans' best hope lay in yielding to the inexorable attraction exerted on them by the United States. In his view every treaty or agreement transacted between the two nations served merely to avert or delay direct annexation, the indirect control of a protectorate being the preferable option for Americans in so far as it afforded "the advantages of annexation without its responsibilities, without the undesirable feature of bringing into our body politic a people foreign in race, language and customs."[13] Schoenrich sees no sadness in this inevitable fate, for he expects it to bring greater benefits to Dominicans than they could possibly imagine. Indeed, only under the tutelage of the United States could Dominicans aspire to achieve peace, without which no prosperity could come; "all the troubles which have befallen the Dominican Republic" stem "directly or indirectly" from "the state of civil disorder which has so long been the bane of the country."[14] The American military rule of the Dominican land had, he thought, ended violent strife among political factions vying for control of the country. "When we think of the vast resources of Santo Domingo . . . we must be glad that the clouds which have so long shrouded the land in darkness are definitely dissipated at last and that the sun of peace and prosperity has begun to shine. . . . A new era has begun for beautiful Quisqueya, which, under the protection of the Stars and Stripes, is destined to enjoy a greater measure of freedom, progress, and prosperity than its inhabitants have ever dreamed."[15]

The Dominican Republic did not "become one of the richest gardens of the West Indies," as Schoenrich had predicted. When the Americans relinquished the government of the country in 1924, the nation still had grave economic and social problems, and violence remained a constant element of political life. The difference was that now the power to perpetrate such violence lay principally in the hands of social sectors trained or favored by the United States, since the occupying forces had succeeded in disarming the civilian population and enhancing the effectiveness of the armed forces. Thus, in February 1930, less than six years after American rule formally ended, General Rafael Leonidas Trujillo came to power and initiated a thirty-year reign of terror. He had been trained by the National Guard the occupying forces had created. From 1916 to the present, there has been more bloodshed, corruption, and cynicism in Dominican society than during all prior years of republican life. Since 1916, however, as a result of the celebrated disarmament, the power of coercion and destruction has resided almost exclusively with the most conservative sectors of society. This includes, not incidentally, economic violence, which is primarily responsible for the great exodus of Dominicans from their homeland and the emergence of Dominican immigrant communities in the diaspora.

Early American Images of Dominicans

The perception that Dominicans would secure their future by embracing North American control and protection was preceded by a stage in the public discourse that saw in the Dominican land the chance for U.S. citizens themselves to realize their future. More than four decades before Schoenrich, W. S. Courtney, in a book suggestively entitled *The Gold Fields of Santo Domingo,* had announced "the development of the vast mineral, agricultural, manufacturing and commercial resources of the Spanish part of the Island of Santo Domingo" as an ideal outlet for the "surplus of mental and physical energy" of the people of the United States.[16] The author warded off any suspicion that the people of Santo Domingo might, by virtue of their tropical habitat, be deemed "semi-barbarous." He insisted, instead, on their civility, politeness, and affability, their quintessential honesty, citing the complete absence of robbery or theft "within the limits of the State." The following passage is illustrative: "Travelers, utter strangers to each other, meet at the inns, lay their money, watches and other valuables together on the table, swing their hammocks in the same room, retire, some rising to pursue their different journeys, while others sleep, and a single instance of a larceny under such circumstances of temptation has never been known."[17]

Lurking behind Courtney's benign representation of the Dominican character was a sense of Dominicans as good-natured, noble savages, devoid of human complexity. They had neither vice nor virtue. They would not harm others, but neither could they help themselves. Without the "mental and physical energy" of the Anglo-Saxon, people in Santo Domingo, Courtney found, "wholly lack that thrift and industry necessary to their own material well-being, and redemption of their country from the desolation into which it has fallen."[18] With a temperament inherited from their Spanish ancestors, Dominicans seem apathetic about the demands of capital accumulation: "No allurements of wealth will arouse them from their indolence and lethargy." Americans, offspring of the Anglo-Saxon race, with "its herculean energies and its inherent genius and skill," are urged to take advantage of this land that Providence has brought forth for them. But in addition to being a highly profitable enterprise, adding the Dominican land to the arena of American maneuver was for Courtney a historical inevitability. "That this gem of the Western Sea will sooner or later, through the enterprise of the Anglo-American, be rescued from desolation, its valleys and plains transformed into Elysian gardens and blooming fields, its mountains made to yield, its golden stores and its now solitary rivers and pensive bays thronged with commerce, is inevitable."[19]

Many enterprising Americans did view the Dominican Republic as the land of opportunity. In the last century Joseph Warren Fabens and William Leslie Cazneau in 1859 negotiated with Dominican President Pedro Santana a concession of land on which to build houses for Americans, in order to encourage migration from the United States.[20] Cazneau's wife, Jane Maria McManus Cazneau, who was part of the entrepreneur's dealings, authored under the pen name Cora Montgomery a small book entitled *Our Winter Eden* (1878), in which she recreated the pastoral experience of living in Santo Domingo as an American settler. Fabens' *In the Tropics* (1863) purports to show the success of a young American after twelve months of working the land there. The editor's introduction calls attention to the book's utility in teaching the reader "what Nature—not the stern old parent of Our North, but Nature young and prodigal and Eden-like brings forth in the charmed circle of her tropical home."[21] The author, for his part, observes that "hundreds of the working classes are seeking new homes in countries where *intelligent* labor can best be made to supply the want of capital."[22] In a subsequent edition, published under the title *Life in Santo Domingo* a decade later, the editor enhanced the Edenic scenario by adding a supplementary chapter about the Samana Bay Company of Santo Domingo, "inaugurated in this country, with headquarters in the City of New York, on a large and comprehensive scale, by a number of our leading capitalists"—thus anyone wishing to travel to "the island for the purposes of husbandry" now "will go literally among his countrymen, and will receive protection and all necessary aids in founding his new home."[23]

Fabens and Cazneau were partners in various economic ventures in Santo Domingo. The most curious was the importation of thirty camels to ensure good transportation in the Monte Cristi area.[24] More enduring was a project to annex the Dominican Republic to the United States, an idea that had interested various American presidents but reached the level of a passion with Ulysses S. Grant. The American Civil War hero, in collaboration with Dominican President Buenaventura Báez, invested much energy and time in pursuing the acquisition of the Dominican

territory. To that end he appointed his personal secretary, General Orville
E. Babcock, commissioner in the Dominican Republic.

At times, the commitment to annexation meant that the U.S. government took sides in political struggles among Dominican factions. On July
10, 1869, Secretary of the Navy George N. Robeson ordered Com-
mander Owen of the U.S.S. *Seminole* to capture a steamer used by General Gregorio Luperón, a nationalist insurgent leader who opposed the
Báez government: "This vessel has been interfering with American commerce and sailing upon the high seas without legal authority," Robeson's
despatch contended.[25] But the ulterior motive was to protect Báez's government and secure a safe course for the annexationist scheme. Indeed,
the American Commercial Agent Sommer Smith lost his position in the
Dominican Republic for holding "unfavorable opinions" regarding annexation, just as his substitute, Major Raymond H. Perry, would be permitted to resign when he too proved to be less than cooperative.[26]

Such was the urgency to finalize the proceedings that in February
1870 the steamship *Albany* took possession of the Province of Samana in
the name of the United States. Babcock appointed Fabens the American
agent there. Grant's nemesis, Senator Charles Sumner, the chairman of
the Senate Committee on Foreign Relations, led the opposition that ultimately defeated the project. "Báez," Sumner declared, "was sustained in
power by the government of the United States that he may betray his
country."[27] He denounced Cazneau and Fabens as "political jockeys" who,
along with Babcock, were conspiring to defraud both the Dominican
Republic and the United States.

The image of Dominicans as an essentially mild breed, easygoing,
good-natured, and too indifferent or lazy to interfere with any foreigner
eager to reap the wealth of their land survived this uproar and recurred
often in the American press and travel books of the nineteenth century.
Journalist D. Randolph Keim puts it succinctly: "The character of the
people, generally, is that of an easy, thoughtless, inoffensive set who
would prefer to live in listless forgetfulness of the duties or responsibilities
of life. Their notions are exceedingly primitive, and their wants exceedingly few."[28] When President Grant sent a commission to the Dominican
Republic to study the viability of annexing it, the members found stated
"the physical, mental, and moral condition of the inhabitants of Santo
Domingo . . . to be much more advanced than had been anticipated."[29]

Dominicans appeared denormalized in the public discourse of nineteenth-century America—a portrayal that remained current until the early
part of the present century. They were "an honest and inoffensive people"
according to a "sketch" published in New York in 1906 to garner support
for a pending treaty whereby President Roosevelt sought to formalize U.S.
financial control of the Dominican Republic.[30] Indeed, in trying to present

Dominicans as a good, harmless people, American authors often construed them as predominantly Caucasian to make them acceptable to white American readers at a time of rampant antiblack racism. Thus the 1906 sketch states that while "the black race is in complete ascendancy" in Haiti, among the Dominican people "white blood preponderates."[31] Henry Hancock, another supporter of the treaty that would subsequently be known as the Dominican-American Convention, declared that in the Dominican Republic the "inhabitants are, with very few exceptions, white."[32]

The Colonizer, the Colonized, and the Individual

Nineteenth-century images for the most part falsified the Dominicans' collective profile. The practice may be inherent in the interaction between colonizer and colonized, as one gathers from Frank Bonilla's discussion of U.S. government spokespersons' appraisals of Puerto Ricans after the American occupation of 1898. Puerto Ricans saw themselves "coldly assessed by various agents of the overlord," through images that invariably rendered them devoid of human complexity. In the eyes of these official witnesses, Puerto Ricans were either "a gentle, patient, uncomplaining lot, living in ignorance and penury, generally polite, and willing to work in a plodding, undemonstrative way," as perceived by a certain Captain Macomb, or, in the contrasting image advanced by a Lieutenant Blunt, "lazy and dirty," but "very sharp and cunning."[33] Bonilla places these depictions within "a mind warping exchange that has disfigured and scarred mentalities among both rulers and ruled. This fragmentary and distorted self-knowledge constitutes a crippling heritage from which, I believe, none of us has so far achieved more than partial deliverance."[34]

   We have not yet mapped the dimensions of the scar produced by the images of Dominicanness articulated and disseminated by the agents of the overlord. One might suppose the disfigurement to be less extreme in the Dominican Republic, a virtual protectorate, than in Puerto Rico, where the Northern neighbor executed a classic colonial regime. But one notes a striking resemblance between the logic of U.S. observers and that of the Dominican ruling elite in the discourse on progress, native resources, race, ethnicity, and the role of foreigners in national development. Even the language Dominicans used to assess their interaction with Haitians may have been modulated by a logic introduced by American overseers in the nineteenth century. This chapter is not the place to pursue the implications of this "crippling heritage" for people in the Dominican Republic. Rather, I shall conclude with some thoughts on its implications for the Dominican diaspora in the United States.

   The early images of Dominicans formed by U.S. observers were hardly complimentary, but they were not bitterly disparaging. The predominant depiction is friendly in a paternalistic way. It reflected only disrespect; out-right scorn and violent defamation would come later. At the time, Americans went to the Dominican Republic to pursue their own interests, which were chiefly economic, strategic, and political. But since they did not undertake to colonize the country formally, they could sever their tie to Dominicans at their convenience. This loose arrangement, in which Americans had much to gain and hardly anything to lose, did not foster the kind of tension that generates adversarial sentiments. Within such a context, it would not seem odd or unnatural for individual Dominicans to gain ascendancy in the United States, even become stars of American society.

The Dominican María Montez came from Barahona to New York and rose to stardom in such successful Hollywood productions as *Arabian Nights* (1942) and *Cobra Woman* (1943), which elevated her to "world cult status."[35] In the late 1940s New York's high society followed the adventures of Porfirio Rubirosa, a Dominican who developed an international reputation as a playboy by romancing wealthy and famous women. His conquests included the tobacco heiress Doris Duke, the actress Zsa Zsa Gabor, followed years later by her sister Eva, and Barbara Hutton, granddaughter of the founder of Woolworth. The fashion designer Oscar de la Renta and the legendary pitcher Juan Marichal, already inducted into the Baseball Hall of Fame, are also Dominicans. All four, coming to the United States as individuals, were able to pursue their interests and ambitions unimpeded by anti-Dominican feeling. However, sociohistorical events of the past three decades have reduced significantly the opportunities for Dominicans to attain visibility outside of ethnic considerations. Once Dominicans emerged in the United States as an ethnic minority vying for political and economic space, they challenged entrenched sectors whose own political and economic fortunes have become less secure as a result of the quest for empowerment by Dominicans and other Latino communities.

Migration and Demonization

The death of the dictator Trujillo (1961), another American military invasion (1965), and congressional passage of the Immigration Law of 1965 paved the way for the massive exodus of Dominicans from their homeland to the United States. Today, Dominicans are one of the most numerically significant communities of new immigrants in the United States. In New York they are the most recent minority group, the second-largest Latino subgroup, and the fastest-growing national community. From 1982 to 1989, the Dominican Republic ranked seventh among countries sending migrants to the United States, and Dominicans ranked ninth in naturalization as U.S. citizens (43,333 in the 1982–89 period).

In New York during this period, Dominicans outnumbered all other communities in their naturalization rate (27,587), made up 42 percent of all Caribbean immigrants settling in the city, and, along with the Chinese, accounted for 58 percent of all new immigrants in the borough of Manhattan. Between 1983 and 1989 Dominicans moved into the neighborhoods of Ansonia, Cathedral, Hamilton Heights, Washington Heights, and Inwood in larger numbers than any other national group of immigrants.[36] Impressive as they are, these statistics tell an incomplete story about the numerical significance of Dominicans in the United States and in New York. A large portion of Dominican migration to the United States has been undocumented or through informal channels. The actual size of the Dominican immigrant population can only be approximated.

As was the case with earlier immigrants, the rapid growth of Dominicans has provoked xenophobia from the mainstream media. For some years now, Washington Heights and its mostly Dominican inhabitants have been associated in the city's press almost exclusively with drugs and violent crime. The *New York Post* has frequently devoted pages to news articles that speak of Dominicans as "a community where three of the biggest sources of income are drugs, loan sharking, and money laundering."[37] Defamatory portrayals of the community, which date back no more than ten years, have increased in frequency and virulence since the summer of 1992, when the death of José "Kiko" García at the hands of an officer from the 34th police precinct sparked three days of upheaval in Washington Heights.

The journalist Mike McAlary has painted the community as follows: "The Dominican Republic has always exported talent to the United States. The sports pages are filled with statistics of Dominican baseball heroes in the Major Leagues. But for every George Bell and Pedro Guerrero, Stan Javier and Julio Franco thrilling American audiences, there are now a dozen lethal drug dealers from San Francisco de Macorís terrorizing neighborhoods in upper Manhattan."[38] To illustrate the prevalence of crime among Dominicans, and its roots in the homeland, McAlary, with the backing of the *New York Post,* took a four-day trip to the Dominican Republic. He assessed the prevailing moral climate of San Francisco de Macorís this way: "There is a hint of dark evil in every gold-toothed smile, and the sound of sinister laughter in the pock-marked streets."[39] In April 1994, when officers from the 30th precinct were arrested for various forms of corruption, including collusion with drug dealers, it turned out that one member of the "dirty dozen," Alfonso Comprés, was a Dominican. This sufficed for McAlary to shift the focus of his coverage from corruption in the New York Police Department to Dominican criminality. The title of his article for the *New York Daily News,* "The Tragic Legacy of a Narco Village," alludes to the city where Comprés was born, and where he presumably planned to return:

"if the cops moved in, he could always go back to San Francisco de Macorís. This is the way of the Dominican York."[40]

Dominicans have endured slanderous representations from public figures as important as Staten Island Borough President Guy Molinari, police union boss Phil Caruso, and the director of the Hispanic Society of America, who decried the location of his high-brow museum in Washington Heights. In his campaign to unseat Mayor David Dinkins, the present New York City mayor Rudolph Giuliani condemned his opponent's expression of sympathy for a Dominican mother whose son had died at the hands of the police. Giuliani construed the gesture as siding with "urban terrorists."[41] These examples reveal the vulnerability of Dominican immigrants, who must, for the time being, endure slanders without being able to challenge their detractors. The turning point will come, one expects, when the Dominican community has gained so much economic and political power that it is no longer expedient to denigrate its members. One also hopes that by then Dominicans will have penetrated the media and, through access to the columns of English-speaking newspapers and the cameras of mainstream television, will have a say in the construction of their public image.

The negative image of Dominicans, bespeaking, as it does, weakness and vulnerability, may have a deleterious effect on efforts to build alliances with other Latino subgroups. During a literary colloquium at Ollantay Center for the Arts in Queens in the late 1980s, the Puerto Rico fiction writer Ed Vega highlighted the inevitability of intra-Latino division so long as the current economic scenario prevails: "If all Latinos were from Ecuador the same thing would happen because the question is economic. In other words, 90 percent of the wealth is controlled by 10 percent of the population. Then, a few crumbs are given to 90 percent of the people so they can fight amongst themselves."[42] Dominicans face, in addition to intra-Latino animosity, the danger of a tension with their compatriots at home. Powerful Dominicans from the homeland, without a clear knowledge of or identification with the diaspora, may find it easier than immigrant spokespersons to obtain a hearing in important sectors of American society—government, foundations, or corporations. This might well provoke the resentment of U.S. Dominicans against their brothers and sisters back home, particularly since this immigrant community already has experienced its share of rejection in the homeland.[43] Nor can we at present ensure that the negative images of Dominicans currently prevalent in public discourse in the United States will be rejected when they are reproduced in the media of the sending country. These tensions are all the more worrisome when we consider that in a restructured, global economy, Dominicans in the United States and those in the Dominican Republic may find themselves increasingly in a position of rivalry.

Chapter 10

The Legacy of Conquest and Discovery: Meditations on Ethnicity, Race, and American Politics

Gerald Torres

> *They are the color of Canary Islanders, neither black nor white.*
> CHRISTOPHER COLUMBUS (CRISTÓBAL COLÓN),
> NOTEBOOK, NOVEMBER 10, 1492

> *American society has no social technique for handling partly*
> *colored races. We have a place for the Negro and a place for the*
> *white man: the Mexican is not a Negro, and the white man*
> *refuses him an equal status.*
> MAX S. HANDMAN, "ECONOMIC REASONS FOR THE
> COMING OF THE MEXICAN IMMIGRANT" (1930)

Mestizaje

In *The General in His Labyrinth,* Gabriel García Márquez has Simón Bolívar painfully reflecting on his failed dream to unify South America as one nation and drive out the Spanish overlords.[1] Plagued by feverish nightmares, unable to sleep in the days before leaving Bogota on the Magdalena River, as near to collapse as his dreams, the General can only mutter: "Nobody understood anything."[2] Bolívar's dreamed-of unity splinters into feuding and competing national identities that become the demons in his nightmares: "There is no other alternative," he says. "Either unity or anarchy."[3] The polarity of his vision continues to infect the idea of the nation-state, the liberal analog for the construction of "a people." The construction of "the citizen" supplants the notion of "the subject" and through the construction of rules of inclusion broadens the notion of who belongs. By separating the idea of the nation-state from the idea of a people, a broad unity may be achieved. Our nightmarish horrors are Bosnia and Rwanda. The polite version is Quebec. The terror of dissolution and chaos is always real and always with us.

The construction of the liberal nation-state posed the question: How can we organize ourselves to make liberty and solidarity two aspect of the same phenomenon?[4] Yet for the United States a different question has emerged. Domestically, instead of competing nationalities, has race recreated the divide that drove Bolívar mad and that de Tocqueville noted? Has the problem of race in domestic politics so corrupted the possibility of dialogue that all ethnically based interest group politics must mimic the structure that racial politics has created?

I want to address these questions in the context of contemporary Hispanic political identity, and in the context of my thesis that Bolívar's dream of a united "pan-Hispanic" identity may ultimately be fulfilled in North, not South, America and in response to competing racial, not national, identities. To address these questions, however, requires some concern with the problems of conquest and discovery.

As will be evident, there is an irony in the topic I have chosen because there is irony in the dream that the various national cultures of Latin America could, by driving the Spanish imperialists out but retaining the Iberian culture, be combined to produce a non-nationalist (in the sense of local nation-state) pan-Hispanic identity. It is a dream that is as old, certainly, as Simón Bolívar.[5] García Márquez's novel about Bolívar's last days summed up his frustration at the failure to establish the South American Union. Jose Martí expressed this dream of Latin American unity as well. The General's dream will undoubtedly first be achieved north of the Rio Grande. That is the principal irony. The combination of the national cultures of Latin America into a version of pan-Hispanic identity will probably be achieved in North America before it is achieved in South America (where, except for the various trade alliances, the dream died with Bolívar).

Rather than continue here with a historical overview and analysis of the conquest and discovery of America, I want to bring Bolívar's problem up to date. The change in location of the dream is critical, but it is a virtually identical dream that animates the attempt to generate a stable unity in the face of the centrifugal forces of diverse national identities. My general argument is as follows:

1. A pan-Hispanic identity forged from the many national cultures of Latin America makes sense in the context of the history of ethnicity in the United States.[6] Indeed, I want to suggest why such a result may be compelled by the structure of North American thinking about racial identity.[7]

2. If my hypothesis is correct, the creation of a generalized Hispanic identity may be compelled as well by the structure of interest group politics in the United States. That is, liberal interest group pluralism, when imbricated by deeply held conceptions of race and identity, may produce a set of rational responses that result in the construction of ethnicity in the concrete ways that we have witnessed in the past forty years. I want to suggest a less commonly observed point as well: that the complexity of the component national identities creates the subversive poten-

tial, ultimately, to undermine the structure of racial and nationalistic politics in a positive way.[8]

3. Finally, I want to speculate on what all this might mean for the organizing principles of North American political culture. At the risk of seeming hopelessly optimistic, I suggest a vision of democratic politics that is at odds with the corrosive nationalism that plagues us today. The evolution of Hispanic identity in North America gets its democratic strength from processes that lead, ultimately, to the reduction of nationalism as the organizing principle for political action.[9] I take these ideas, pull them together, and demonstrate just how the processes they describe work to produce the very idea of a multicultural Hispanic identity.[10] I also show how that new multicultural identity works to produce changes within the paradigmatic racial politics of our age.[11] My central idea in this chapter is that national identities can be suppressed only through the imposition of a more encompassing identity or a new national identity. This is the essence of the assimilationist model of ethnic life in the United States. But what I am arguing here is that in America there is an intermediate state that is dictated by the structure of American politics. What we observe first is the creation of a faux ethnic category; then, because for Hispanics this has meant a largely nonwhite grouping, the ethnic category is transformed into a faux racial category.

Culture, Politics, Law: Prolegomenon to a Democratic Faith

I will take it as a given that the idea of "*the* Hispanic" or "*the* Latino" is a problematic notion for those of us of one or another Latin American heritage who find ourselves here in the United States.[12] I recall a conversation with Oscar Hijüelos, who told me that the first time he saw the word "Hispanic," all he could see was *his panic*. I must say I share his anxiety. The pan-Hispanic idea is problematic because it requires those of us who were colonized by Iberian imperialists to begin, first of all, to conceive of ourselves as having an identity that overlooks or supersedes the various national cultures that give vitality to a specific ethnic identity.[13] Many Mexican-Americans, for example, identify far more closely with their Indian roots than with their Spanish roots, despite the relative attenuation of that connection and the continued vitality of the Spanish language in Mexican-American life.[14] Such a valorization of Indianness is either rejected or less prominent in other Latin American cultures. The layering of abstractions is a feature of modernist national creation at work within the context of domestic politics.[15] It is not unique to the United States, but a feature of our time.

Let me be a little more specific. "Hispanic" is an abstraction in a different way than the idea of "Cuban" or the idea of "Mexican." "Hispanic" is an abstraction in the way that nationalism is. To say that the idea of the Cuban or the Mexican is an abstraction is correct, but those categories have real, empirical, intersubjective (that is to say, communal) and localized roots. To claim to be a Hispanic is to make some claim about the ways in which one's specific Latin American ethnic heritage is made concrete within the general culture of the United States.[16] The power of this dynamic was brought home to me one day some time ago when my mother, who made me understand what it is to be Mexican, described herself to me as a Hispanic. This is something I could not conceive my grandmother doing. Further, it is not as though the hard-bitten Mexican community of my youth, where my mother still lives, compelled this transformation—it does not have that kind of cosmopolitan ambiance. Even the modern world of Univision and Telemundo are merely the current versions of the Mexican television of the 1960s that was broadcast from Los Angeles. Yet it is certainly true that the panethnic dynamic of modern Spanish-language television would have invaded my old neighborhood. I admit to having been somewhat taken aback at the time my mother chose that self-description, but I realized that she was merely subject to a less assimilationist variant of the same pressures I was both knowingly and unknowingly subjected to from the time I went away to college. She never left the Mexican community, but her sense of the community she belonged to changed. I, on the other hand, did, but the consequences of that departure were at once immense and invisible to me. Not to my mother. Slightly more than fifteen years before her "Hispanic" remark, one spring day when I was home from college, she told me, with great prescience, "Gerald, you are white in ways that you don't even know."[17]

The specific features of a particular national category fall away in the face of the corrosive process of domestic ethnic creation.[18] Since that process is essentially political, the elements of identity that matter are not those that are the essence of a specific culture, but those that can be converted to a more generalized representation of an ethnic type. (The focus on language is an example of this phenomenon.) This creates many opportunities and many problems, some of which I explore in the sections that follow. Suffice it to say at this point that the problems and opportunities mirror the "assimilationist/pluralist" split that has dominated discussion of ethnic identity in the United States. In order to more fully explain this process, I turn next to an exploration of the problematics of creating an ethnic category for a nonethnic identity.

Four Ideas About Discovery and Identity

Let me propose four ideas about why there is an emergent Hispanic identity and why the process of its creation is in some measure the consequence of that set of circumstances we have come to call the discovery of America by Columbus. I am here using "discover" in the sense I refer to below. Columbus, after all, is celebrated as an Italian hero, but, of course, he sailed for Spain and "discovered India" for the Spanish crown. That he should be celebrated in the United States at all is interesting. He is credited as a foundational figure though he represented a culture that has little foundational significance for the United States except in an oppositional way. One might even characterize him as the representative of the anti-Enlightenment forces in power in Europe at that time. Yet Columbus is important for the process he has come to symbolize. His actions are used as a shorthand for the massive western expansion of Europe into North and South America. That physical expansion was an extension of both the nation creating that was occurring in Europe and the adoption of Christianity as one of the foundational models for civil society.[19] If one is able to collapse the discovery of America into the generalized process of nation creating, then it will be easy to understand the existence of a Hispanic identity as the furthest extension yet of that process.

When I began to write this chapter, I thought it offered an important opportunity for me to address the idea of multiculturalism and Hispanic identity. I also thought that the animating organizing conception would be a meditation on the significance of conquest and discovery in the making of America. Perhaps the idea came to me because I originally started thinking about these themes during the year of the quincentenary of Columbus's voyage. I think the idea also appealed to me because of the centrality of those twin concepts to our conception of race and otherness in law and politics. They are central because they place our national genesis squarely within both the tradition of European colonialism and the idea of American uniqueness. The idea of *discovery* elides the issues of "by whom?" and "of what" and also avoids examining the narrative structure within which such an event occurs. *Conquest,* to the contrary, locates both a legal and national starting point for the story. In fact, discovery mediates the implications of conquest and colonialism. Discovery as a thematic device negates, in part, some of the coarser implications of conquest and colonialism and contributes to the creation of the myth of a benevolent process. This is especially true when discovery proceeds from a priori conviction of what there is to be found.[20] If you expect to find subjects of the Great Khan, but instead find natives who "would make good and industrious servants," either capable of conversion to Christianity or fit for slavery, this "discovery" justifies the path of conquest.[21]

Much that is problematic about our understanding of the role of race in domestic politics and law can be revealed by examining other grounding myths of our national creation. This means going beyond the generally sterile originalism and natural law controversies that have dominated the law reviews and policy debate over the last decade.

Contemplating the twin ideas of conquest and discovery within the context of Hispanic political identity really means contemplating the creation of the idea of America. While conquest has always had a place in the American national imagination,[22] discovery has been more problematic,[23] despite its inclusion in our annual celebration of both Columbus and Thanksgiving. Except for the legal doctrine of discovery that was used to justify the assumption of plenary federal jurisdiction over Indian tribes (and assert for the federal government its right to a place at the table of the family of nations),[24] anyone who invokes the idea of discovery in American iconography has always had to account for the interaction with the Indian people who were found here. Importantly, those Indian people were implicated in the survival of the early colonists whether during that first winter in Massachusetts or through the intervention of Pocahontas.[25] The first important thing to notice about discovery is that the discovery was not just of a place, but of the need to reconfigure the known world: politically, religiously, and physically.[26]

The compelled reconfiguration would entail a profound change in the place and role of Europe in the world. The world had, literally, to be redrawn. Each country in Europe could assert a new centrality. The blankness of the new map allowed the European nations to rewrite themselves: New England, New Spain, New Amsterdam. This nomenclature did not reflect a failure of imagination, though it might seem to; it was, instead, a form of national redemption. The wealth of the new world promised new power. The crown could be somewhat more forgiving of deviance in exchange for the promise of gold and the spread of Christendom. The new world caused the countries of the colonizers to recharacterize themselves. The Castillians, for example, became Spanish in part through the designation by Cortés of the newly colonized territory as "New Spain."[27] The limitations of Europe could be redeemed by the wealth and novelty of what their sailors, soldiers, and clerics had found. Modern time could begin.[28]

As I have already noted, the adventurers did not find empty land. They found a land peopled with what they could only call "Indians." Even as they proclaimed the "New Englandness" or the "New Spanishness" of the "new world," they could not count the people they found there as "New Englanders" or the "New Spanish." Initially, there was doubt whether they were to be counted as people at all.[29] The Catholics differed from the Protestants on this point, believing that through the redemption of the human soul the Indians could "become human" if they converted. Yet even before the discoverers and their sponsors could theologically, philosophically or ethically address that question—and there did develop a vast literature on that point[30]—they had to confront the concrete existence of millions of indigenous people. One initial approach was to exterminate or enslave those they found. That policy would prove unstable.[31]

The inscription of Europe in the Americas was riven at its inception by the great divides of Europe. Columbus represented southern Europe, with its Iberian culture and Catholicism, in opposition to the Teutonic/Germanic culture and Protestantism of northern Europe.[32] The significance of this distinction between the European north and south lies in the way in which social and economic life was organized within each broad cultural grouping, the distinct motivation for exploration, and the nature of the colonization program.[33]

The distinct processes and nature of the conquests of the north and the south led to a fundamental distinction between the nations of the north and those of the south that arose from the union of national identity with racial identity.[34] Because of the conception of civil society that the largely northern European colonizers brought with them, the northern version of racial identity is essentially bi-polar: the races came in two colors, white and non-white. The exclusion of the original inhabitants of the Americas from civil society and its notions of humanity, in conjunction with the introduction of the slave trade, reinforced this bi-polarity.[35] The early treatment of European immigrants, whom we would all today identify as "racially white," reflects this bi-polar conception of race.[36] Regardless of the class occupied by the immigrant, the racial codes were designed to maintain the distinction between those who were white and those who were legally excludable from civil society.[37]

This conception of racial otherness was different in Latin and South America. It was challenged in those areas colonized by southern Europeans through the creation of a specific and identifiable third type: the mestizo.[38] Although whiteness was the norm and the hierarchical ranking of people on the basis of color was not unknown in Latin America, the mestizo must be distinguished from the categories of racial identity created in the North. Here, I specifically mean categories like mulatto, quadroon, octoroon, and the like. Those categories were created and defined specifically in relationship to whiteness, whereas mestizo is a term of relation not to whiteness, but to other distinct and "pure" types. The purity of the type is a fiction, of course, because the mestizo is the product of the *mestizaje*. The Indian who could not be conquered and the European who could only reproduce the culture and the "race" by mixing

produced this third type. This was a group that was joined to the new world and the old through the common link of the culture of Spain and the peculiar form of imperialism that flowed from that culture. This linkage will be critical in the modern (and postmodern) iteration of Hispanic group identity.

Creating a National Presence

The first idea I propose for your consideration posits a very simple explanation for the existence of a Hispanic identity in the United States. The pressure of responding in a coherent way to the politics of national identity defined in terms of interest group politics—that is, pluralism as expressed in American political culture—has led to the creation of an umbrella group that subsumes individual national cultures.[39] The "discovery" of Hispanic identity is a coherent and rational political response to the structure of American politics.[40] Let me demonstrate what I mean.

Imagine that you are a member of a specifically identified cultural subgroup, say Mexican-American or Puerto Rican or Cuban-American.[41] Imagine further that you have surveyed the political landscape. After your review you ask: How can my group organize in a way that gets the issues we are concerned about onto the national political agenda? The obvious answer that you come to is that it can only be done if your group establishes a national political presence.

Seeing the answer, of course, is only the first step. The critical question is: How is that national presence created? Looking at the distribution of Hispanic national cultures in the United States, you discover very quickly that there are Puerto Ricans, Cubans, and Dominicans in the East and in the Southeast. In the Southwest there are Mexicans, Guatemalans, Salvadorans, and other Central Americans. In Chicago there are Mexicans, Puerto Ricans, Cubans, and some other South American groups. Your observation reveals that the various groups made up of distinct national identities are highly dispersed. You also note that the dominant cultural subgrouping tends to replicate itself in ways that define all members of cognate subgroups as part of the dominant group. Thus Latinos in Los Angeles tend to adopt the general characteristics of Mexicanness in public life, whereas in Miami the dominant Hispanic identity is Cuban. Observing this you note that one way to establish a national presence within the context of American interest group politics is to try to subsume those national identities within a broader identity. At that point the question becomes: What is that identity going to be?

One possible source of transnational identity is to organize according to the identity of the colonizer. This is a good ploy because it creates an immediate distinction between you and those who were colonized by the

British and the French. Moreover, there are specific variants of this historical experience that can be called up or repressed as needs be. We can call this identity "Hispanic." Hispanic identity has both a linguistic and a historical pedigree. This identity can then become a point around which to organize specific political interests.

Unfortunately, any alert reader will recognize that this first premise has embedded within it specific notions of representation that I will decline to elaborate here, but which will be explored in the context of my fourth idea. This first premise also subsumes, without engaging critically, the assumption that group identity is an organizing political force—that is, that at some level people participate in politics and seek representation as members of "a group." This first premise also elides the problems of conflict between the elite and the popular base and between the national and the local and the elites that each arena creates. This complex of conflicts is critical, and my failure to discuss it fully here should not be understood as an attempt to minimize the consequences of those conflicts. This complex of conflicts is derived from the general American predisposition to make all politics national, despite the admonition of people like the late Tip O'Neill that all politics is local.[42] The current debates over federalism really mask the national nature of American politics. We see all politics as national because, unlike most other Western democracies, we have the virtually direct popular election of the chief executive. We think of ourselves as coming together as a people in the symbol of the presidency and, through it, the national government. While Americans are resolutely antistatist in rhetorical predisposition, there can be no denying that all politics, however local, is pushed through a sieve of national identity.

Bi-polarity and Racial Politics

The idea of using Hispanic identity as an organizing principle is a coherent response to the management of cultural difference in the United States. I am suggesting by this assertion, of course, that cultural *difference* is only salient for some groups and triggers a management response by the governing elites.[43] By "management response" I mean a patterned reaction based upon learned techniques for minimizing political conflict that is threatening to the ruling elites. One management practice is to express political difference based on culture along a black/white axis.[44] That is, cultural difference in the United States for political purposes is defined principally in racial terms. This is a critical technique for managing ethnic conflict. It works because race in the United States is bi-polar: black and white or white/nonwhite. The consequences of this bi-polarity are significant.

Such racial polarization is another example of the residue of embedding the concept of discovery in the founding mythology of America. The colonization of what is now the United States was accomplished primarily by the British.[45] People from the Iberian peninsula were chiefly responsible for colonizing Latin America. In Latin America, the discoverers were confronted by much more numerous, and in some instances more systematically organized, native cultures than confronted the discoverers of the North.[46] The presence of these imperially organized cultures meant that the colonizers had the structures for the centralization of access to the material wealth of the new world already in place, as well as the political structure to manipulate that accumulation.

These facts, especially the number and organization of the native population, had a substantial impact on the use of chattel slavery.[47] In the North, the attitudes toward native people were markedly different from those in Latin America. The felt need for and use of slavery also meant that African people would be imported into North America, primarily the United States, in large numbers and for a longer period than in Latin America.

In the North, the "discoverers" brought their families. This fact (along with their religious predisposition) facilitated the decision to exclude native people from the sphere of civil society. In the South, to the contrary, the invaders were priests and warriors, by and large without women. These men set about creating immediately, through either rape or marriage, a mixture of "bloods." At the root, in the foundation, of "New Spain" in Latin America, the idea of mixture is central. By "mixture" I do not necessarily mean blending, but something like a suspension. The European cultural identity was embedded in a non-European reality. The proof of this is the extent to which the indigenous political forms were used to solidify Spanish control. Yet, as we all know, the transformer is rarely untransformed. Moreover, the forces for the creation of a pan-Hispanic identity in South America are less compelling because there is no opposition to Iberian cultural hegemony except that of the natives and to some extent the descendants of manumitted African slaves.

In the United States having produced a civil society that by and large excluded natives,[48] colonists proceeded to suppress native religious practices with no immediate systematic attempt to Christianize them[49] (the converse of which is another distinctive feature of the colonizing of the South). Regardless of the reasons for this exclusion of the existing native population, the dominant outsider was the African slave. In some sense, the African slave was incorporated into the political economy without having a social existence in the dominant civil society.

These facts, combined with a constitutionally established status as other,[50] installed bi-polarity in the description of racial identity that was at the core of American civil society at its creation. Thus, pushed forward to contemporary politics, a pan-Hispanic identity implies that we have already subsumed all these various national cultures. Finding ourselves in the United States responding to pluralist interest group politics, it makes sense to use a panethnic term that creates, in effect, a faux racial category. This move effectively counterfeits a race in a way not normally conceived of in contemporary sociological terms. It defines ethnicity in racial terms and conceives of a political identity that can be organized around the racial bi-polarity (white/nonwhite, with blackness as the model for non-whiteness) that exists in U.S. politics today.

Despite the rationality of this response from political elites this strategy is unstable. In fact, as I will presently argue, the bi-polarity of racial politics is under stress precisely because of the "racialization" of ethnic politics. The rational response that I have described creates a resulting tri-polarity that subverts the idea of race itself.

Racial Mixture and Racial Management

Once this move in identity politics creates a pan-Hispanic "ethnicity," ethnic groups that find themselves within that pan-Hispanic identity (Mexican, Cuban, Colombian, Peruvian, Puerto Rican, etc.) gain a space and a technique to deal with the racial distinctiveness and conflict that is internal to their own cultures. For instance, once you define Hispanics as a political interest group it makes sense for a black Puerto Rican to be Puerto Rican Hispanic rather than American black if the specific political advantages of being a Puerto Rican outweigh anything that could be gained by trading in an ethnic identity for a racial one. (The process is exactly reversed for "racially white" ethnic groups, who as a result of becoming white normalize their ethnicity.) This analysis implicates the idea of intersectionality in several ways—not least in that, if my first premise is correct, then even if "Hispanics" ultimately desire assimilation, they must first be "black" in order to establish their national political identity.

Yet, the very process I have described destabilizes the idea of race as a bi-polar category. Pan-Hispanic ethnicity within the structure of American interest group pluralism creates a form of political discipline that allows (this analysis suggests *requires*) ethnic groups to work out their own racial politics under the rubric of Hispanic identity. A failure to do so will show the category "Hispanic" to be empty and thus render it incapable of providing a foundation for specific political action. Moreover, it would make the nationalization of ethnic politics along that vector impossible or subject to the kind of race-baiting that we have seen in recent political contests.

Exploring a country like Mexico, for example, exposes this process at work. In Mexican culture, the idea of mixture is one of the primary elements. The complexity arises, in the sense of working out racial politics within ethnicity, where "Indianness" is valued primarily in mixture and devalued in isolation—except, that is, for conventional reference to the heroic pre-Columbian past. Even the most European-looking Mexicans (that is, Mexican nationals in Mexico)[51] point to the mixture of their roots, no matter how thin that mixture may be, as a way to authenticate their ethnic identity and to work out the problems of racial subordination that have taken place over 500 years.[52] Even facing the reality that Mexico has not worked out its problems of race, the existing political system has historically based its legitimacy on portraying the transfer of power from the colonial rulers to the domestic elites as on the continuum of imperial power that was rooted in the Mayan, but especially the Aztec, period. But my argument is that in North American politics, the type of identity politics I am describing creates a different space for racial politics to be played out. It creates a sphere that is outside the structure of bi-polar (white/nonwhite) racial management. This "ethnic identity" creates the idea of Hispanic in quasi-racial terms in relation to the white/nonwhite axis, but as an absolutely nonracial term internally. The Hispanic identity is not internally racial, instead, it is an ethnic identity that has racial valences within domestic politics.

The Social Construction of Racial and Ethnic Identity

My fourth premise is in tension with the third because I am making a complicated, almost contradictory, claim. That claim is that the manipulation of ethnic identity described in my first premise was conceived of as a tool of elites. Yet, for it to function as a way for ethnic elites to capture goods (power, rent, etc.) it must return some concrete benefits to the local groups represented by the elites. Thus the local ethnically specific subgroups participate in the identity of Hispanic to the extent that it allows access to the national political agenda (and thus to the national distribution of social goods). This participation, however, transforms the local groups to the extent that the fiction must be maintained, because the fiction is structurally "American." By "structurally American" I mean that the creation of an overarching group that erases local specificity causes the local groups to define their issues in a way that corresponds to the structure that national elites have constructed. This is emblematic of contemporary liberal interest group politics in the United States.[53] The hope for positive social transformation lies in the belief that the tension created in the redescription of the polity will result, as well, in the redescription of race.

The fourth idea is that the politics represented by American interest group pluralism carries with it an implicit promise. It is a promise that is hard to work out in the black/white equation, but easier to work out in the Hispanic version of the white/nonwhite equation. The promise held out to ethnic groups is an old one: you can escape the bi-polarity of racial categories by assimilating into the generalized culture of the United States. That is, you can participate in the distribution of economic, cultural, and political power if you organize politically in the way I have outlined, and if you recognize that racial bi-polarity is central to the stability of national politics. This requires, however, that you recognize that the ultimate goal of organizing politically in the way that I have outlined is to erase the polarity between Hispanic and white. The racial bribe held out to Hispanics is a form of cultural assimilation that eliminates the power of a specific political-ethnic identity. This kind of offer is possible because of the intrinsically nonracial foundation for the category "Hispanic." But it is a form of assimilation that remains quite problematic for African-Americans. Their history of being enslaved is unique among nonwhite groups in the United States. As a consequence of both the process and the mythology of the discovery of America, African-Americans stood outside the development of the nation, and that process denied to them, even on the level of theory, the ability to be assimilated. Perhaps most simply, their color and the political and social responses to it for most of the history of this country foreclosed the ethnic model of assimilation.

Admittedly, the issue of color and the persistent racialist notions about both Indians and Latin Americans raise the question of whether some groups, even faux racial groups, are assimilable. This is particularly true for Mexican-Americans in the Southwest, where the proximity of the border contributes to a continual refreshing of the Mexican culture within the United States. This process prevents the development of a specifically locatable romantic past or a nostalgic scrim through which to view and construct an ethnic immigrant narrative.

The central irony is that Bolívar's dream is really coming true in the United States because there is a space that allows and, I have argued, requires that Latin American cultures work out their differences and unite. But it is a space defined by American politics, that is outlined both by the racial history of the United States and the racial dimension of politics in the United States.[54] Unfortunately for those who would like to use the racial bribe, the racial mixture that characterizes the national cultures that make up the "Hispanic" grouping complicates a clear articulation of Hispanic ethnic politics as a modern expression of the white ethnic experience within cultural pluralist/interest groups politics. This is true because of the distinctly "nonwhite" make-up of large segments of the "Hispanic" population. That means that those Hispanics who opt to be "white" within the meaning of the conventional immigrant construction must, in some important political way, opt out of being Hispanic. It may be a strategy for individual assimilation, but it is not a strategy for political empowerment.

There is a dual promise at work. What I foresee is not the fulfilling of the promise as I have described it: that if Hispanics adopt this strategy the result will be total assimilation. (Some would argue that this was the strategy LULAC, the League of United Latin American Citizens, pursued in its early days.) Instead, a fully textured working out of a complex Hispanic identity creates the opportunity to break down the idea that there is a racial dimension to citizenship.[55] This idea persists even though it is not official and is contrary to the national liturgy.[56] The hope of that promise lies in my third premise: that this pan-Hispanic identity creates a space, one might say a model, for the "safe" working out of racial differences within the American ideal.

If the construction of Hispanic identity requires the constituent groups of that broader category to come to grips with their own racial politics in order to maintain the vitality of the national political project, then there is hope that the historic racialization of domestic interest group politics will provide the seeds of its own undoing. This will only be possible where color ceases to be the central organizing principle of social groupings. Feminists have faced this problem, but without the force of nationalist cultural traditions to overcome the barrier of having to choose one paramount source of identity, and the power of racial politics in the United States has largely prevailed.[57] The Hispanic project is a case study of the social construction of racial and ethnic identity. It has also rendered claims of racial essentialism unstable. The fact that Hispanics can be of any "race" suggests that *what* you think and even *who* you think you are is determined by more than who you look like. Combined with the realities of power, that is a basically hopeful claim, but not one that promises a smooth line out of the bog of our racial history.

I would like to suggest one final hypothesis. The ultimate consequence of the discovery of America may be that Columbus's misadventure set in motion the concatenation of events that will lead to the transformation and end of nationalism as we have known it. I am not suggesting that this process will be quick—after all, we are still laboring with the reverberations of the European entry into the Americas some five hundred years after the first landfall in what is now Hispaniola. The racialization of domestic pluralist interest group politics arose when our liberal traditions took root in a culture of conquest dressed up in the mythology of discovery. Conquest provided one justification for colonization carried out with arms. The colonization of indigenous people by Europeans through conquest not only resulted in the creation of a new race, but signaled the superiority of the European. Discovery provided an alternative justification. The moral consequences of discovery are markedly different, since sovereignty is declared by law rather than mere arms. But it also created a locus of resistance. The mestizo and the new-world-born Spanish resisted the hegemony of Spain by declaring a new national identity. They resisted initially by facially complying with the commands of the crown but ignoring them in practice. They dismissed the directives with the excuse that they would not work in local conditions.[58] It was not rebellion, but common-sense obedience.

The gradual reconciliation of the two traditions of discovery and conquest has shaped the structure of contemporary politics. The one has long led to a distribution of the spoils that the other argues is unjust. What I have described in this brief chapter is one aspect of the working out of that prospect, and I have, some would argue, taken too rosy a view. I have tried to make coherent the tangle of impulses expressed in political terms at all levels of the political process and across almost all political issues. The issues are no longer cabined in the box called "civil rights."[59] Nor, I have argued, are they restricted to an increasingly unstable black/white axis, even where that structure has provided the model for political organization and accommodation.

A colleague at another institution related the following story, which I take to be an instantiation of my thesis. In a seminar project in which the women of color were asked to gather at one end of the room, the first two to sit were a Cuban-American and a Mexican-American. The class had been meeting for six weeks, and both had publicly identified themselves in class discussions as Latinas. Two Asian women, trying to figure out where the women of color were meeting, looked over at the corner where the two "Latinas" sat and became confused. They saw two white women, because both of these Latinas are descriptively white. One Asian woman subsequently said that she was delighted that these women identified themselves as women of color—she now understood that this term had political rather than just descriptive power. One of the Latinas said that this exercise had helped create a new sense of community between the various women of color in the class. The recognition that the designation was more than a physical description, that it was a political identity, was like an electric charge running through that subgrouping.

Several questions are raised by my hypothesis and by this story. One aspect of my hypothesis is that the black women in the group felt empowered by the broadening of their community of color. Suddenly, to their surprise, white-looking people voluntarily became colored. In this sense, the meaning of the story is that race is a political rather than a natural category and that black people, the most "raced group," will benefit by the expanded category.

On the other hand, the truth remains that color is a powerful determinant of many aspects of social life. You have to hold both truths in your mind at once. The fear of black members of this expanded community is that the whiter members will accept the "racial bribe" and eventually abandon them. Thus their former alliance will be used against them to reinforce the idea that the general society is not racist and that there is room for the right kind of people. Tokenism is used as a justification for continued white-skinned privilege, and white people can use the example of the formerly colored people to reject the need for more dramatic and broadly inclusive change. In a temporary alliance of convenience, as soon as the costs outweigh the benefits, those who can defect will. This might include those light-skinned blacks who can leave without fear of opprobrium. The temporary advantage has the risk of becoming a long-term disadvantage. The fear is that anyone who voluntarily agrees to be black is in some sense not really black, because our culture has defined blackness as something that you can never escape.[60]

How does one respond to those fears? One response is that political action often requires strategic though temporary alliances. However, my hypothesis and this answer raise another question: Why should black people, even if empowered temporarily, engage in the creation of this new space? The answer to that question has to lie in a commitment to a truly democratic polity. The enlarged polity is more likely to make decisions, including profound structural reform, in response to organized pressure, especially when it is broadly representative. I do not want to overstate this point or to sound unduly optimistic. Yet part of the allure of this new definition of community is that it requires changing the rules about the construction of the polity, and that process itself is valuable.

In a recent conversation, Peterson Zah, the former president of the Navajo Nation (Dine), told me that he likes to go fishing, and when he does, he likes to drop a stone into the water. Once you drop the stone into the pond, he added, you cannot move faster than the ripples and still maintain the symmetry of the expanding rings. Perhaps the process of transforming national identities is like the slow movement of concentric circles intersecting after many stones are dropped into the pond. Our efforts are merely like the dropping of many stones in the pond. The patterns they create have their own pace and scale

Then again, perhaps there are more suitable metaphors for the process. One might be Cortés's burning of his boats, his concrete recognition that you cannot retreat from the discovery of the new world. Or perhaps the ceremonial inside-out wearing of the sacrificial victims' skin in the Mexica[61] tradition captures the way in which each new identity is really part of the old. To become "Hispanic" is to turn the idea of an ethnic identity inside out, because it is ultimately to shed any specific identity in the hope of participating in this life as an American.

Chapter 11

Transnational Political and Cultural Identities: Crossing Theoretical Borders

María de los Angeles Torres

Political borders—a defining feature of nation-states during the twentieth century—are changing, being reinforced at the same time that they are eroding. These increasingly porous frontiers suggest that, like economies, the nature of politics and of political participation may also change.[1] One reason is that people, particularly in diaspora communities, are affected by decisions made by governments in which they have only a limited voice or no voice at all. In home countries, governments make decisions that affect diaspora communities residing beyond the state's geographic jurisdiction. In host countries, diaspora communities often have a restricted role in public affairs because of their newcomer status. Ironically, while some countries are extending voting rights to their communities abroad, most host countries are limiting or even reversing some of the avenues immigrants have used to express their opinions in the past. There are few analytical and legal concepts that go beyond the nation-state as the parameter for political participation, making it difficult to envision immigrant political participation in both host and home countries.

In addition, the cultural identities of diaspora communities are not only informed by the host country, but also have many points of reference to home country culture. Past cultural and familial connections are not severed by crossing political borders. Immigrant flows from home countries have added new layers to existing diaspora communities. Yet the prevailing social science framework used to study the immigrant experience assumes that the nation-state is the principal organizational unit of politics and cultural identity. In this framework, public power is organized and contested within the geographic boundaries of nation-states, which also define the economies and social organization of societies. It is the state that regulates the affairs of the nation.

Citizenship: Who Is Entitled?

The notion of citizenship is deeply interwoven with the rise of the nation-state. With the formation of nation-states came a new set of conditions that defined the rights of individuals, particularly in relation to the state.

169

These included a definition and legal categorization of who was entitled to these rights. Citizenship became something to be granted or denied by the state. Although there are many legal variations in how citizenship is acquired—for instance, under German law it is passed from parent to child, while under Spanish, French, and British law the place of birth is the determining factor[2]—nation-states make citizenship and residency a requirement of political participation.

Furthermore, citizenship assumes loyalty to a state. In order to acquire U.S. citizenship, for example, emigres must swear an oath of exclusive allegiance to the United States. Yet the identities of many immigrants are too complex to allow this. Diaspora communities often reside in multiple states or have traveled through them. Restricting loyalty to one state flattens immigrants' experiences and limits their political options, particularly when they are affected by the decisions of many states.

The "nation" side of the nation-state concept also carries built-in assumptions. In regard to citizenship, the nation was conceived from the start as socially and culturally homogeneous. Those who are citizens are assumed to have a common cultural base. Even in the United States, where property, gender, and race were used initially to define who was included in the body politic, a romanticized abstraction of the androgynous, raceless citizen prevailed. Naturalized citizens—that is, those not born in the United States—were expected to leave their homeland behind when it came to public affairs.

Those born in other countries are not automatically entitled to U.S. citizenship. The state can choose whether and when to grant this right to those who apply. Moreover, participation in public affairs depends on one's legal status. Undocumented residents and legal residents who are not naturalized are not allowed to vote, nor do they enjoy the same rights as citizens.

The Assimilation Model: Politics and Identity

Assimilation, the prevailing model of immigrant political development, is shaped by a geographically determined definition of political space and agenda. The assimilation model predicts that recent immigrants do not participate in politics immediately after their arrival in the host country because they are still preoccupied with home country issues and with trying to adapt to a new environment. By the second generation, ties to the homeland have weakened. Political involvement begins at the local level, moving to the national level within another generation. By the third generation, the political agenda of immigrant groups may include international issues; by this time the focus of international affairs is not confined to the country of ancestry because the connection with the homeland has effectively been broken. Although there is a distinction between assimilation (becoming the other) and acculturation (adapting to the other), assimilationist views now dominate the public discourse.[3]

This view of political participation fit well within a pluralist framework that conceived of politics as a product of individual and organizational effort. Individuals organized to exert pressure on the political system, which provided outputs needed by the community. This model of politics was based primarily on the experiences of immigrants who came to the United States at the turn of the century—a time of extraordinary industrial growth and relatively weak government structures, particularly at the local level. Communities first became integrated economically, facilitating their political incorporation. (It is not clear whether these earlier immigrant communities genuinely cut their ties to the homeland or whether such ties simply were difficult to maintain. For example, in a study of ethnic Chicago, historians of various immigrant communities noted a persistent interest in homeland issues even at the turn of the century.[4] Models of political development that suggested an assimilationist path to political participation have failed to explain this persistence.)

The assimilation model is less useful in explaining the political development of groups that came to the United States at a time when the economic structure was different and the state had become much more expansive. European immigrants and emigres from countries in neocolonial situations—countries that were politically or economically dominated by the United States, like many in Latin America and the Caribbean—have had different relationships to the United States. When emigre communities did not succeed in achieving formal political incorporation, the unquestioned validity of this model forced social scientists tended to focus their inquiries not on what was wrong with the model (whose validity was unquestioned), but on what was wrong with these communities. The answer usually was that they resisted assimilation. A group of Latino political scientists set out to disprove this claim by documenting the attitudinal similarities between "Americans" and immigrant groups, such as Mexican-Americans. As a result, for years the study of Latino politics sought to dispel the importance of ethnicity as a factor in political mobilization and to counter the assumption that home country issues were part of the agenda for such immigrant communities.[5]

How is the political identity of diaspora communities evolving in light of changes in the nation-state? Identity is a social construction that requires continuous negotiation among the individual, the community, and the society at large. Social and political identities have at least two important dimensions: how societies construct an individual's or a group's identity, and how the individual or community constructs its own identity.

Social and political identities are closely tied to each other precisely because the nation and the state are coupled. The nation embodies culture, history, and social structures, while political identities are defined and regulated by the state. The concept of citizenship does not exist in a vacuum; rather, it is related to other aspects of a society, particularly when a society is marked and divided by racism and when race and national origin have determined who is awarded citizenship. Nor is the definition of citizenship isolated from questions of politics, as is the case in totalitarian regimes, which demand loyalty not just in return for citizenship, but in return for a national identity. It is in this intersection that social identities, including ethnic and national identities, become critical in understanding who has access to a political system.

The assimilationist view of immigrant identity predicts that, by the second generation, immigrant communities will have lost their affective and cultural ties to their homeland and identify themselves with the host country. In the United States, the second generation will have become "American." However, many first-generation Latinos, their children, and even grandchildren retain a level of interest in home country politics and culture. Like the political assimilation model, the prevalent model of identity assumes a singular identity tied to one geographic space. It also assumes that this identity is fixed and does not change over time.

The notion of assimilation itself assumes not only that integration is desirable, but also that it is possible. Shedding one's ethnicity is taken as a sign of leaving behind that which is old and replacing it with something new. This act suggests that individuals and communities can somehow discard their past and incorporate into a new culture. But this predictive model does not take into consideration the fact that in many host countries, immigrants are neither welcomed nor allowed to assimilate socially or, at times, even legally.

Another serious limitation of the assimilation model is that it cannot explain the persistence and reappearance of ethnicity and the desire to reconnect with the homeland in the sons and daughters of immigrants. These movements may be stronger in the second and third generations, particularly at times when anti-immigrant feelings are on the rise. Such has been the case, for instance, for third-generation Mexican-Americans born on Chicago's South Side. One of the country's strongest and most vibrant neighborhood museums, the Mexican Fine Arts Museum in Chicago's Pilsen neighborhood, was founded by the grandchildren of Mexican immigrants who had come to work in Chicago's steel mills. Their struggles to provide education to the Mexican community included bringing to that community the art and culture of their country of ancestry. (Later on, the museum's goal expanded to include bringing to Mexico culture created by Mexicans in the United States.)

In addition, reconnecting to the identity of one's parents may be more important at certain stages of the life cycle. The passage from adolescence to adulthood is generally accompanied by a reassessment of one's heritage and values. For second-generation immigrants, this can manifest itself as an awakening of interest in the homeland and culture of one's parents.

The prevailing vision of politics and identity insists on a uniform public culture while permitting political pluralism. While a wide array of cultures and even languages is permitted in the private spaces of U.S. society—religious, private educational, and cultural institutions—public (political) discourse demands cultural homogeneity.

The assimilation model itself may be a myth that developed in the United States between the two World Wars. Immigration to the United States from Western Europe was at its peak. When the United States went to war with Europe, patriotism and loyalty to the United States were expected. People rallied publicly under the banner of "Americans." Ethnic communities, particularly those from countries with which the United States was at war, such as Germans, Italians and Japanese, suffered varying degrees of repression. It was during this period that the public myth arose that immigrant communities actually had cut their ties to the homeland and were now as "American" as the native-born. (Curiously, Mussolini's government was the first to develop a state-sponsored project to reach out to Italian communities abroad and encourage them to influence U.S. policies toward their home country.)[6] But racism persisted. For example, after World War II Mexican-Americans formed organizations of veterans to show their loyalty to the United States. But racism was so severe that even Mexican-Americans who had been killed in the war were not buried in the same cemeteries as "white" soldiers. In response to such discrimination, organizations like the GI Forum and the League of United Latin American Citizens (LULAC) began advocating for equality and integration.

The Emergence of Alternative Views of Latino Reality

History and Homeland: The 1960s to the Mid-1970s

Integrationist movements of the post–World War II era failed to bring equality and were met with disdain. Although the federal government eventually responded to internal and international pressure to abolish segregationist laws, racism remained entrenched in states and local communities. The persistence of racism contributed to the emergence of more radical movements. In the United States, the civil rights movement of the 1960s led communities that had been excluded from the political process on the basis of race or national origin to demand inclusion on the same grounds.

Unlike the integrationist movement of the 1950s, which sought entrance and equality, the movements of the 1960s sought to change the rules of the game as well. This included a vision for transforming the cultural and political spaces in which immigrant communities exist.

Instead of trying to prove that they were loyal Americans, immigrant organizations in the 1960s sought to define their identities in terms of difference. Difference was celebrated in a search for roots that had been severed by oppression and denied by shame. One of the results of this search for identity was an affective return to the homeland. Some groups, such as the Colorado-based Crusade for Justice, founded by Corky González, initially sought a mythical homeland, Aztlan; and even organizations with a U.S.-based agenda, such as Raza Unida, later sought relations with Mexico. In the Cuban exile community, groups like the Antonio Maceo Brigade and Areíto sought connections to Cuba.

At the same time, radical movements in Mexico and Puerto Rico reached out to communities abroad. For example, connections were established between Mexican-Americans and the Mexican left after governmental repression in Mexico forced many political activists to flee to the United States. Organizations like Central de Acción Social Autonóma (CASA) represented the merger of the struggles against repression in Mexico and racism in the United States. Pro–Puerto Rican independence organizations bridged communities on the island and the mainland.

Radical politics in the various Latino communities challenged the prevailing paradigms of identity and politics by crossing borders. Scholars became critical links in this crossing as they began to redefine the paradigms within which the politics and identity of Latinos in the United States were studied. Chicano scholars, for example, played an important role in challenging ahistorical accounts of the origins of the Chicano community.[7] The recovery of history led to a growing awareness in the Southwest of the connections between the Chicano community and Mexico.[8] Alternative frameworks like the internal colonial model looked at the connections between the U.S. conquest of Mexico's northern territory in the mid-1800s and labor exploitation to understand the persistence of poverty and racism in the Southwest.[9]

Parallel critical studies emerged in the Puerto Rican and Cuban exile communities. Studies of Puerto Rican labor migration to the United States examined the connections between the colonization of the island and the migratory response of labor.[10] Cuban exile scholars sought to understand how U.S. foreign policy toward Cuba influenced the formation of Cuban communities in the United States.[11] Yet many of these studies were still bound by nation-state perspectives. An exception was the geopolitical model Carlos Forment suggested to analyze terrorist politics in the Cuban exile community.[12] In this model the unit of analysis is the region, and hegemonic politics finds expression through regional blocs. In the field of sociology, Marisa Alicea's dual-home-base model began to depart from the culturally accepted notion that immigrants have a single "home."[13] (Bi-national experiences were seen under the assimilation model as potentially destructive to the formation of community. Indeed, the ability to move back and forth from the island to the mainland was often cited as the reason for Puerto Ricans' low wages and low voter turnout.)

In addition to the search for homeland, another phenomenon emerged. Various groups of similar national origins began to come together as a means to mobilize community and political resources. Félix Padilla initially documented this phenomenon in Chicago, the first U.S. city to witness the coexistence of communities from several Latin American countries.[14] While retaining its individual ethnic identification, under certain circumstances a community would also adopt the label of "Latino," a broader ethnopolitical identity that coexisted with other ethnic identities.

In 1984 four university-based research centers dedicated to the study of the Latino experience in the United States came together to form the Inter-University Program for Latino Research.[15] This was the first academic endeavor to bring together Latino scholars from different disciplines and communities. Underlying many of its research projects was the assumption that Latino groups in the United States share a common legacy because the United States had intervened in some way in their countries of origin. Yet each group, and each subsequent immigration wave, was unique.

Growing organizational unity at the community level also found expression nationally. Organizations such as the National Association of Latino Elected and Appointed Officials (NALEO) and the Hispanic Institute (the research arm of the Congressional Hispanic Caucus) attempted to present a unified voice in national politics. Since it was harder to find consensus on foreign policy than on domestic issues, these organizations often avoided the former. Other groups, such as Policy Alternatives for the Caribbean and Central America (PACCA), the Southwest Voter Registration and Education Project, and the Cuban American Committee, advocated changes in U.S. policies toward Mexico, Central America, and the Caribbean.[16]

Ambivalent Homelands: The 1970s to the Mid-1980s

Just as attempts to assimilate to the host country encountered limits, so did movements to reconnect with countries of origin. For example, U.S.-based Mexicans experienced a mixed welcome in their homeland, where they were often referred to as *pochos* (wetbacks), and where they found the government's repressive politics intolerable.

Nevertheless, as the number of Mexican-Americans taking part in

U.S. political life rose, the Mexican government began to consider the possible implications for its interests in the United States, hoping to create a Chicano lobby similar to the Jewish-American organizations that supported Israel within the United States. In the 1980s, the Mexican government institutionalized this interest in an office dedicated to the *Mexicanos de Afuera* (Mexicans Abroad) in its Ministry of Foreign Relations.[17] This office was responsible for developing and maintaining ties with Mexican-American communities in the United States; activities, organized through Mexico's consular offices, included cultural events and arranging for scholarships to study medicine in Mexico.

Cuban exiles, called *gusanos* (worms) in their homeland, had similar experiences with the island government, although this relationship unfolded within a much more politicized climate, both on the island and in the United States. Cuban exiles who tried to return to their homeland were told by government officials that they would better serve the interests of the revolution by remaining abroad and arguing for the lifting of the U.S. embargo imposed on Cuba in the early 1960s.[18] The Ministry of the Interior was put in charge of the Comunidad Cubana el Exterior (COCUEX) project.[19] Like Mexican-Americans, Cuban exiles found that their relationship to the homeland was placed within the context of state interests, particularly foreign and security affairs. Both homeland governments considered those who had left not as nationals, but rather as resources to be used in the "national" interest.

The relationship of Puerto Ricans on the mainland to those on the island was also ambiguous. Although the independence movement at times has been stronger in U.S. cities such as Chicago and New York than in Puerto Rico, those on the island arguing for independence did not support efforts to include Puerto Ricans living in the United States as part of the electorate. On this issue, supporters of independence found allies in the pro-statehood forces, who were also leery of the politics of U.S. Puerto Ricans. When the question of a referendum on the island's status was debated in 1990, groups on the island, including the *independentistas,* lobbied against allowing mainland Puerto Ricans to vote. It became clear that home country governments and political organizations ultimately held a very narrow definition of who was to be considered part of the nation.[20]

The movement to reconnect with homelands failed just as the assimilationist path had. Homeland governments were mainly interested in the political clout, symbolic or otherwise, that their communities abroad could offer. Even when remittances sent home by immigrants began to provide critical economic resources—in some cases becoming the most important or the second most important contribution to the gross national product—communities abroad were still not entirely welcome in the body politic. In many cases, the resentment deepened.

Identity Redefined: The 1980s to the Mid-1990s

Latinos had found that while they shared some common ground with their countries of origin, there were important differences as well. Being in and out of place in both home and host country gave rise to the exploration of border identities. Border identities are unique because they contain elements of various cultures coexisting side by side. Community organizations have played a central role in the creation of border identities, but it is artists and writers—unconstrained by the slow production mode of academia or the structures of the electoral arena—who have redefined the parameters of the debate and offered more radical notions about identity and, consequently, politics.

In the Southwest, Gloria Anzaldúa proposed the notion of border identities, which forced a reexamination of the prevailing rigid categories of ethnicity and gender that had emerged from the 1960s.[21] In Cristina García's novel *Dreaming in Cuban,* Pilar returns for a visit to the forbidden island to reconnect with her grandmother Celia, who gives her the task of remembering not just for the exile community, but for the nation as a whole.[22] This proposition stands in sharp contrast to the passive role ascribed to diaspora communities by most home countries. The same theme is echoed in Guillermo Gómez-Peña's work. Not only does he call for a mutual recognition of home country and diaspora through a radical dialogue, but he also suggests that Mexicans in the United States have developed unique cultural and political skills as a result of the struggles they have had to wage against racism. Furthermore, Gómez-Peña argues, home countries can rely on these skills in developing cultural and political projects that offer an alternative to the pervasive and often popular global market culture.

Rubén Martínez, a Mexican/Central American writer in East Los Angeles, explores the multiple sources of his identity and loyalties in *The Other Side*.[23] For Martinez, *Latinismo* is embodied in himself. He does not suggest, however, that a hybrid identity represents a smooth synthesis; rather it is a continual and sometimes painful process of confrontation where there is always another side with which to contend.

Visual artists also have vividly explored migratory identities. The Puerto Rican artist Bibiana Suárez questions the contradictory images of herself held by her home and host countries through two self-portraits, one in which she is black and another in which she is white. The message is unmistakable: the dominant society in the United States views immigrants from the Caribbean as nonwhite, while on the island her blond hair and green eyes make her *blanquita.* Iñigo Manglano-Ovalle challenges the legitimacy of identities prescribed by political borders in his series on "illegal aliens." Enlarged photographs of detained aliens' thumbprints are accompanied by text containing personal recollections of their journeys to the United States. Included in the exhibit is a resident alien card with the picture and name of Christopher Columbus.

In contrast to the proposition of single nationality (for example, *either* Mexican *or* American), the notion of border identities recognizes the presence and synthesis of many cultures. In this conception, one does not have to deny the existence of the other, and ambiguity is accepted as an essential element of identity. Ambiguity provides flexibility and, consequently, the potential for movement and development. In contrast to the negative notion of ambiguity Richard Rodríguez documents in *Hunger of Memory*,[24] those who emphasize border identity see ambiguity as a fertile zone.

The concept of border identity is also distinct from the hyphenated proposition of ethnicity found, for instance, in Gustavo Pérez-Firmat's *Life on the Hyphen: The Cuban-American Experience*.[25] In this conceptualization, two fixed identities are linked by a hyphen. The direction of change is unilinear, from the identity being left behind to the new American identity, and the emphasis is on the "American"—that is, people supposedly retain some ties to their ethnic background but function as Americans within the society. The hyphenated model complemented the idea that an individual must be loyal to only one state. In contrast, a border identity that is multiple may imply multiple loyalties. Furthermore, the hyphenated model assumed fixed identities on both sides of the equation, while, in reality, home country cultures were becoming more and more "Americanized" at the same time that U.S. culture was becoming more "Latinized."

The cultural border zones that had been so clearly demarcated by political borders eroded as consumer products and cultural images crossed borders with ease. Border identities are ambiguous and constantly changing. They emerge at the margins and define themselves as hybrid creations of distinct forces. The notion of *Chicanismo* is closer to the concept of border identity because it assumes fusion; however, in *Chicanismo* identity was viewed not as a process but as a goal. Indeed, the Chicano movement saw itself as a unique nation in search of a state.

Similar reconstructions of identity have occurred in other Latino communities. The border (in airspace) between New York and San Juan brought forth debates concerning the identity of Puerto Ricans in New York ("Newyoricans") and Puertoriqueños. Fear that U.S. colonization of the island had destroyed its culture contributed to the rejection by island residents of Puerto Ricans who lived in the United States. At the same time, Puerto Ricans were not accepted as "Americans." The response was a hybrid construction ("Am-e-rican") that encompassed both identities and reasserted itself in the eyes of both the host and the home country.[26]

The highly politicized aquatic wall between Cubans in Miami and

Havana provoked its own debates. For the island's government, *Cubanía* belonged to those who were committed to the political project of the state. But this rigid notion of who was Cuban was later modified as the Cuban government made moves to open up to its communities abroad. After the collapse of the Soviet Union, exile remittances became the second most important source of cash for the Cuban government, which made efforts to reach out to the exile community at the same time that it continued to exclude it from the homeland. In the meantime, the second generation of Cuban exiles in the United States continued a process of attachment to both host and home country culture nurtured by the unprecedented exodus of artists and intellectuals in the late 1980s who sought a "third option"—a cultural and political space beyond the political borders of the island and the exile community.[27]

The search for a more complex understanding of identity was in part a response to the rigid categories of identity that emerged from the radical movements of the 1960s. It was also a response to the postmodern prediction that, as cultural spaces became increasingly homogenized through easy transportation and communication, all human beings would in effect move toward a single identity. Instead, communities at the "margins" came to witness an accelerated fragmentation of identity. As nation-states eroded, they were not replaced by a homogeneous superstate or a single identity. Rather, societies became more diverse as immigration from one part of the world to another rushed ahead, giving rise to the movement for a recognition of the multicultural character of societies. At the same time, receiving societies became less open. While the 1960s movement for equality—that is, political and civil rights—asked for representation in the host country, and the movements of the 1970s witnessed demands to reconnect with the homeland, the multicultural movement of the 1980s sought to transform the public spaces in both home and host countries.

Institutionalization and Backlash

The backlash against the multicultural movement emerged in the late 1980s and early 1990s at a time when U.S. society was witnessing a major transformation of its economy as well as its position in the world. The new service-based economy provided few high-paying and many low-paying jobs, a structure that exacerbates social inequality. At the same time, an unprecedented number of minorities had begun to enter what had been previously almost exclusively "white" institutions, signaling the end of white dominance within them. A backlash ensued, met by newcomers' demands for the transformation of these institutions. Racial and ethnic tension in the United States increased.

Minorities entering U.S. institutions played a critical role in demanding their transformation. But their demands were met with hostility, even by traditional allies, such as supporters of the civil rights movement of the 1960s. In universities, for example, white progressives were insulted when the African-Americans and Latinos they had helped bring into the academy demanded radical change. For many progressive whites, the question of equality was defined as one of representation, not necessarily sharing power with minorities.

In some universities, administrators embraced the rhetoric of multiculturalism. New faculty members were allowed to create courses and even programs devoted to the study of minority communities, although these generally were not funded at the same level as traditional programs. Ethnic studies often have been marginalized or exoticized, with universities and other institutions packaging courses about minorities, women, and gays under the banner of multiculturalism. Instead of mainstreaming these topics, this process marginalized these communities further. The reduction of "otherness" to an exotic location in academia tended to distort the discourse. Instead of deconstructing "otherness," such strategies reinforced it.

Furthermore, conservatives unleashed a backlash against diversifying the public sphere. Many conservative intellectuals have questioned whether democratic societies could have a multicultural public space. For example, Richard Bernstein, an early promoter of the phrase "politically correct," maintains that there should be a separation between private identities, which can be diverse, and the public realm.[28] In part, he bases his vision on the need to keep religion and ethnicity out of the public space, noting that historically (as in the European Jewish experience) when religion has entered the public discourse, it has been used for repressive purposes.

Arthur Schlesinger, Jr., views the multicultural movement as dangerous to democracy because it sabotages the unity of the nation. In *The Disuniting of America*,[29] he presents the argument that democracies need a uniform public identity in order to grant equal status to all citizens. But while in theory all individuals are equal, citizens who were not white, rich, and male historically have not had equal access to the political system. Schlesinger's vision of the United States thus ignores the fact that many communities were never considered part of the unified whole. Similar arguments have been made in Great Britain by John Rex,[30] who sees multiculturalism as incompatible with a democratic state. Like Schlesinger, he equates the public persona to the "citizen," who in theory should have a shared cultural identity, and calls for "privatization" of other aspects of identity.

For proponents of the idea that citizens should share a cultural identity, the basic unit of politics is, again, the nation-state: the public persona is defined as a citizen of a specific nation-state. Individuals who are not born in the nation-state where they reside may or may not be eligible to obtain the status and protections of citizenship.[31]

Many opponents of the multicultural movement also call for the closing of borders, arguing that increased immigration poses a threat to a culturally unified nation. The same forces call for English-only policies. What began as a conservative intellectual backlash in the 1980s found expression at the voting booth a few years later. In the early 1990s, candidates from both the Republican and Democratic parties ran successfully on anti-immigrant platforms with distinctly racial and ethnic overtones. Only mayors of large urban areas like Chicago and New York spoke up in defense of immigrants. In these cities, the undocumented population included significant numbers of European immigrants.

Transnational Cultural and Political Identities

The alternative to the notion of a culturally homogeneous public space confined within the border of a nation-state is the multicultural paradigm. In this paradigm, the public space can accommodate many cultures; the teaching of a variety of cultures and languages is encouraged and it is recognized that the imposition of any one culture oppresses the others. Even so, the multicultural paradigm in its first instance proposed a transformation of the public space within the confines of the nation-state, leaving unchallenged the notion of the nation-state itself.

Increased worldwide immigration coupled with ease of transportation has brought people into more direct contact with multiple cultures. In addition, rapid changes in communications and transportation have contributed to a global economic transformation. Political institutions thus far have resisted these changes. Nonetheless, paradigmatic changes in the definition of identity and the resulting vision of politics are taking place.

With increased contact between people and cultures, we may be witnessing the rise of transnational identities. Such identities are likely to be more visible in communities where people have crossed many borders. Diaspora communities where people are grounded in multiple cultures also produce hybrid identities.[32] The notion of a transnational or hybrid identity presents an interesting personal and political vision for diaspora communities. It proposes not only that communities be transformed, but that their host *and* home countries undergo transformation as well. Both home and host countries are often leery of these propositions.[33] This proposition would also encourage a political hybridity that expands not only the objects of politics, but the forms as well.[34] A transnational framework that accepts hybrid cultural formations brings to the forefront questions of what is home and what is exile. It also creates what others have called a "third space" beyond the confines of any one nation-state.[35]

Such a transnational framework also raises the problem of political bi-focality. Purnima Mankekar, for instance, asks "how we conceive of a political space that enables us to subvert the binaries of homeland and diaspora, while simultaneously allowing us to build alliances with struggles for social justices in both places?"[36] Throughout the 1900s, various immigrant communities have participated in both home and host country politics. Sometimes homeland issues have taken priority, while at other times host country problems have dominated the agenda. The contestation of power has crossed borders. The Southwest Voter Registration and Education Project has struggled with this dilemma for years. On questions involving the encroachment of U.S. foreign policy on Mexico and Central America, it has been an ally of the Mexican government; on questions of human rights, it often has challenged that government. In the Southwest, the project's ongoing work to increase voter registration and mobilize Chicano voters has often pitted it against local power structures.

The expansion of the political space to include multiple states suggests that the concept of a citizen bound to a single nation-state also must change. A transnational political identity, or citizenship, would better accommodate the rights of individuals who for a myriad of reasons cross the frontiers of multiple nation-states and whose lives are affected by decisions made by more than one state.

This discussion raises enduring dilemmas. For one, the realm of the political is still organized along the lines of nation-states, and within the international order, some nation-states are more powerful than others. This means that discussion of a global society or a global notion of rights emerging from more powerful nation-states can be read as another form of domination. Nonetheless, regardless of how the language of "globalness" is used by those in power, the reality is that there are human rights that do cross the borders of nation-states, and these need to be protected. Against the backdrop of an interconnected world, it would be shortsighted simply to dismiss any discussion of global rights as impossible to conceptualize. Such a discussion, of course, will involve difficult questions. What is the balance between specific national or ethnic rights and global human rights? Who determines the limits of such rights? Through what institutions are these issues to be discussed and decided upon?

What is clear is that, today, much of what is done in one part of the world affects other parts of it. Because of their transnational experiences, diaspora communities have long struggled against the restrictions of "one identity, one state." The reconceptualization of identity and power emerging from these communities is an important point of departure for a broader discussion that challenges the nature and exercise of power in this century.

Part Four

Reaching for the Civil Society on a Global Scale

Chapter 12

Popular Movements and Economic Globalization

Jeremy Brecher

Social movements are crucial vehicles through which non-elite groups express their values and interests, especially when these are imperfectly represented within central institutions. Economic globalization has had a profound impact on both the present condition and the future options for social movements around the world. In this chapter I explore some aspects of globalization that are significant for social movements and then discuss new responses that are emerging from such movements. I hope the chapter will confirm the important role of links between U.S. Latinos and Latin Americans in forging a constructive response to globalization.

Until recently the focus of my work has been far more local than global. For the past fifteen years I have studied the Naugatuck Valley, a deindustrializing region in western Connecticut.[1] Only gradually have I been forced to recognize that in order to understand the Valley's deindustrialization, it is necessary to pay attention to the dynamics of globalization, of which the Valley's decline is a part.

I carry in my mind a symbol of the impact of globalization on the Naugatuck Valley's sizable Puerto Rican community. In the early 1980s, the Brass Workers History Project, of which I was a part, interviewed Alejandro López, the first Puerto Rican to work for what was then one of the Valley's largest employers, the Scovill Manufacturing Company. Our 1982 documentary, *Brass Valley*, opened and closed with shots of López working in the Scovill brass mill.[2] Just last year I suggested that he be interviewed again for a documentary on the history of Puerto Ricans in Connecticut.[3] He was—standing amid the bulldozed rubble of the plant in which he used to work. When I speak in generalizations about the impact of globalization on Latinos, it is Álex López who haunts my vision.

Globalization

Modern capitalism developed within a system of territorial states. Trade and investment between countries were important, but they usually were conducted by companies rooted in a single home country. Some companies had large holdings abroad, but usually as part of an imperial system in which ultimate authority remained at home. National governments controlled treasury departments, central banks, trade and labor policies, taxation, commercial law, and other key economic institutions, thereby retaining the ability to manage their national economies.

This system of nation-based economies is evolving rapidly toward a global economy. Computer, communication, and transportation technologies have slashed distances, making possible the coordination of production and commerce on a global scale. Lowered tariffs have reduced national frontiers as barriers to commerce, facilitating transnational production and distribution. Corporations are globalizing not only to reduce production costs, but also to expand markets, evade taxes, acquire knowledge and resources, and protect themselves against currency fluctuations and other risks. "As almost every factor of production—money, technology, factories, and equipment—moves effortlessly across borders," former U.S. secretary of labor Robert Reich wrote in 1991, "the very idea of an American economy is becoming meaningless, as are the notions of an American corporation, American capital, American products, and American technology. A similar transformation is affecting every other nation."[4]

Three hundred companies now own an estimated one-quarter of the world's productive assets.[5] Of the largest one hundred economic units in the world, forty-seven are corporations—each with more wealth than 130 countries.[6] International trade and financial institutions like the International Monetary Fund (IMF), the World Bank, the European Union (EU), and the new World Trade Organization (WTO) have developed powers formerly reserved for nation-states. Conversely, national governments have become less and less able to control their own economies.

This transformation is what is often referred to as globalization. At the core of globalization lies a sharp increase in capital mobility, the capacity to move capital around the world. New transportation, communication, and production technology helped make this possible, but the process has been driven largely by a wish to lower the costs of production. Mobility makes it possible for corporations to move to low-cost areas, thereby pitting people in different communities and countries against each other.

Capital mobility is supposed to increase economic efficiency, but under current conditions its effects can be malignant. An unregulated global economy forces workers, communities, and countries to compete to attract corporate investment. Each tries to accomplish this by reducing labor, social, and environmental costs below the others. The result is often "downward leveling"—a disastrous "race to the bottom" in which conditions for all tend to fall toward those of the poorest and most desperate.[7]

Downward leveling is not limited to low-skill, low-tech jobs; it increasingly affects high-skilled professionals as well. A software programming center in Bangalore, India, for example, services thirty global corporations at half the price the same work would cost in the United States or Western Europe.[8] Company officials can communicate with employees around the world by satellite as easily as they can with workers in the building next door. Nor is downward leveling a problem only for developed countries; corporations like Nike pit the poorest countries—for example, Mexico, Indonesia, and China—against each other in the most brutal fashion.[9]

The race to the bottom has unintended side effects that multiply its impact. As each work force, community, or country seeks to become more competitive by reducing its wages and social and environmental overheads, incomes and social and material infrastructures deteriorate. Lower wages and reduced public spending mean less buying power, leading to stagnation, recession, and unemployment. As corporations move jobs that paid ten dollars an hour to countries where they pay one dollar an hour, workers can buy less of what they produce. As each country tries to solve its own problems by producing and exporting more products even more cheaply, the result is a downward spiral. This is reflected in the loss of good jobs and the rise of insecure, part-time, low-paying jobs in many parts of the world.

The tendency of market economies toward downward leveling and downward spirals was long countered by policies of national economic regulation that set minimum standards and stimulated economic growth. Large corporations once encouraged such regulation, but beginning in the 1970s they saw it increasingly as an obstacle to their emerging strategies. They and the think tanks and economists associated with them began to develop a new public policy agenda—what might be called a new "Corporate Agenda"—designed to encourage downward leveling.

Proponents of this Corporate Agenda encouraged governments to use high unemployment to fight inflation. They promoted cuts in wages, public services, and environmental protection to reduce businesses' production costs. When unemployment and falling real wages led to declining buying power, they no longer supported efforts to counter this through government policies. Instead they forced groups that might protest against downward leveling into the margins of the political arena.[10]

Meanwhile, backers of the Corporate Agenda supported the development of international economic institutions to administer the global economy.[11] Some of these are global, like the World Bank, the IMF, and the WTO (formerly GATT, the General Agreement on Tariffs and Trade); others are regional, like the North American Free Trade Agreement (NAFTA) and the EU. The WTO and regional trade groups like NAFTA have made rules that largely implement the Corporate Agenda, while the World Bank and IMF have imposed it on most of the world's poorer countries as a condition for receiving loans and investment.

International economic organizations increasingly set the rules within which individual nations must operate, and they increasingly cooperate in pursuit of the same objectives—objectives generally indistinguishable from those of the Corporate Agenda. For example, they have set ceilings for consumer, environmental, health, labor, and other standards; reduced business taxes; and facilitated the movement of capital to lower-wage areas. This new system of global governance is not based on the consent of the governed. It has no institutional mechanism to hold it accountable to those its decisions affect. For that reason, this emerging system of undemocratic power is calling forth new forms of opposition.

Popular Movement Response

The triumph of globalization and the Corporate Agenda has generated an unanticipated and largely unrecognized backlash. Developed and developing countries alike have suffered the results of downward leveling, meaning that popular pressures for change have been generated nearly everywhere.

Slowly at first, then with increasing speed, popular movements have emerged in many parts of the world to resist the effects of globalization. Their immediate goals have included saving jobs, restoring wage cuts, stopping toxic dumping, preserving small farms, subsidizing necessities, redistributing land, blocking or revising trade agreements, winning labor rights, preventing privatization, and preserving minimum wages and job security. Their tactics have included electoral politics, strikes, civil disobedience, marches, demonstrations, letter-writing campaigns, legislative lobbying, and even armed uprisings.[12]

These movements often have been marked by the formation of extraordinary coalitions. The struggle against NAFTA in the United States, for example, brought together the labor movement and a substantial part of the environmental movement—often antagonists in the past—as well as farm, consumer, and other groups.[13] The campaign against World Bank funding for destructive development in the Amazon rainforest united indigenous Amazonian rubber-tappers, a global network of environmentalists, and native peoples throughout the Americas.[14] Labor rights efforts have linked human rights advocates, trade unionists, and antipoverty activists in the First and Third Worlds.

These activities are without doubt responses to local conditions—but local conditions that are themselves in part the product of global forces. Resistance is developing within two superimposed but radically different spheres: the long-established nation-state system and the emerging global economy. This leads to a continuing ambiguity, a peculiar intermixture of left and right, nationalist and internationalist strands.

In the Third World, resistance has been manifested in so-called IMF riots in countries from Egypt to Brazil in response to the imposition of structural adjustment programs; in general strikes from India to Bolivia; in electoral rejections of austerity programs, as in Venezuela; and in armed uprisings, as in Chiapas.[15] In newly industrializing countries like Korea, South Africa, and Brazil, it has been seen in the emergence of militant trade unionism, often centered in the burgeoning export sectors, and in powerful political movements and parties linking the new labor base with large sectors of the urban and rural poor.[16] In the formerly Communist countries, it has been reflected in the electoral defeat of "shock therapy" programs in Russia, Poland, Slovakia, Lithuania, Hungary, and elsewhere.[17] In the First World, resistance has been seen in mass student and worker protests and social disruption against elimination of the minimum wage for young workers in France; general strikes against cuts in social programs and labor protections in Italy, Belgium, and Spain; in the unexpectedly widespread resistance to the Maastricht, NAFTA, GATT, and other treaties promoting economic globalization; and in strikes like those at Caterpillar and Bridgestone against the cuts in wages and working conditions demanded in the name of "global competitiveness."

Such responses are part of a tradition of popular social action far older than contemporary globalization. Farmers, workers, consumers, and citizens threatened by downward leveling have long organized themselves at local and national levels to resist the malignant effects of competition. They have encouraged governments to adopt environmental, labor, and social policies that block the descending spiral.

Globalization, however, has put the effectiveness of such vehicles into question. As corporations have become increasingly global, and as supranational institutions like the IMF, World Bank, and WTO have become increasingly powerful, the powers that people have established in the national arena have been largely outflanked. Today, if governments and work forces fail to provide labor, social, economic, and regulatory conditions to corporations' liking, corporations can go elsewhere, leaving economic devastation in their wake.

Globalization itself, however, is beginning to generate responses that cut across national borders. This can be seen most clearly in the movements that have developed in response to international trade and financial institutions. One example is the growing struggle against the policies of the World Bank and IMF, which began with battles over the Bank's role in the destruction of particular regions like the Amazon rainforest and the Narmada Valley in India, developed into a broader critique of structural adjustment, and in 1994 seriously spoiled the party for the World Bank and IMF's fiftieth anniversary with the "Fifty Years Is Enough" campaign.[18] Other examples include the cooperation that developed continentally among opponents of NAFTA and worldwide among critics of the Uruguay Round revisions of GATT.

Why is such transnational cooperation occurring? Downward leveling is creating a lose/lose, negative-sum game for a majority of people in all parts of the world. In a race to the bottom, nearly all lose. Globalization is therefore producing a common interest in resisting downward leveling among diverse constituencies. It has brought about alliances of environmentalists and labor unions; farmers and public health activists; advocates for human rights, women's rights, and Third World development; and others whose interests might seem to be in conflict. Downward leveling similarly produces a common interest among people in different countries and regions of the world—an interest in halting the race to the bottom.

Such efforts are creating an alternative to the globalization of capital, an alternative that might be called "globalization-from-below."[19] While it has no single definitive statement, the general outlines of globalization-from-below have been articulated in many forms by a wide range of movements and programs around the world.

Globalization-from-below begins with the fundamental premise of democracy—that people should be able to make the decisions that affect their lives. It therefore argues, in sharp contrast to the Corporate Agenda, that global institutions must be democratic, transparent, accountable, and accessible to the public.

Globalization-from-below recognizes the need for transnational rules and institutions. But it advocates far different functions for such institutions than the Corporate Agenda. Globalization-from-below opposes global rules designed to force downward leveling, while supporting global rules that, for example, protect labor and environmental rights and standards.

Globalization-from-below rejects the effort of corporations to take non-elite groups in different countries and play them off against each other. It sees the upward leveling of the conditions of those at the bottom as a common interest of all who are not in a position to exploit cheap labor, environmental, and social costs. The ability of people in each country to organize and raise their standards is beneficial to people in other countries. The advocates of globalization-from-below believe that, if corporations are going to cooperate worldwide to pursue their interests, ordinary people must also do so. Accordingly, they put a strong emphasis on building cooperation among popular organizations and movements across national borders.

As an alternative to downward leveling, globalization-from-below proposes "upward leveling"—raising the standards of those at the bottom, thereby reducing their downward pull on everyone else. Upward leveling means a cumulative increase in both power and well-being for the poorest and least powerful: poor and working people, women, marginalized groups, and their communities. The advancement of those at the bottom is crucial to blocking the race to the bottom. Upward leveling involves many different kinds of activity: grassroots rebellions, local coalition-building, transnational networking, and creating or reforming international institutions.

NAFTA, GATT, and similar agreements are often described as "rulebooks" for the international economy. Unfortunately, the rules they lay down are almost entirely rules to prevent citizens and governments from doing things corporations do not like. Instead, the global economy needs rules that protect ordinary people and the environment from corporations and corporate-dominated governments by establishing minimum rights and standards.

One way to establish minimum standards is to set rules for global companies through corporate codes of conduct. For example, religious, environmental, labor, Latino, and women's organizations in the United States and Mexico drew up a *"Maquiladora* Code of Conduct" for U.S. corporations operating along the Mexican side of the U.S–Mexican border. The code spells out provisions for environmental protection; requires that workers be notified of hazardous materials; bans employment discrimination based on sex, age, race, religious creed, or political belief; requires equal pay for equal work; protects workers' right to organize; and demands disciplinary measures against sexual harassment.

The Coalition for Justice in the Maquiladoras, which developed the code, has engaged in a series of campaigns to pressure such companies as the Stepan Chemical Company, the Ford Motor Company, and the hypodermic syringe manufacturer Becton, Dickinson to comply with it. The coalition's exposé of toxic flows from General Motors plants into the Mexican water supply was largely responsible for GM's 1991 decision to spend $17 million to build water treatment facilities at its thirty-five *maquiladora* plants.

Such codes can be incorporated into national law and international agreements. For example, during the struggle against South African apartheid, the U.S. government enacted a code of conduct that included recognition of unions and support for the black workers' movement, and required all U.S. companies operating in South Africa to follow it. An International Labor Code has been developed by the International Labor Organization (ILO), which is part of the United Nations system.[20] The code is made up of conventions that cover such subjects as freedom of association, abolition of forced labor, elimination of discrimination in employment, minimum wages, social security, occupational safety and health, rights of women workers, and many other aspects of the labor agenda. The conventions are legally binding only on countries that have ratified them, but the ILO code provides a widely accepted definition of labor standards.

Since the early 1980s there has been an international movement to include international labor rights in national trade law and international trade agreements.[21] U.S. trade law in 1988 defined denial of internationally recognized labor rights as an unfair trade practice against which unilateral action could be taken under international trade rules. The rights to be protected, drawn from key ILO conventions, included the right of association, the right to organize and bargain collectively, a prohibition on the use of any form of forced or compulsory labor, a minimum age for the employment of children, and acceptable conditions of work with respect to minimum wages, hours of labor, and occupational safety and health.

A possible model for imposing pro-social rules on the global economy comes from the EU. Wary that jobs might rush to the poorest regions of an integrated Europe, the EU decided to include a "Social Dimension" in its rules. Minimum labor standards are spelled out in a Social Charter. The Social Dimension also includes "structural funds" that provide resources to compensate poorer member states for the possible costs of meeting EU standards.[22] The combination of minimum standards and compensatory funds for poor regions is a good starting point for thinking about what kinds of rules and policies would begin to bring about upward leveling, rather than downward leveling, in the global economy.

Halting the race to the bottom and encouraging upward leveling require minimum standards worldwide. These can be incorporated in both national law and international agreements and institutions. The cumulative effect would be to establish a worldwide social charter setting a floor under environmental, labor, and social conditions.

Proposals for corporate codes of conduct, global social charters, and the like seek to provide environmentally and socially sustainable win/win solutions for ordinary people in different parts of the world. These proposals grow out of a dialogue rooted in a diversity of groups and experiences. They can serve as building blocks for a "Human Agenda" embodying interests that are threatened by the Corporate Agenda, but shared widely by people all over the world.

Despite the emergence of common interests, many conflicts undoubtedly remain. Bridging these will require a creative search for mutually beneficial compromises. I would like to discuss one example in which linkages between Latin Americans and Latinos in the United States could play a crucial role.

The example concerns the various calls for minimum global rights and standards to protect human and labor rights and the environment. While rules would protect poor as well as rich countries from the race to the bottom, they have real costs for poorer countries whose products would be made more expensive by such requirements. The Mexican political scientist Jorge Castañeda has proposed a "Grand Bargain" between

First and Third World countries that would respond constructively to this conflict. Such a Grand Bargain, he writes, "must entail a return to nonreciprocal policies and differentiated market access, in compensation for the implementing of environmental and social policies in the Third World that deter jobs from fleeing en masse from the high-wage countries to the low-wage ones, while at the same time ensuring more job creation and investment in the Third World countries than would occur otherwise. . . . In exchange for not leaving their markets totally unprotected . . . the nations of Latin America should establish social and environmental controls in their export sectors conforming to norms followed in the industrial nations. Exports would grow at a reasonable pace, domestic markets would remain protected in some areas, and not so many jobs would be displaced from North to South. The added benefit of such a compromise is that it might make sustainable development possible."[23]

A Grand Bargain does not have to wait for the initiative of diplomats in national capitals; it can start with the "popular diplomacy" of individuals and social movements with ties that cross national and North-South borders. For example, in the early 1990s a meeting of textile and garment trade unionists from throughout the Americas developed a joint position paper embodying an alternative to the running battle over the admission of Third World exports to the United States. It proposed that the unions of the hemisphere agree that such imports will be allowed if—and only if—basic human and labor rights like the right to organize and bargain collectively are protected in the location where the products are made.[24]

It takes more than a position paper to resolve a deep historical conflict, but this example illustrates the kind of creative search for win/win solutions in which popular movements are beginning to engage. And it indicates why U.S. Latinos with links to Latin American labor and popular movements are well situated to contribute to a broad transnational alliance advocating a Grand Bargain to encourage upward leveling.

Chapter 13

The New Synthesis of Latin American and Latino Studies

Pedro Cabán

Academics and administrators are—for a variety of reasons—promoting the integration of traditional Latin American Studies and Latino-oriented programs and departments. Although the dynamics of these mergers will differ, some generalizations are possible: Latin American and Latino Studies have distinct academic histories, are positioned differently in the intellectual hierarchies of the university, and have evolved as separate fields of inquiry with quite divergent perspectives on the link between knowledge and action. In the following pages I discuss the competing analytical traditions, normative orientations, and epistemologies, as well as the contrasting political projects and policy concerns, of the two fields. In the context of recent demographic and economic changes that are affecting the political dynamics of the United States, I want to examine the link between national politics and policy and their relationship to the possible synthesis of Latino and Latin American Studies.

The university is reassessing the research and policy objectives of Latino and Latin American Studies in the context of globalization and resulting domestic reconfigurations. As a consequence of a transfigured global economy, rapid demographic changes, the evaporation of traditional military threats to national security, and deteriorating material conditions of the citizenry, the U.S. state must redefine its domestic and foreign policy. Policy-makers are confounded by the predicament of how to preserve a patriotic construction of nationhood and the legitimacy of political institutions in the midst of economic deterioration and the relative numerical decline of the Euroamerican population. The current policy dilemmas are debated within the university, and these discussions have a bearing on curriculum and research issues. Deeply engaged in discussing and analyzing the processes that are continually transforming U.S. society, the university often has prescribed remedies for policy-makers.

Global Change and Domestic Reconfiguration

The United States is presently the fifth-largest Latin American nation, and Latinos constitute the fastest-growing population within U.S. borders. So state the authors of a 1990 Trilateral Commission report, which warns that "extremely large, extra-legal and potentially inassimilable immigration flows cause resentments, burden social services and spawn criminality."[1] Implicitly the authors are warning of the existence of an alien nation within the United States, thereby implying that Latinos, despite their U.S. citizenship, are not "authentic" Americans. A National Defense University report called *Security in the Americas* echoes the same fears, noting the "realization among the policy making community in this country that, with continuing immigration and refugee flows, the United States is facing a challenge of major proportions."[2]

According to these reports the United States is experiencing an irreversible racial and cultural reconfiguration, impelled by approximately 21 million U.S. citizens of Latin American and Caribbean origin, in addition to the multitudes who do not appear in official registries. These policymakers fear that the social fabric of the United States can ill afford continued infusions of similar foreigners. *Security in the Americas* warns that large contingents of Latin American "aliens" will corrode U.S. cultural institutions and foster ideological confusion. The study draws explicit links between Latin American migrations and drug trafficking: "The massive potential impact of immigration and uncontrolled drug trafficking is a factor in national political cohesion. . . . Although immigration is argued by some as adding a positive human resource, the countervailing impact of the drug culture on American society possibly negates the positive impact of new migrants."[3]

These reports feed popular apprehension about the threat of unrestricted Latin American migration and the prolific growth of resident Latino communities in the United States. Written at the start of the 1990s, they are also surprisingly perspicacious in identifying issues like uncontrolled immigration, fiscal burdens on local and state government, crime, resistance to assimilation, and the ambiguous nature of Latino national identity, each of which has a particular poignancy for Latin Americans and Latinos.

Admittedly, U.S. hysteria about foreigners is nothing new. Ronald Takaki's *A Different Mirror* has amplified public knowledge of the character and function of racism in the construction of U.S. society.[4] *Security in the Americas,* however, postulates the novel idea of a foreign Latin American nation residing in the United States, and warns of the threat this nation within a nation poses if its growth is not checked. Proposition 187, restrictive immigration policies, recent congressional action to eliminate funding for bilingual education, and the virtual dismemberment of social welfare will undoubtedly impede the expansion of immigrant communities.

U.S. postwar economic expansion was fueled in no small measure by large contingents of cheap immigrant labor. In the current era, permanent or provisional reserves of surplus labor are no longer required for U.S. economic growth, and this surplus population is seen by policy makers and the public as an economic liability. Politicians argue that the threat to employment lies not with free trade but with undocumented immigrant labor. The United States has sought to remove barriers to U.S. investments and trade with Latin America, as it simultaneously attempts to restrict immigration by creating a hostile political climate and enforcing sanctions against undocumented workers.[5] In its quest to impose free trade and promote globalization, the U.S. government has deftly overcome trade union, environmental, and community-based challenges, as well as the plaintive pleas of noncompetitive sectors of domestic capital, to the North American Free Trade Agreement (NAFTA).

Globalization has undermined the ordered global system of production and trade the United States had imposed at Bretton Woods, Vermont, where the United Nations Monetary and Financial Conference was held in 1944. Globalization has also compelled the state to abandon its self-proclaimed (but fictional) role of regulating the behavior of capital in the interests of national development. Major U.S. multinational corporations that want to reestablish a preeminent position in Latin American have compelled the state to dismantle barriers to trade and investment, including renewing the sale of advanced weapons.

Some fear that the state is losing its capacity to sustain a national community as it assumes a more aggressive posture in promoting U.S. transnational corporations. David Held has observed that in the "age of imperialism the cultural experience of those in core countries was stabilized by the imagined community of the nation state."[6] National identity once afforded cultural security to the populations of core states. But, as John Tomlinson has noted, "When people find their lives more and more controlled by forces beyond the influence of those institutions which form a perception of their specific polity, their accompanying sense of belonging to a secure culture is eroded. The average European or North American probably no longer experiences the cultural security their national identity used to afford."[7] This secure culture was a racially exclusive democracy, which, according to Alexander Saxton, was "democratic in the sense that it sought to provide equal opportunities for the pursuit of happiness by its white citizens through the enslavement of Afro-Americans, extermination of Indians, territorial expansion largely at the expense of Mexicans."[8] (I would add to the list the colonial domination of Filipinos and Puerto Ricans.) Historically, a racially exclusive democracy existed in relative harmony with an economic structure that privileged white male Euroamericans at the expense of the enslaved, vanquished, and colonized. What is novel in the current situation is the erosion of the ideological hegemony of a particularly Euroamerican construction of U.S.

national culture that was enforced on a matrix of racial diversity. This erosion is a function not only of the disordered domestic economy, but also of the durability of alternative cultural realities and their expanding presence in the public sphere. The U.S. state is struggling to sustain what Held calls a "national community of fate"—an imagined community that was overwhelmingly European, male, Christian, and militantly nationalistic in its construction.

The passage of Proposition 187 in California is only the most recent manifestation of political elites' efforts to foment racial polarization to their advantage. Politicians play on the fears of a vulnerable working class and deliberately misinform workers that their economic well-being is threatened by the virtual slave labor of Mexicans and Central Americans. Proposition 187 affirms Andrew Hacker's observation that "a politics purposively permeated by race has consolidated enough white Americans as a self-conscious racial majority. This is not to say that they are bigots or racists. It is rather that they are threatened, not always in ways they understand."[9]

The state has developed a two-track response to shifting racial demographics and the requirements of U.S. transnational corporations. Domestically, the state provides an arena for nativist forces who decry the existence of a foreign menace that must be kept at the margins of political power. In this case citizenship provides a semblance of protection to racial minorities but does not privilege these "aliens" beyond the formal legal canon, which seldom is universally enforced. Given the virtual criminalization of non-U.S.-citizen status, the most vulnerable are those lacking citizenship—overwhelmingly foreign-born people of color. Latinos constitute the largest of these contingents of legal and nonlegal peoples in the United States. Resident communities of Latin American peoples have politically as well as economically "thrown into sharp and invidious relief the differential status of citizen and noncitizen[,] . . . rekindled nativism among some sectors of the population and led to policy debates that touch the very nature of community and polity in the United States."[10]

The domestic consequences of globalization have increased the vulnerability of the Euroamerican working and middle class. In this context Latinos, African-Americans, and Asian-Americans are portrayed as posing a moral threat to the established cultural order and undermining the economic vitality of the nation. Their growing numbers impart further anxiety to a Euroamerican citizenry that already feels threatened by economic reconfiguration and the related uncertainties that lie ahead.[11] At the same time, these groups have fought to purge themselves of degrading and destructive self-identities imposed by the dominant culture and are striving to gain political access.

The University Setting

This is the context in which the university operates. A microcosm of the society in which it is embedded, the university recently has come under attack by critics voicing, "often from mutually contradictory intellectual and ideological presuppositions, the widely felt sense of disappointment or downright betrayal."[12] This highly ideological attack also cites the academy's supposed radical bias and the intellectual idleness of its faculties. Books with inflammatory titles such as Charles Sykes's *Profscam: Professors and the Demise of Higher Education,* Roger Kimball's *Tenured Radicals: How Politics Has Corrupted Our Higher Education,* Bruce Wilshire's *The Moral Collapse of the University,* Page Smith's *Killing the Spirit: Higher Education in America,* and Dinesh d'Souza's *Illiberal Education* have undermined the credibility of the university. State legislatures have reacted to this convenient neoconservative outburst by demanding that the public universities and colleges provide an accounting of their performance and assessments of their faculties' productivity.

Far from harboring an army of tenured radicals, universities have, in fact, actively developed relationships with private industry in such fields as biotechnology and pharmaceuticals. The competitive market environment and culture of the corporation permeate universities,[13] as new structures of centralized, top-down decision making displace the collegial model that was the hallmark of academic life. As universities appropriate the new culture of the corporation, links with industry and government become more complex and varied. And their role as corporate service providers, in turn, generates additional pressure on them to serve as guardians of the canon.

Universities have always been engaged in the pressing social policy debates of the day. Not only an arena for dialogue and reflection, universities support research that often influences the formulation of public policy. Research collaboration with the federal government is the product of a process that began during the waning days of World War II and intensified during the Cold War.[14] The United States emerged from World War II as the world's dominant economic and political force and launched a campaign to contain communism. One instrument to oppose European penetration was pan-Americanism, a longstanding goal based on the untested idea that Latin American aspirations and U.S. objectives were relatively harmonious.[15] Understanding the dynamics of the region was the key to realizing U.S. strategic and economic goals. After the launching of the first Sputnik and the expansion of the Soviet Union's influence in the Third World, the U.S. quickly enacted the National Defense Education Act of 1958. This became the principal conduit through which the federal government financed university-based basic and applied research, particularly on the Third World. Title VI of the NDEA established area studies centers throughout the United States, funded language training programs, and financed the acquisition of specialized foreign collections and materials for the major private libraries.[16]

But the modern era of Latin American Studies reached its "take off stage . . . when the growth of the profession coincided with the Cuban Revolution and Alliance for Progress."[17] In 1962 the Ford Foundation began providing support for training Latin Americanists and for Latin American Studies programs. These initiatives were cosponsored by the American Council of Learned Societies (ACLS) and the Social Science Research Council (SSRC).[18] An international meeting of the directors of centers that received Title VI funding and Latin American scholars whose work was funded by the Ford, ACLS, and the SSRC led to the creation of the Latin American Studies Association (LASA) in May 1966.[19] Latin American Studies centers in Latin America—primarily in Chile, Mexico, Brazil, Argentina, and the Andean countries—were also supported during this period. International academic collaboration between U.S. scholars and their counterparts in Mexico and South America increased dramatically during the 1960s and 1970s. According to Joseph S. Tulchin, a former editor of *Latin American Research Review,* "The focus of concern among students of Latin America has shifted perceptibly to issues with heavy public policy dimensions."[20]

During the last thirty-five years, the social science component of Latin American Studies has experienced considerable intellectual unrest. Until 1968 modernization theory, with its focus on economic growth and institutional development, dominated the field. The following decade dependency theory, which drew much of its theoretical inspiration from the scholarship of Latin Americans, emerged as the dominant critique of modernization. The hold of dependency theory eroded for reasons that ranged from ideological to methodological. Since 1980 the field has been characterized by a theoretical eclecticism and concerned with more modest middle-range propositions.[21] Postcolonial studies, and postmodernism, Latin American feminism, and literature-inspired cultural studies have occupied the energies of increasing legions of young scholars in the field. During this thirty-five year period, formal academic training improved dramatically, while the amount of social science research and the number of publications on Latin America vastly increased. The number of Latin American specialists soon outpaced the available positions in the academy, government, and the private sector as the importance of Latin America as a security concern declined.

During the 1970s some of the most important Latin American policy research was undertaken in established think tanks or research centers.

These centers served as a forum where academic researchers and foreign policy specialists from both the United States and Latin America could exchange ideas and findings with policy-makers, business executives, and military officials. The universities' link with these centers was either direct, in that they were formal units of a university, or indirect, in that universities provided the centers with intellectual expertise. More recently the enactment of NAFTA and the Summit of the Americas renewed interest in Latin America, by heralding the demise of post–World War II U.S.-Latin America relations driven by Cold War fears. John D. Rockefeller's $11 million endowment to Harvard University to establish a Latin American Studies Center is indicative of a new wave of concern. Prominent centers, such as the North–South Center of the University of Miami, continue to generate important policy-oriented research and serve as forums for sustained dialogue between academics and policy-makers.

Latin American Studies was always a contested arena. It was a field of study whose practitioners were multidisciplinary in training and relied on field research for their scholarship, at a time when discipline-based social scientists sought to develop general theories and rejected the context-bound approach of the area specialists.[22] The generous government funding of area specialists and their centers led to rivalries and tensions with colleagues in traditional departments. Moreover, many academics were convinced that the growth of Latin American Studies was directly related to a U.S. policy goal of using Latin American allies to contain the expansion of Soviet influence. Empirical research on the dynamics of Latin American society was also essential to identify possible challenges to U.S. interests in the region. Thus, Latin American Studies was often perceived as lacking the intellectual roots and analytical detachment of a true discipline. Latin American Studies were certainly not part of the canon.

After the field's rapid expansion in the 1960s and 1970s, Latin American area studies encountered internal contentions. Although the field itself was multidisciplinary, some individual scholars were often steeped in their disciplines. Tensions between these specialists and the multidisciplinary generalists surfaced in the scholarship as well as in LASA conferences. In addition, close contact with Latin American populations who had been victimized by militarism, economic exploitation, and political repression radicalized many Latin Americanists. Proponents of a critical and activist theory challenged the logical positivists who tended to populate Latin American Studies programs. Some Latin American scholars generated critical analyses that challenged U.S. imperialism and intervention in Latin America. During the 1980s U.S. university-based Latin Americanists worked with community and church organizations to marshal public opposition to the U.S.-sponsored wars in Central America. Publications such as *Latin American Perspectives* and *NACLA Report on the Empire* provided an important space for critical scholarship.

The field of Latino Studies occupies a distinct niche in the academic hierarchy and is characterized by a profoundly different set of analytical and political concerns. Latin American Studies was a top-down enterprise promoted by government agencies, university administrations and large foundations. In contrast, ethnic studies programs were interested in studying the "Third World within" the United States, and linking these studies to the "Third World without."[23] The genesis of Puerto Rican and Chicano Studies departments was virtually the polar opposite of that of Latin American Studies. The fields came into being during a period of social ferment and were parts of an attempt "to uncover the occluded and submerged, to liberate the repressed in the process of shaping people's history. Their project was to redraw the boundaries, to affirm the autonomy of the internal colonies (barrio, reservation, inner cities) and thus recover the space for the exercise of popular democracy."[24] From their inception, Puerto Rican and Chicano Studies questioned the role of the university as a neutral, universal seat of learning. Josephine Nieves, an early proponent of Puerto Rican Studies, observed "that the era of social upheaval, community conflict, and demands for institutional change gave these ethnic programs a stamp and character of social practice and theory building different from most other university programs." These programs engaged in "a critique of the way social science theory and methods had served to legitimize our colonial history."[25] In particular, proponents of Puerto Rican Studies equated the scholarly and politically emancipatory goal of the academic enterprise. According to Frank Bonilla, this critical stance was based on one "simple premise":

> Puerto Rican Studies now exists in the United States because consciously or intuitively enough of us reject any version of education or learning that does not forthrightly affirm that our freedom as a people is a vital concern and an attainable goal. We have set out to contest effectively those visions of the world that assume or take for granted the inevitability and indefinite duration of the class and colonial oppression that has marked Puerto Rico's history.[26]

Puerto Ricans and other Latinos resisted the university-sanctioned education because many felt that "the projection of an inferior or demeaning image on another can actually distort and oppress, to the extent that the image is internalized the supposedly neutral set of difference-blind principles of the politics of equal dignity is in fact a reflection of one hegemonic culture."[27] The significance of mounting and sustaining a research agenda grounded in progressive social objectives was forcefully articulated by the National Association for Chicano Studies:

We recognize that mainstream research, based on an integrationist perspective which emphasized consensus, assimilation, and the legitimacy of societal institutions, has obscured and distorted the significant historical role which class conflict and group interests have taken in shaping our existence as a people to the present moment.[28]

The relationship between the university and ethnic studies departments, Puerto Rican Studies in particular, was infused with antipodal pressures. Almost a decade ago I wrote:

From the outset departments of Puerto Rican Studies were assigned an inherently contradictory task. On an ideological level they served to legitimate the urban university and to diffuse the intensity of student activism by directing it into the classroom. But on the social and political level the departments were invariably propelled toward a troubled relationship with the university administration. Those of us who view pedagogy as inherently political recognized that our task was to reinterpret the distorted and culturally denigrated history of our community, to directly repudiate entrenched notions that our community consisted of a passive and subservient people, and to demolish the racist stereotypes which demeaned our past and discredited our presence in United States.[29]

Latino Studies departments were unwelcome and relegated to practical exile in the margins of the university's intellectual life. Twenty-five years after their establishment, these departments remain understaffed and underfunded, accepted as the price the liberal university has to pay to sustain a facade of tolerance. Many university administrators recognized the vitality and volatility of these "academic enterprises as social movements," and sought to channel them into less politicized avenues.[30]

In contrast to the policy payoffs and effective social engineering that Latin American Studies promised, Latino Studies held out the troubling prospect of a sustained critique of traditional disciplines. The cultural and social representations inscribed on racialized categories of people and the methods used to construct these representations were the early targets of ethnic studies departments. New research led to reconstructed political memories that gave students the intellectual tools to inform their political visions. Ethnic studies departments rejected the notion that knowledge is divorced from the institutions and social relations of power. This stood in contrast to the problem-solving, data-gathering orientation of many Latin American Studies centers.

Discussions of unifying Latino Studies and Latin American Studies are taking place in the context of a growing recognition that borders and territories are no longer the exclusive markers of political and national identity. Moreover, the Latino identity is imbued with social, cultural, and political values that are resilient against the homogenizing impulses of the economically and politically dominant society. The interest in linking Latin American and Latino reflects the growing official view that Latinos in the United States and Latin American and Caribbean people form an essential community, whose ties of language, culture, religion, and history are very durable and have effectively frustrated efforts at "melting them in the pot."

Three themes should be considered in any discussion about the synthesis of Latin American and Latino Studies: historical constructions, essentialism, and transnationality/ globalization. The import of these themes in the development of Latino Studies is very pronounced, but they have also been a factor in the evolution of Latin American Studies from a policy- and basic-research oriented academic enterprise to its current status as a relatively eclectic multidisciplinary field.

Historical Constructions

The first issue to consider is the historical construction and representation of colonized and postcolonial peoples. Specifically, what historiography will inform the research and pedagogy of a united Latin American and Latino Studies field? When materially and socially dominant actors inscribe marginalized communities with attributes that validate their subjugation, the project requires the imposition of historical amnesia. A potent malady that is inflicted on the powerless to preserve a particular order, historical amnesia also preserves the academic canon by preventing alternative and contestatory interpretations from being debated.

A precondition for constructing and imposing a homogenizing national identity among culturally heterogeneous populations is the destruction or concealment of the latters' history. It is this concern that informs Kelvin Santiago's study of U.S. colonialism in Puerto Rico, which offers observations on "how colonized subjects are historically constituted: as presumably unitary but shot through with endless contradictions, as the apparently homogeneous target of useful domination fragmented into multiple embodiments, as . . . driven to the margins yet . . . producing . . . myriad resistances."[31]

Citizens of Latin American origin constitute a large and growing segment of the U.S. population. This "minority," in combination with the African-American and Asian "minorities," actually approximates a majority of the citizens of the United States. Most of these people are not recent migrants, but have lived, loved, and toiled in this country for many years, if not centuries. The Mexican presence in what is now the territorial United States preceded what Carlos Fuentes has called one of the first waves of illegal aliens—the Pilgrims who disembarked on Plymouth Rock. The point is that Latin Americans have been an indelible part of the history of the United States and have been active agents in its social and cultural formation.

The denial that people of color in the United States had a history worthy of discovery, accompanied by the belief that they are merely subjects lacking a social consciousness or memory of any consequence, facilitated the creation and imposition of a world view that legitimized their subordination. Similarly, the transmission of European and Euroamerican scholarship as sovereign demeaned alternative scholarship and implicitly portrayed it as devoid of value and authenticity. Ethnic studies invariably undertook its projects of historical reconstruction as acts of affirmation: "In a culture without a historical memory, where the crisis of identity and the crisis of memory are coterminous, remembering is itself a central category of the ethnic project."[32] Popular memory, according to E. San Juan, Jr., is "one of the necessary means for oppressed peoples to acquire a knowledge of the largest context of their collective struggles, equipping them to assume transformative roles in shaping history."[33] The historical reconstruction of a collective moment has been an essential component of the intellectual production of Latino Studies programs. The university has long resisted the challenges that such research poses to the reigning scholarship and has proven resistant to these countervailing intellectual currents.

In the 1960s and 1970s, African-American, Chicano, and Puerto Rican college students rebelled against this orthodoxy and rejected the notion that only university-sanctioned knowledge should inform their educational experience. The establishment of Chicano and Puerto Rican Studies departments followed quickly in the wake of this intellectual and political challenge. Not surprisingly, these ethnic studies departments and programs were deprived of the resources to undertake the kind of substantive research that could be used to challenge the prevailing orthodoxies. For nearly a quarter-century the vast majority of the undergraduate programs in African-American, Chicano, and Puerto Rican Studies have subsisted in the margins of the university, languishing because of neglect and academic denigration.

Puerto Rican Studies departments were viewed by traditional departments and the administration as devoid of academic integrity and invariably portrayed as myopic and hopelessly insular. Operating as isolated academic units and lacking internal sources of political and administrative support, the departments emerged as relatively weak bureaucratic actors. Budgets were minuscule, faculty and instructional staffs were minimal, and tenure track positions were few. Moreover, service functions added an extra burden.

Through their scholarship and pedagogy, Puerto Rican, Chicano, and Latino Studies programs have sought to decenter the dominant representation of U.S. national history. The field elaborates a race- and class-based analysis that situates domination, subordination, and colonialism as essential elements in the formation of U.S. society. Latin American Studies programs, in contrast, generally have not taken as a central purpose of their intellectual project the discovery and explication of the history of oppositional struggle. Much of the scholarship on Latin American society, though valid, has conformed to the disciplinary regimen of positivist social science and has lacked the oppositional and emancipatory substance of Latino Studies' intellectual agenda. Latin American Studies programs may indeed generate the empirical information upon which to build a more liberating and empowering analysis of the formation of racial communities in the United States and hemispherically. Recent history suggests, however, that Latino Studies programs are more committed to this goal, and more willing to take the necessary risks to realize it.

Latino Studies departments have persevered because of the intellectual output of their faculties, the emergence of professional associations, continued student support for their curriculum, and the links they have nurtured with their constituencies inside and outside the university. It is their insistence on recovering missing episodes in the formation and experience of Latino reality that has prompted a vociferous reaction by the conservative academic establishment. Arthur Schlesinger, Jr., warns that ethnic studies programs pose a threat to liberal education, plunging U.S. culture into "incoherence and chaos." He dismisses their academic validity and emancipatory project by arguing that "the use of history as therapy means the corruption of history as history." In the process, he muses that the proponents of ethnic studies glorify groups' achievements and bury their less favorable episodes, while emphasizing their victimization at the hands of Europeans.[34] Schlesinger and his colleagues want to eradicate ideas that challenge cultural and ideological hegemony within the academy by linking the work of critical scholars of color to the specter of social decomposition. The affirmative representations elucidated by ethnic studies programs and critical theorists overtly challenge the highly selective and sanitized versions of official history. It is the erosion of hegemonic discourse by this alternative scholarship that provokes the guardians of the canon.

Essentialism

Much of the social research on Latin America, as well as popular views of Latin Americans, is informed by the deliberate construction of essentialisms. According to Barry Hindess, essentialism refers "to a mode of analysis in which social phenomena are analyzed not in terms of their specific condition of existence and their effects with regard to other social relations and practices, but rather as the more or less adequate expression of an essence."[35] The essence is the basic element that constitutes the real or ultimate nature of a being. It is indeed common for hierarchically arranged societies to construct essentialisms that abbreviate the identity of marginalized or subaltern populations to disparaging codes.

Latinos in the United States are portrayed as a distinctive racial minority that refuses to assimilate, that preserves its Spanish language and cultural identities, and that harbors fervid loyalties to the country of origin. Thus, the Republican Party ideologue Pat Buchanan, articulating the concerns of U.S. groups that oppose granting statehood to Puerto Rico, warned in 1990 that Puerto Ricans manifest "a defiant refusal to surrender their national identity, to dissolve themselves in a great American melting pot."[36] Forcing statehood on Puerto Ricans would create a Quebec within the United States, Buchanan argued, conjuring up images of rampant terrorism by Puerto Rican separatists. Portrayals of Latinos typically are portrayed as intrinsically opposed to the dominant culture and resistant to its modernizing, progressive, and cosmopolitan influence, alien entities who choose to reside on the socioeconomic margins of the United States by clinging stubbornly to a parochial cultural identity.

The concept of the melting pot is predicated on the assumption that exposure to superior Euroamerican culture will eventually, but inexorably, result in the eradication of immigrants' cultural identity. Once cleansed of undesirable foreign traits, new immigrants will appropriate the cultural constructs of a supposedly homogeneous culture that permeates U.S. society. Given this perspective, it is not surprising that the totality of the Latino historical experience is reduced to artificial essences concocted by others. Thus, we are told that Latinos reject the homogenizing and democratizing currents that are designed to acculturate and assimilate the foreigner. This seeming refusal to assimilate has been portrayed not as a conscious act of resistance and affirmation, nor as a culturally derived form of incorporation that deviates from the script, but as a function of their intellectual, if not genetic, inability to apprehend the superiority of the North. For many Latinos, to assimilate means to accept a narrow conception of participation. The assimilation model is built on the premise that functional participation involves passive citizenship, acceptance of hierarchy, an assigned niche in an economically stratified society, aggressive patriotism, and above all English language proficiency. To participate responsibly in the body politic, one must not organize on the basis of racial/ethnic or class critiques of the prevailing social and political order. Strict adherence to melting pot notions of assimilation invariably means the suppression of the unique in the service of a synthetic and totalizing construction of a uniform national culture.

Even if African-Americans and Latinos buy into the myth of assimilation and internalize the right behavioral codes, their inclusion is always provisional. The recent resurgence of fallacious theories linking socioeconomic and educational attainment to genetically determined physiological capabilities is testimony to the resilience of notions of racial superiority. It is frightening to realize that this pseudo-scientific nonsense enjoys currency. Whether stated openly or not, the socialization process in the United States implicitly portrays African-Americans and Latinos as lacking the genetic or hereditary material to attain the highest levels of social, economic, and political power.

In this context, affirmative action loses its original rationale as a legal device by which society ameliorates the consequences of entrenched and institutionalized racism, becoming instead a bureaucratic device to privilege unjustly those who lack the behavioral and intellectual capabilities to succeed. Charles Murray and Richard Herrnstein therefore condemn as "overly optimistic" the "premise that interventions can make up for genetic or environmental disadvantages."[37] Thus, the state intervention to achieve equal access to education, employment, or housing is futile, since some groups of people, usually categorized by ethnicity and race, are cognitively incapable of competing with the Euroamericans and achieving the same level of success. The negative essentialisms assigned to people of color are now fortified by theories that purport to document their genetic limitations.

Proponents of modernization theory often worked, implicitly or explicitly, with notions about the culturally derived limitations of Latin American and Caribbean people. The golden era of modernization theory coincided with the expansion of the Soviet Union's influence in the Third World and Cuba's transition to its own variant of socialism. With rare exceptions, Latin American history, institutions, and people were portrayed in essentialist terms, often with the aid of value-laden analytical perspectives and methodologies infused with ethnocentrism. Implicit in much of the modernization literature was the notion that Latin American countries were prone to perpetual political instability and rampant corruption. Latin American civilization was fashioned by an authoritarian and Catholic tradition grafted onto the cultures of indigenous peoples who were submissive and fatalistic. Latin Americans lacked the energy, enterprise, and drive to achieve there were characteristic of Euroamericans. The prospects for democracy and market capitalism were virtually nonexistent on a continent shackled by an antiquarian culture dominated by a landed elite content with preserving its wealth and opposed to modernization. These and similar essentialisms permeated much of the thinking and writing of that time.

Yet, when democratic institutions did function to the benefit of the working class, the United States was quick to intervene to preserve the privilege of the reigning elites. The arrogance of empire was most candidly revealed by Secretary of State Henry Kissinger, who, in a display of imperial contempt, said, "I don't see why we need to stand by and watch a country go communist due to the irresponsibility of its own people." In his review of U.S. attitudes toward Latin America, George Black observed:

> Going in, to do for the hapless natives what they seem incapable of doing for themselves, has been an ever present temptation since 1898, the natural outgrowth, as Louis Hartz wrote, of Americans' unshakable belief in their own moral rectitude, and the universal appeal of the U.S. political system. All of the United States' major policy initiatives in the region have been presented in part as grand rhetorical gestures and in part as technical exercises in problem-solving. After all, as Hartz has pointed out, "It is only when you take your ethics for granted that all problems emerge as problems of technique.[38]

The methodology of social science inquiry, imbued with the bias of essentialism, thus reduced a rich, varied, and complex history into readily digestible racial and behavioral categorizations.

Transnationality

Recent scholarship has developed new insights into the dynamics of Latino communities in the United States. Scholars are examining the transnational characteristics of Latino identities and assessing how history and globalization affect their construction. In place of interpretations of immigrant communities as engaged in a quest for assimilation, researchers are discovering dynamic communities that preserve much of their cultural distinctiveness and sustain and nurture relationships with their countries of origin.

Globalization has resulted in the disintegration of rigid barriers that impede the international movement of cultural and material commodities, intellectual property, information technologies, and people. The growth of a vital Latino-American culture and reality in this country and the blending with it of presumably more authentic cultural practices from homelands are partially the result of globalization. This mobility threatens communities that are primarily determined by reference to geography or territoriality. For Latinos in particular, however, the unifying force of globalization has been enhanced by geographical proximity to their countries of origin. While the development of communication technologies has contributed to the building of transnational communities, internationalization of production has led to demographic transitions that fuel their expansion. "Internationalization is setting in motion new flows of worker circulation that start out as temporary but generate conditions in which families and whole communities are compelled to anchor economic survival simultaneously in more than one national space."[39]

Globalization for some is not a value-laden concept. Unlike imperialism, "globalization suggests interconnection and interdependency of all global areas which happens in a far less structured or purposeful way . . . as a result of economic and cultural practices which do not aim at global integration, but which nonetheless produce it."[40] But the concept of globalization lacks the analytical precision and theoretical grounding of imperialism; since it can mean whatever the user wants, it is a concept of limited analytical utility. Not surprisingly, given its value-neutral pedigree, it has enjoyed great currency in the 1990s. Yet globalization, which involves a high level of interstate coordination and collaboration, is nothing more or less than the most recent and most highly developed form of capitalism as a social relation of production on the global level. Jeremy Brecher and his colleagues have argued that the last two decades "saw a multifaceted globalization and fragmentation of power. U.S. economic institutions hemorrhaged into a global economy of transnational corporations, world markets and an integrated 'global factory.'"[41] This has resulted in the relative decline of U.S. global economic power and has forced nation-states to redefine their role as policy-making institutions that regulate the operation of national capital in the international economy.

Globalization does not diminish the role of the state as an agent of capitalist expansion; rather, the role of the advanced capitalist state in creating international institutions has been redefined. Leo Panitch has argued cogently that "states act as authors of a regime which defines and guarantees through international treaties with constitutional effect the global and domestic rights of capital."[42]

Capital's aim is the homogenization of the world's population into an undifferentiated mass of consumers. To achieve this, corporations will require the legal and constitutional guarantees that only states can provide. This latest stage of capitalist development eventually will encounter limits to its expansion. One impediment to globalization will be popular resistance as states face ever-greater challenges to managing the domestic political economy. Globalization also has had the effect of solidifying cultural identities and historical affinities and elucidating the interconnectedness of social formations across boundaries.

How are transnationalism and globalization treated in the research agendas of Latino and Latin American Studies programs? Chicano and Puerto Rican Studies since their inception have conceptualized the interconnectedness of Latino communities and their countries of origin. The Mission Statement of the LASA Task Force on Latino Issues makes this point clearly:

To be Latino, or Latino-Americano, in the United States entails a complex cultural and social construction that bridges two realities. Identity is not delimited by territorial boundaries or a cultural hegemony that presumably imposes a benign uniformity in all spheres of a social and political life. Yet, the Latino reality in the United States is frequently analyzed as either comparable to "other minorities" because of the common experiences of marginalization, or in contrast to these populations because of its distinctive culture and history. Seldom is the discussion of Latinos situated in the broader international dimension, contextualized by reference to transactional dynamic between Latino communities in the U.S. and Latin America. The transnational feature of Latino formation is only now entering the discourse of the academy.

Traditional scholarship has rarely, if ever, contemplated the notion that Latino communities in the United States and Latin American and Caribbean communities abroad constitute a continuum of peoples, cultures, ideas, and language. Duality of identity has long characterized U.S. conceptions of Latin Americans. Latinos are portrayed as U.S. citizens of Latin American origin who constitute a distinct, culturally uniform, homogeneous subsector of the population, but one that has resisted acculturation. The work of Chicano and Latino Studies scholars has compelled many to question the accuracy of longstanding notions that Latin Americans and Hispanics living in the United States are two different historical and social entities, spatially separated and profoundly insulated from each other, and therefore incapable of influencing each other's formation as agents of change.

Social science researchers wedded to the notion that the nation-state is the unit of analysis assumed that communities were static and fixed formations. Migration was thought to be either a temporary movement precipitated by labor market opportunities or, if the migrants settled permanently in the United States, as the beginning of a process of assimilation into the dominant cultural and social system. This perspective reigned in earlier sociological and anthropological studies of Latino populations and was entrenched in the comparative method of Latin American Studies. It stood in marked contrast to the theorizing and empirical work of scholars in Puerto Rican and Chicano Studies, which was informed by their communities' experience as colonized, migrant, and marginalized peoples. That Puerto Rican, Chicano, and other Latino communities are "simultaneously engaged in a struggle for inclusion and ethnic affirmation within the United States while they seek to maintain some voice in affairs 'back home,' has only recently been 'discovered' by the traditional disciplines that purport to understand the Latino reality."[43]

Events precipitated in large measure by the domestic restructuring that has accompanied this new phase of the internationalization of capital challenge the conventional wisdom. The Los Angeles uprising (which Mike Davis called the first U.S. multicultural *intifada*),[44] the enactment of Proposition 187, the active role of Latino community and advocacy groups in the NAFTA debate, the longstanding contribution of Cuban-Americans in shaping U.S. foreign policy toward Cuba, and the efforts by Puerto Rico's political leadership to mobilize support among U.S.-resident Puerto Ricans for fiscal measures favoring transnational corporations that invest in Puerto Rico—these are merely some of the more visible indications of the interconnectedness of Latin American and Latino experiences. It remains to be seen how globalization will further reconfigure these transnational communities, making more evident the myriad linkages that nurture both immigrant and homeland communities.

Considerations

Despite the shortcomings of "Latino" as a cultural and political label, it nonetheless has attained currency among peoples of Latin American and Caribbean origin who reside in the United States. "Latino," like "Chicano," is a label of self-identification, claimed by these communities in opposition to the "Hispanic" or "Hispanic-American" label enshrined in federal government statistics. "Latino" states that the identities of Latin American peoples living in the United States are also nourished by the cultural traditions, historical experiences, and social interactions of their countries of origin.

Admittedly, the label offers an essentialist notion of Latin American reality by emphasizing the homogenizing and leveling force of Spanish influence in the Americas. Spanish colonialism left a legacy of resilient Iberian cultural institutions, Catholicism, religious and cultural syncretism, the destruction of indigenous peoples and civilizations, African and Chinese slave labor, and the Spanish language. But these elements of historical and cultural commonality are also superficialities that mask the complexities, particularities, and diverse formations of Latin American communities.

"Latino" derives its essential meaning from experiences and myths that are at variance with, if not opposed to, the hegemonic culture of the United States. The label is readily shed when Latin American and Caribbean people are among themselves, an arena in which we identify ourselves on the basis of country of origin. A Chicana, a Dominicano, and a Puertorriqueña may seek to unite as Latinos in order to confront institutionalized racism, build electoral alliances to acquire local political power, or simply gain space within an institution. But once exclusively in the company of another Latin American, we jettison "Latino." It is a label that facilitates collaboration among peoples whose experience has been overwhelmingly one of marginalization, economic exploitation, and political disenfranchisement. Latinos may also be guilty of an essentialism, but it is an essentialism adopted to gain a tactical advantage in a broader strategy of empowerment. This tactical essentialism cuts across class categories.

Global interdependence has spawned profound tensions and inequalities. Novel integrative institutions have been devised by a regionally based capital–state nexus to facilitate capitalist interaction. New accords like NAFTA have engendered profound disruptions that evoke the prospect of deepening social immiseration and marginalization on one hand and the potential for cross-national popular organizing and resistance on the other.[45] Legions of researchers and organizers have taken on the task of assessing and interpreting this transfigured regional economic calculus and its attendant social disruptions.

The subtext for much of this work is the declining explanatory significance of national territory and the nation-state. Boundaries that separated Latin American from Latino Studies are eroding as rapidly as the *fronteras* (borders) among nation-states in the Western hemisphere. The logic of integrating the research agendas and institutional resources of Latin American and Latino Studies seems self-evident in the context of evolving globalization and the demise of assimilation theory. But how will the distinct fields of study be harmonized? And will the merger of these two epistemologically divergent fields be beneficial to either?

Clearly it is this last question that will provoke the most controversy in the ongoing debates within the university. As liberated zones within the academy, Puerto Rican and Chicano Studies undertake to expose traditional research as a tool of oppression. Involved in this enterprise of understanding Latino histories through Latino lenses was the quest to acquire agency in constructing a collective identity. Research and education were embedded in an explicit political project to transform the university. No doubt the demands of academia moderated the political activism inherent in many Latino Studies programs, while the requisites of tenure injected strictures unanticipated by young Latino scholars when they first appropriated a space in the university. These realities have weakened the community affiliation that was the hallmark of many Latino Studies programs. Some are concerned: "Ethnic studies faces a crises: will it continue to conform to the disciplinary regime of the academy? Or will it try to recuperate its inaugural vision as part of wide-ranging popular movements for justice and equality, for thoroughgoing social transformation?"[46] Yet, these tensions are what has sustained the dynamism of the Latino research agenda. The seemingly contradictory quest to balance a need for an emancipatory pedagogy and scholarship with critical research that is informed by rigorous methodologies and theoretical precision has compelled the university grudgingly to accept the validity of the enterprise.

Can we say that Latin American Studies confronts a comparable set of tensions? I argued earlier that the growth of Latin American Studies was related to U.S. policy goals in the region. But Latin American Studies has also experienced intellectual ferment as critical theorists have challenged the dominant position of the "policy wonks" in the university and profession. As a consequence, the research pedigree of Latin American Studies is also contested, although traditional scholarship that claims objectivity and value-neutrality is acknowledged and rewarded, and still sets the standard for tenure in the university. The public policy thrust of prestigious Latin American Studies centers has not abated; rather, it has intensified precisely because of the renewed salience of Latin America for the U.S. state and capital.

Puerto Rican and Chicano Studies departments were established almost exclusively in the public university. Latin American studies programs have tended to flourish in the private university, although there are notable exceptions. University officers have responded to their fiscal crises by eviscerating those programs that contest traditional scholarship. Clearly, Puerto Rican and Chicano Studies have fallen, and will continue to fall, victim to the budgetary surgery now being administered across the country. This reflects not only a clear class bias, but also an ideological impetus. Latin American Studies programs whose faculties have been adherents of critical theory are also subject to budgetary reductions and even dismantling. Thus, a fiscal logic based on criteria of efficiency and economy may drive the integration of Latino and Latin American Studies in various public universities.

I suspect that Latin American Studies programs in key private and flagship state universities will be shielded from draconian budget cuts. The sheer weight of the existing scholarship on transnational communities and their role in the unfolding process of globalization means that these centers are in actuality supporting research on Latino communities. In such a setting, however, research on Latino transnational communities will, most likely, be sanitized, deprived of its critical edge and its objective of reconstructing political memory. It is likely that Latin American Studies programs will reassert a "hegemonic pluralism" that "seeks to reconcile incompatible interests, class and gender differences, within the idea of a national culture or a synthesizing American identity."[47]

The battle lines between Latino and Latin American Studies programs are more fluid and negotiable in the public university. Yet here, too, the epistemological underpinnings of Latin American and Latino Studies are distinct, if not oppositional. These programs have occupied very different positions within the intellectual hierarchy of the university, and their respective institutional power bases and access to funding vary greatly. It seems clear that the domestic dynamics of transnationalism and globalization will occupy debates on curriculum transformation and the research agendas of the synthesized Latin American and Latino Studies programs. I anticipate that the research and pedagogical missions of the combined departments will be the most difficult area to negotiate.

Will these departments be plagued by profoundly disconnected and internally contradictory pedagogical and research objectives? What will be the defining characteristics of the integration of intellectual traditions that have been in opposition? How will these programs seek to make sense of an altered domestic political and economic reality that is giving sustenance to a nativist and reactionary social agenda? And, most critically, will such a combined department preserve the mission of Puerto Rican and Chicano Studies—to treat neglected histories and current political struggles for inclusion and representation as legitimate areas of inquiry and instruction?

Chapter 14

Rethinking Latino/Latin American Interdependence: New Knowing, New Practice

Frank Bonilla

The Intellectual Legacy

The conference in Bellagio that generated this volume was in many ways a culmination of a process extending over at least three decades. Yet the foregoing chapters only hint at the range and complexity of the roles individuals and organizations have assumed in bringing into being the substantial research and policy apparatus that now supports undertakings of this scope. The group was assembled with an eye to the inclusion of individuals with distinctive individual career paths coupled with a record of organizational innovations in knowledge creation and use. A full ac- count of the underlying resource base and potential for action present at those sessions is clearly beyond the reach of this chapter — it would require a close tracking of the individual trajectories of all who shared in those deliberations as well as a thorough mapping of the institutional legacy they have helped put in place. What follows is a broad account, anchored in some key developments since the early 1970s, of Latino endeavors to develop a vision and organizational base for research on our own condi- tion along with a comprehensive critique of prevailing modes of policy- oriented inquiry concerned with social equity.

For many Latino academics and students, the late sixties and seventies proved a major turning point. In those years, they plunged into the strug- gle to establish within U.S. universities a space where the intellectual work of our communities might be accomplished. The campaign for Puerto Rican Studies emerged, paralleling struggles by Chicanos, other Latinos, Latin Americans, and African-Americans. A 1972 quarter-long seminar at Stanford University produced a landmark volume entitled *Structures of De- pendency* and defined the parameters of the enterprise then being launched.[1] Interestingly, critical aspects of the Stanford program were echoed in the plans for the Bellagio sessions.

By the 1990s, the Inter-University Program for Latino Research (IUPLR), a consortium of ten university-based Latino research centers in the United States and an equal number of issue-focused national research teams, was actively promoting (with the Social Science Research Council, SSRC) several programs to support training and research on Latino issues. In 1993 the IUPLR and the SSRC jointly called for a review of "the applicability of current research and theoretical paradigms in the humanities and social sciences to Latino populations." About the same time an independent initiative by the Gulbenkian Foundation was calling for a comprehensive "Restructuring of the Social Sciences."[2] To a number of the prospective Bellagio participants, that call conveyed the true scope of the issues at stake today as Latinos in the United States seek to consolidate a university-based research and policy capability of their own.

The projected Gulbenkian restructuring sought to respond to three historical developments: the emergence over more than a century of the "three cultures"—the natural sciences, the humanities, and the social sciences; the division of the social sciences into distinct "disciplines"; and the breakdown in the years since 1960 of the intellectual consensus supporting both sets of boundaries—the ones around the domains of the distinctive scientific "cultures" as well as the proper fields of the main social science disciplines. The result, according to the Braudel announcement, has been "massive world wide drifting, in which more scholars feel dismayed at the state of the social sciences, but very little is being done collectively to change the situation."

At about the same time, SSRC president David Featherman, having recognized the scope and seriousness of this challenge, spoke out independently on this theme. In a 1993 issue of the SSRC newsletter *Items,* he wrote:

> We at the Council—indeed, all of us in higher education—face a
> fundamental dilemma. How do we instill the capacity to analyze and to
> recommend tractable solutions for the complex problems of the 21st
> century if the most important step is problem finding? As early as 1971,
> a report in *Science* magazine concluded that the most intellectually
> path-breaking and practically useful research was most frequently based on
> a pooling of disciplinary knowledge. This research more typically rejected
> the tendencies of individual disciplines to define solutions for a problem in
> terms of extant disciplinary paradigms.

And equally to the point:

> How should we design our universities and our curricula in higher
> education in order to bring the skills of analysis, problem finding, and
> problem solving more in alignment with the problems and solution
> strategies that will be encountered and required in an increasingly
> transnational world?[3]

Home Country Roots, Metropolitan Models

It may be worth remembering that as the movement for racial and ethnic studies got under way in U.S. universities in the late 1960s, social research in Latin America, and especially research in which U.S. Latin Americanists were principal actors, was undergoing a deep crisis. Some of these tensions have only recently come to the fore as Latino Studies begins to command a new role in terrain heretofore seen as privileged turf for U.S. Latin Americanists and their special institutional apparatus. Dissension has surfaced on numerous campuses and within professional organizations such as the Latin American Studies Association, where a newly constituted Latino Studies section has begun to make itself heard, playing a prominent role at LASA's 1997 conference in Guadalajara.

Yet, as a study of Cold War foreign policy and democratic politics in the hemisphere observed a generation ago, "American government frightens and bewilders its friends and enemies alike."[4] Project Camelot, a Defense Department–sponsored multicountry study of civil insurgency and its control, was terminated in mid-1965 after protests by the State Department and the Chilean parliament. Any hope that social science research might contribute to useful human purposes in Latin America foundered. The shadow of suspicion fell on all U.S.-based academics and Latin American nationals trained at or associated with U.S. institutions.[5] Yet policy-oriented research seemed to require grappling with the most sensitive aspects of individual and group political attitudes and behaviors if it was to enhance the possibility of overcoming longstanding barriers to collective consensus and action on social problems. Then as today, here was what many saw as the vulnerable underbelly of social ententes and paths to progressive change in countries confronting grave challenges, including external manipulations.

By the 1960s, political leaders in Latin America had been increasingly won over by ideologies of development—that is, industrialization and modernization. However, none of the plans had been notably successful, and most were unmistakable failures. The explanation appeared simple. Political conditions did not permit the ready implementation of programmed economic change. Therefore, theory built on research from disciplines concerned with human behavior should be brought to bear on economic policy problems. The Massachusetts Institute of Technology's Center for International Studies and Venezuela's Center for Studies of Development (CENDES) at the Universidad Central joined forces in an unprecedented attempt to apply the most advanced resources of empirical data gathering, analysis, and synthesis to the study of nation building in societies undergoing a grinding flux of internal contention.[6] Briefly, the project involved independent samplings of opinion among some thirty population groups ranging from traditional farmers and agricultural wage workers to urban squatters and on through a score of working- and middle-class occupations to government officials and business executives. Separate hours-long qualitative interviews with nearly one hundred members of the political, business, and cultural elite as well as sociometric data pinpointing the number and strength of linkages among them sought to map the operative structure of power and influence. Computer simulations of the processes shaping the building of conflict and consensus on major issues drew, in various ways, on all these data, applying both statistically derived "empirical" laws as well as theoretically grounded "arbitrary" laws to determine outcomes.

The point of this extended aside is that the concepts, methods, and practical apparatus for assembling massive and complex arrays of information to facilitate analysis, synthesis, disciplined speculation, and invention concerning the social and political dimensions of the policy process were essentially in place nearly thirty-five years ago. Though probably much enhanced at present, these resources have largely lain fallow or been used selectively in ways that further fragment and obstruct a timely sharing of knowledge and rational coordination across social groups within nations and, more recently, with respect to transnational operations.

The Venutopia computer simulations of the late 1960s regularly predicted new crises and breakdowns peaking in the 1980s in the search for policy consensus in Venezuela. The factors that seemed to sustain renewed dissension and social conflict in that setting have since then proliferated throughout the hemisphere and are now manifest in the United States itself. The "periphery" is now said to have penetrated the "core," even though it is widely perceived that processes originating within that core are largely shaping destructive outcomes both domestically and abroad within a new framework of "asymmetrical interdependence."[7]

Conditions among Venezuela's elite had considerable weight in the model's bleak predictions. The nation's top corporate, government, and cultural leaders, the study found, were largely out of touch with one another, out of touch with their constituencies, and finally out of touch with the major issues then confronting the nation and most of its citizens. Most groups, but especially the poor, felt isolated, marginalized, and alienated from political organizations and government at every level. No institutions or mechanisms able to bridge these deep divisions rose to the challenge of putting the massive and sensitive self-knowledge generated by the "diagnostic approach" (as it came to be called) to work toward solutions. The experience brought home that any effort at integrating policy and planning techniques with social science inquiry must maintain an inordinate self-consciousness concerning its own operations. Every phase of research, each step in consultation, and dissemination with significant publics, becomes part of a complex process of self-definition and discovery. The following statement by an MIT professor with reference to the current demands of transnational research is thus particularly refreshing:

> The support required for this within the university is not just hortatory; university administrators have to demonstrate the will to commit scarce resources, to overrule other initiatives that ignore, neglect, or conflict with goals of internationalization, and to create an environment for faculty and students that responds to more than discipline based incentives and rewards.[8]

When people ask today, as Latinos have done for nearly a quarter-century, what role the university should play in the solution of pressing social problems, we are more than ever aware that we are really asking what we must demand of each other and our disciplines to give such endeavors effective substance.

Grounding the Movement for Latino Studies

Two decades ago a youthful ferment drove the demands for the inclusion within the university of Latino concerns. The movement for Latino Studies is still represented in some quarters as no more than that—a naive enthusiasm and self-assertion by newcomers within a centuries-old institution whose structures and traditions they only dimly understand. Yet, as we have seen, questions at the center of debate and organizing efforts in Latino communities in the seventies reached not only back to Latin America but across the full range of disadvantaged U.S. minorities. The concern was as much to find common elements in the structures of inequality affecting each group as to pinpoint the particulars of each group's condition. The story of one such initiative will convey part of the process through which the starting mission and agenda for Latino Studies came into being.[9]

This returns us to the 1972 research seminar on dependency theory organized by graduate students and faculty at Stanford University. The seminar was intended to permit the simultaneous exploration of a variety of issues: questions of theory, method, research practice and the political uses of intellectual work. It therefore unfolded as a complex event bringing together many strands of thought, feeling, and purpose in sometimes confusing and conflictual profusion. The conditions and objectives the group set for itself were as follows:

1. The multinational and multiethnic composition of the group was an essential ingredient. A primary goal was to provide politically concerned Third World students and professors of diverse origins

(in the present case chiefly Latin Americans and blacks, Chicanos, and Puerto Ricans) with an opportunity to explore the possibilities of establishing a common framework for the analysis of inequality and dependence among and within nations.

2. Students and professors were to work full-time during the quarter (ten weeks) as a loose collective of small research and discussion teams. A half-dozen subgroups functioned during the seminar, with cross-cutting memberships among the twenty principal participants.

3. Recent Latin American formulations concerning dependency were taken as a point of departure. The aim was a critical assessment of the historical scope of these concepts and the range of national and subnational situations they covered, and the extension of the economic structures and processes they described to other aspects of social organization.

4. To effectively meet the requirements set out in point 3, the seminar team was to be not only multinational and multiethnic but also interdisciplinary.

5. The seminar considered the degree to which the dependency framework could be specified and formalized in a computable economic model with sociopolitical extensions. However, it gave primary emphasis to the implications of the dependency approach for research practice and operations, and especially for the generation, communication and uses of research-based knowledge.

6. Participants asked whether, within the framework of such a seminar, a much desired reconnection of theory, research methods, and social relevance could be partially achieved in social training (especially for minority and Third World students and professors).

The seminar produced a volume with some sixteen separate contributions. Only a handful of these can be mentioned here. A lead paper on the economy by Fernando Henrique Cardoso set out the new dimensions of capitalist expansion that, in his view, required a reconsideration of the Marxist and Leninist analysis of this phenomenon in the late nineteenth and early twentieth centuries. Cardoso proposed that new combinations of internal and external factors were prolonging and intensifying dependency and producing development benefiting selected local sectors. He emphasized moving beyond mechanistic inferences from economic structures to political behaviors or from material interests to motivations, and setting guidelines for the study in depth of specific, variant structures of dependency as they were taking form in Latin America.

The political discussion focused on the significance for national politics of the structural constraints stemming from the network of international economic ties consolidated after World War II. However, contributors expended much more energy in critiques of leftist diagnoses and strategies for liberation originating in Latin America than in challenging or exposing the insufficiencies of development theories emanating from the United States. Still, the task was not merely to recapitulate, with the benefit of hindsight, the shortcomings of earlier left-nationalist, Marxist and structuralist (Economic Commission for Latin America) analyses, but to weigh the meaning for Latin Americans of the broad-gauged internationalization of elites and institutions already under way. Because of the composition of the group, discussion gravitated toward the Brazilian case and focused on the controlling role of the military, technocrats and bureaucracies, on authoritarian politics, demobilization, and restrictions on participation, and on repression and manipulation as corollaries of development in the dependent mode. Nevertheless, the group also noted the elements of continuity, partial efficacy and attractiveness to key groups of the regime in power, as well as its achievements and goals. Dependency theory as it then stood exposed certain contradictions in existing structures, and policies designed to sustain those structures as well as in some strategies intended to transform them or bring them down. The dependency framework also shared specific limitations with other academically grounded, substantially deductive schemes of social analysis, especially with regard to questions of popular participation and mobilization.

The problems confronted in the political sphere loomed even larger when the group addressed issues of culture and ideology. Indeed, the group remained largely unsatisfied even with the questions it was able to formulate. What kind of cultural and ideological superstructures do dependent economies and political systems generate and support? What kind of leverage over dependent economic and political-social formations can be obtained through attempts at cultural or ideological construction? The team responsible for this component set out to map specific elements in the process of cultural production and the socializing influences being deployed from the internationalized sectors in dependent nations (educational, occupational, mass media, consumption, and so on). Some sources of cultural resistance and negation were also mapped.

Such complex chains of inference are needed to trace even the most primary forms of cultural interaction that the group ran into something of an impasse. The manner of proceeding sketched above was challenged, especially by those speaking from the perspective of minority cultures in the United States. They saw culture and race as key mobilizing referents of political energies that are turned toward self-emancipation and group liberation through struggle in specific institutional contexts. The mass in U.S. ethnic communities was depicted as a source of energy, insight, and political drive, generating its own intellectual understanding of its situation and political needs through direct action in local institutions and communities. This perception implied a new and unique set of demands and opportunities for intellectuals, especially with respect to priorities in theory and modalities of work. The image of racially and culturally defined groups as embattled collectivities girded for self-defense and active reconstruction of identities, ideologies, and threatened ways of life came across persuasively in separate essays on participating groups.

Latin American participants viewed their own reality quite differently. They saw the Latin American mass as largely passive and perhaps as still shielded from the full onslaught of a leveling international-capitalist culture. They were less preoccupied with preparing to serve a movement of active mass resistance and more concerned with understanding the mechanisms and implications of a cultural penetration that was still focused on elites and the command posts of national institutions. What exactly is at stake, they asked, in the interplay of national cultures in situations of increasing dominance and pressures toward homogenization?

The most penetrating critique of dependency theory was thus a by-product of the effort to assess its applicability to the case of racially stigmatized communities in the United States. Invoking the analogy of colonial dependence (internal colonialism) to explain these cases of group inequality and domination within the developed center highlighted a number of unresolved points in the ongoing elaboration of the dependency paradigm. The most obvious of these shortcomings stemmed from the incomplete and controversial treatment in Marxian analyses of certain key categories: ethnicity, caste, culture, racism and nationalism. It was easy to establish parallels in the economic functions of U.S. ghettos and their inhabitants (e.g., external control of production, capital accumulation, and distribution of surplus; discrimination in hiring, compensation, and consumption; an external apparatus of aid and welfare). The U.S. history of slavery, conquest, and occupation of territories, displacement of populations and patterns of work force migration had clear counterparts in the process of penetration and colonization abroad. Dependency theory saw the nation as essentially flawed and perhaps undergoing a process of dismemberment, but at key points analysis proceeded as though internal homogenization were an achieved reality. In this way, the seminar critique ran, dependency theory failed to come to grips with crucial questions about internal differentiation and the sources of political energies reconstitutive of national formations. At the same time, in keeping with its Marxian antecedents, the theory would dismiss as romantic or regressive those liberation movements within the United States that were organized around claims of racial and cultural emancipation. The difficulty was, of course, that if the processes of selective cooptation and marginalization went forward in Latin America as the theory foresaw, the cause of national affirmation would be left to groups sharing many of the characteristics of U.S. minorities.

Clearly, dissatisfaction with paradigms has reached new heights. My point, once again, is that reflections at this level were central concerns of those of us who were thinking through an intellectual base and practical program of inquiry and self-organization within the academy for Latinos—two decades before these issues were raised, and reluctantly at that, within the so-called mainstream disciplines and research entities that command the attention of policy specialists.

El Centro de Estudios Puertorriqueños

The 1972 Stanford seminar was not only an occasion for developing critical perspectives on theoretical and methodological approaches for inquiry into the conditions of U.S. Latinos and other disadvantaged groups. Participants also generated proposals for research and teaching projects at universities around the country. Very specifically, a faculty and student team closely in touch with community activists in New York and around the country as well as in Puerto Rico worked on a design for a Center for Puerto Rican Studies at the City University of New York. Here again, in order to keep the pertinent discourse of the 1970s in view, I draw selectively from a proposal drafted over that winter quarter and defining the rationales and structure for the center, which was officially launched in February 1973.[10]

> In the last few years, the City University of New York has become a major focus of the Puerto Rican community's drive toward self-realization and institutional articulation. At the moment that this energy is being directed at the University, the institution finds itself hard put to adequately understand and begin to resolve multiple conflicts that have emerged within it in the last decade. In the case of the tensions between the Puerto Rican community and the University, it has been clear that the conflict stemmed essentially from the University's disconnection from this community and its limited comprehension of Puerto Rican needs and aspirations. We view this failure as the product of a deeply rooted and cumulative process that affects the very makeup of the University and its action on many fronts. Very simply, the University has accepted and acted on the definitions and stereotypes of those who have investigated Puerto Ricans as one among many migrants to the city. It has often sought to act quite honestly upon its "scientific" understanding of our community; it has rarely sought to penetrate beyond these abstract conceptualizations to the particularities of the fast changing realities of our existence or our own visions of our place in the city's life.
>
> Much of the new generation, presently entering the city's colleges, finds itself linked to those Puerto Ricans who have chosen to live and work in the U.S. They remain not as assimilationists but as a people who have

seen that the problems of Puerto Rico and other Latin American countries can and should be approached as extensions of problems that we know intimately from within the United States. A potent factor motivating a considerable part of our youth is thus the desire to deepen their comprehension and effectiveness in dealing with problems that affect the Puerto Rican community here in order to intensify and give new content to the dialogue with those on the island tackling the same problems.

Significantly, for many among this generation, the search for a liberating education is closely linked to the parallel struggles of Black and Chicano people. Their experience of U.S. Black culture has been direct and intimate and constitutes a vital strand in an emergent amalgam of criollo and ghetto lifeways with an aesthetic all its own. With the Chicano, Puerto Rican youth share a struggle to maintain a language and culture and to win political autonomy in the face of institutions that have little love or compassion for a people that speak Spanish and intend to continue to do so. The decision of some Puerto Ricans to remain in the United States thus grows out of a commitment to this internal struggle and a partial comprehension of its external ramifications.

Within the university the drive for self-affirmation has been carried forward primarily by students with community support. Because of the nature of the university as a center of learning, this encounter has been both perplexing and revealing. For Puerto Ricans the university was largely defined by the images that the institution sought to project of itself as a site with critical and privileged functions. Since Puerto Ricans as a people had no extensive involvement with U.S. universities, these myths were accepted quite readily. It was only when the university was approached as a natural ally in the effort of collective advance and self-study that other aspects of its operation came into view: its bureaucratism, professionalism, the smugness of its imagined achievements via the cult of excellence, individualism and rigid decorum. When a place was sought in the academy where learning might proceed in ways more attuned to our needs and sense of change, students and community came up against the wall of resistance the university interposes between itself and those who have no power within it and no certified academic credentials.

Thus the principal thrust of present concern with higher education remains centered on the goal of securing a place in the academy where freedom can be won to experiment with new ways of producing and dispensing knowledge that will serve our youth and community. There has in fact been only moderate advance beyond the skepticism and barely veiled arrogance with which early student demands for Puerto Rican Studies were met. Questions continue to be raised as to whether there is enough about ourselves that merits scholarly study and whether any of us have any genuine understanding of what constitutes scholarship. Since the matter at stake, as has been made clear above, is our own survival, a basic lesson has been driven home: we cannot be passive participants in learning and we cannot entrust our intellectual futures completely to the universities. The university has become at best a reluctant ally and at its worst as smooth and evasive in oppressing as it can be elusive in its indifference. We believe a proposal such as the present one must convey as lucidly and emphatically as it can the urgency of our need, the sacrifices that have been made to underwrite our emerging presence in the university and the seriousness of our purpose. To create new knowledge and quickly and comprehensibly transfer it to a long denied community is the principal goal of all our effort undertaken within the university.

Building a Latino Research Base

While the Centro proposal quoted above articulated basic premises, strategies, and a sense of the challenges confronting the Puerto Rican initiative at the City University, parallel formulations were being advanced around the country by African-Americans and, especially in the Southwest, by Mexican-Americans. In that same year, 1972, the National Association of Chicano Studies began to coalesce. In 1974 NACS published a statement of objectives and principles worth citing here, if only to accent the close parallels in the ideas behind these undertakings on both coasts:

1. Social science research by Chicanos must be much more problem oriented than traditional social science. . . . It must be a committed scholarship that can contribute to Chicano liberation.
2. Social science research projects should be inter-disciplinary in nature. . . .
3. Social science should break down barriers between research and action. Research should lead to more effective problem-solving action [and] bridge the gap between theory and action and develop close ties with community action groups.
4. Chicano social science must be highly critical, in the double sense of rigorous analysis and a trenchant critique of American institutions, . . . and it should be a primary task of our scholarship to prepare the ground . . . for a radical transformation of existing institutions.
5. Chicanos must be careful not to unduly limit the scope of our investigations. We must study the Chicano community but within the context of those dominant institutional relationships that affect Chicanos. Our levels of investigation must include the local, the regional and the national, as well as the international dimension.[11]

Putting into place a curriculum, an adequate faculty, and teaching materials for racial and ethnic studies instructional programs was, then as now, as important as mounting the research apparatus necessary to sustain serious scholarship. An obvious void in self-knowledge had to be filled, but this had to go well beyond a "redecorating of the periphery"— that is, a simple rounding out of essentially established accounts of past and current social realities. The side conditions enunciated for the research enterprise set minimal standards for the products to be generated jointly and put to use with and by students and community.

Framing the Paradigm Debate

The decades-long reflections on paradigmatic issues within IUPLR circles have been consistent and productive. This is confirmed by the convergence of concepts and methods in two recent publications—one from an IUPLR working group on Latinos in the U.S. economy and one sponsored by the Social Science Research Council's Committee for Research on the Urban Underclass.[12] The IUPLR volume sought to map the diversity by region and Latino national origin of the modes of incorporation of Latinos into U.S. society. The SSRC volume set out to bring historical perspectives to bear on a critique of the underclass formulation. Both works bring home the need to go well beyond arguments about Latino exceptionalism in assessing the adequacy of the underclass metaphor to address contemporary issues of poverty and inequality. The historian Michael Katz, editor of the SSRC volume, asserts that the effort to give scientific—that is, empirically specific—content to the underclass concept is more problematic than its exploitation in mass media and conservative rhetoric. His closing chapter, "Reframing the Underclass Debate," provides an impressive synthesis of the historical unfolding of social science understandings of poverty in the United States in the course of major economic and other transformations, especially as these bear on African-Americans. His delineation of the interplay of structure, agency, institutional performance, and individual behaviors provides a framework of analysis that dovetails almost perfectly with the perspective developed over recent years by IUPLR researchers seeking a fix on the Latino condition in the United States since World War II. To be specific:

1. Katz proposes as a point of departure a clear portrayal of the context of economic restructuring, demographic change, and residential and work force repositionings that have defined the "postindustrial" city as the key setting for the emergence of the new poverty and race/ethnic polarization. The IUPLR research attempts exactly this in five city-regions of major Latino concentration: New York, Los Angeles, Miami, Chicago, and San Antonio. It uses a matrix of industries and occupations to track redistributions within the work force and also maps spatial rear-

rangements across census tracts. As Katz does, the team stipulates that the underlying dynamic of disinvestment and reinvestment behind restructuring is at once regional, national, and global.

2. Katz points to immigration/migration as a key dimension of demographic transformation that reflects and lends unique characteristics to consequent social resortings of individuals and groups—economic, spatial, social, and cultural. He makes clear distinctions among arrivals from abroad, short-lived or seasonal patterns of movement, and larger regional displacements. This treatment highlights the historical centrality of all of these for African-Americans and other groups, bringing into view, rather than masking, commonalities in the black and Latino experiences. Katz persuasively conveys the historical patterning of these movements ("cycles and circuits of migration") in the generation and reproduction of social stratification. Similarly, tracking the forces behind changes in the origins, magnitude, composition, timing, and end point of migrations has been a central theme of the IUPLR analyses.[13]

3. A historical account of state interventions and the politics of social reform also figures centrally in the Katz framework, bringing into focus the action and inaction of major political agents and the consequences of historical shifts in the disposition and will of governments to address social issues programmatically. Resistance to Latino claims on existing and projected social infrastructures at all points in the political system, as well as in popular attitudes, had, of course, been brought home to IUPLR researchers in this project and in many other settings.[14]

4. Finally, Katz notes the historical tendency in U.S. social analysis to demean the poor and people of color as well as recent immigrants, to cast blame on the disadvantaged for the ills they suffer, and to exonerate social institutions from responsibility, although they are also main agents of social disorganization and failure. Thus the prevalence of bureaucratism and professionalism in major institutions requires constant critical scrutiny. The underclass paradigm, with its behaviorist empirical anchorage, he notes, dictates policies directed toward the micromanagement of behaviors rather than broad programs of social reform. Here again, IUPLR and SSRC analytical slants coincide.

Interestingly, Katz's proposed model treats institutional actors lightly. corporations (and employers generally), unions and other poor people's defense organizations, universities and the knowledge production and policy-making apparatus in general. These have, as I have shown, been prime concerns of the evolving paradigm quest among Latinos, and, especially within IUPLR, for a good number of years. IUPLR's probe into contemporary inequality also brought into view a new parameter of inequality deeply affecting Latinos—toxic and environmental threats in work and residential settings. Nevertheless, there is a striking confluence of ordered thematic prescriptions and shared understandings of systemic processes in the two works cited, despite their independent paths and origins.

The same might be said about the aforementioned Gulbenkian Commission's extended foray into the history of epistemological quandaries in the sciences and their implications for the restructuring of the social sciences today. All science, in the view of that distinguished international body, remains mired in the historical dilemma of reconciling objective as against revealed truths—that is, empirical truth and cultural values rooted in philosophy and religion. Who can unite these in a world system locked in crisis and what role should universities be forging for themselves at this strategic juncture? In lieu of major institutional restructurings and financial commitments based on partially theorized and untested schemes universities could undertake the following: (1) Create year-long interdisciplinary research groups; (2) establish five-year interdisciplinary "institutes" rather than a proliferation of new centers; (3) mandate joint appointments in at least two departments for all faculty members; (4) allow graduate students to pursue joint majors.[15]

These recommendations conform with the agenda that has driven IUPLR and related efforts and that set the platform for our Bellagio session and this volume. The Gulbenkians may be more accommodating to established structures than those long excluded and still marginalized can afford to be. But the awareness of root problems is increasingly shared and manifest across many social boundaries. It is this awareness that is forcing a rethinking of Latino and Latin American interdependence.

Notes

Preface

1. Armando Rendón, "Latinos: Breaking the Cycle of Survival to Tackle Global Affairs," in Chris F. García, ed., *Latinos and the Political System* (Notre Dame, Ind.: University of Notre Dame Press, 1987).

2. *Open the Social Sciences,* report of the Gulbenkian Commission on the Restructuring of the Social Sciences (Binghamton, N.Y.: Fernand Brandel Center, State University of New York, 1995).

3. See Chapters 2 and 13 in this volume by Manuel Pastor and Pedro Cabán.

4. Daniel Bell, "The World and the U.S. in 2013," *Daedalus* 116, no. 3 (1987): 1-31; and "The Year 2000—The Trajectory of an Idea," *Daedalus* 96, no. 3 (1967): 631-51.

5. Murray Gell-Mann, *The Quark and the Jaguar: Adventures in the Simple and the Complex* (New York: W. H. Freeman, 1994), p. 366.

6. Ibid., p. 337.

7. Paul M. Ong and Evelyn Blumenberg, "An Unnatural Tradeoff: Latinos and Environmental Justice," in Rebecca Morales and Frank Bonilla, eds., *Latinos in a Changing U.S. Economy: Comparative Perspectives on Growing Inequality* (Newbury Park, Calif.: Sage Publications, 1993). See also T. J. Lueck, "U.S. Study Finds Hispanic Minority Most Often Subject to Victimization," *New York Times,* November 13, 1991.

8. Abraham F. Lowenthal, "Los Estados Unidos y América Latina en un mundo nuevo," *Norte-Sur: La Revista de las Américas* 2, no. 1 (June–July 1992).

9. William C. Smith, Carlos H. Acuña, and Eduardo A. Gamarra, eds., *Latin American Political Economy in the Age of Neoliberal Reform: Theoretical and Comparative Perspectives for the 1990s* (New Brunswick, NJ: Transaction, 1994).

10. John Brown Childs, "Preliminary Notes for the Utilization of Gramsci in Strategizing Race/Ethnicity/and Political Progress in the Late 20th Century United States," working paper, Chicano-Latino Research Center, University of California Santa Cruz, 1993, cited in Suzanne Jonas and Edward J. McCaughan, eds., *Latin America Faces the Twenty First Century: Reconstructing a Social Justice Agenda* (Boulder, Colo.: Westview Press, 1994), p. 86.

Chapter 1

1. See, for example, María de los Angeles Torres, "Latinos and U.S. Policies

Toward Latin America: A Case Study of the 1988 Presidential Campaign," *Latino Studies Journal* 1 (September 1990): 3-23.

2. Rebecca Morales and Frank Bonilla, eds., *Latinos in a Changing U.S. Economy: Comparative Perspectives on Growing Inequality* (Newbury Park, Calif.: Sage Publications, 1993).

3. Carey Goldberg, "Hispanic Households Struggle As Poorest of the Poor in U.S.," *New York Times,* January 30, 1997.

4. Quoted ibid.

5. Christopher Farrell, Michael Mandel, Michael Schroeder, Joseph Weber, Michele Galen, and Gary McWilliams, "The Economic Crisis of Urban America," *Business Week,* May 18, 1992, pp. 38-43.

6. Daniel H. Weinberg, "A Brief Look at Postwar U.S. Income Inequality," *Current Population Reports: Household Economic Studies,* P60-191 (Washington, D.C.: U.S. Bureau of the Census, 1996), pp. 3-4.

7. Robert B. Reich, *The Work of Nations: Preparing Ourselves for 21st Century Capitalism* (New York: Knopf, 1991).

8. See Rebecca Morales, "U.S. Urban Policy and Latino Issues," *Race Relations Abstract* 19, no. 3 (August 1994): 3-18.

9. Ibid.

10. U.S. Bureau of the Census, *Current Population Reports,* P60-188 (Washington, D.C.: U.S. Bureau of the Census, 1996).

11. Ibid., tables 723, 724.

12. National Commission for Employment Policy, "Training Hispanics: Implications for the JTPA System," no. 27, Washington, D.C., January 1990; Peter Skerry, "E Pluribus Hispanic?" *Wilson Quarterly* (Summer 1992).

13. Johanne Boisjoly and Greg J. Duncan, "Job Losses Among Hispanics in the Recent Recession," *Monthly Labor Review* 117 (June 1994): 16-23.

14. Farrell et al. "Economic Crisis," p. 38.

15. United Nations Economic Commission for Latin America and the Caribbean, *Policies to Improve Linkages with the Global Economy* (Santiago, Chile: ECLAC, 1994).

16. See Chapter in this volume by Manuel Pastor, Jr. and Carol Wise.

17. Albert Berry, "The Challenge of Decimating Poverty in Latin America by 2010," *Frontera Norte,* Special Edition on Poverty, vol 6, no. 1 (1994): 101-19.

18. Oscar Altimar, "Income Distribution and Poverty Through Crisis and Adjustment," in Graham Bird and Ann Helwege, eds., *Latin America's Economic Future* (San Diego: Academic Press, 1994), pp. 265-302.

19. See Jose Maria Fanelli, Robert Frenkel, and Lance Taylor, "Is the Market Friendly to Development: A Critical Assessment," in Bird and Helwege, *Latin America's Economic Future,* pp. 229-63; Eva A. Paus and Michael Robinson, "The Impact of Increasing Economic Openness on Labor: A Comparative Analysis of Latin America and Asia, 1973-1990," paper presented at the 19th International Congress of the Latin American Studies Association, Washington, D.C., September 28-30, 1995; Samuel A. Morley, *Poverty and Inequality in Latin America: The Impact of Adjustment and Recovery in the 1980s* (Baltimore: Johns Hopkins University Press, 1995); and Nora Lustig, ed., *Coping*

with Austerity: Poverty and Inequality in Latin America (Washington, D.C.: Brookings Institution, 1995).

20. United Nations Economic Commission for Latin America and the Caribbean, *Strengthening Development: The Interplay of Macro- and Microeconomics,* LC/G. 1898 SES.26/3 (Santiago, Chile: ECLAC, 1996), p. 13.

21. According to Laura D'Andrea Tyson, *Who's Bashing Whom? Trade Conflict in High Technology Industries* (Washington, D.C.: Institute for International Economics, 1992), managed trade can be understood as "any trade agreement that establishes quantitative targets on trade flows. Managed trade thus lies at one end of a continuum between regulating trade flows through fixed rules and regulating them through fixed quantities or targets" (p. 133).

22. Arthur Okun, *Equality and Efficiency: The Big Trade-Off* (Washington, D.C.: Brookings Institution, 1975).

23. Charles Murray, *Losing Ground: American Social Policy 1950-1980* (New York: Basic Books, 1984).

24. Andrew Glyn and David Miliband, eds., *Paying for Inequality: The Economic Cost of Social Injustice* (London: IPPR/Rivers Oram Press, 1994), p. 2.

25. Torsten Persson and Guido Tabellini, "Is Inequality Harmful for Growth?" *American Economic Review* 84, no. 3 (June 1994): 600-621.

26. William A. Orme, Jr., *Continental Shift: Free Trade and the New North America* (Washington, D.C.: Washington Post Company, 1993), p. 1.

27. Elisabeth Malkin, "Seeking Salvation Through Exports: But the Cheap Peso Alone Won't Be Enough to Fuel a Boom," *Business Week,* March 6, 1995, p. 32.

28. Robert Wade, "Selective Industrial Policies in East Asia: Is *The East Asian Miracle* Right?" in Albert Fishlow, Catherine Gwin, Stephan Haggard, Dani Rodrik, and Robert Wade, *Miracle or Design? Lessons from the East Asian Experience* (Washington, D.C.: Overseas Development Council), p. 70.

29. James R. Golden, "Economics and National Strategy: Convergence, Global Networks, and Cooperative Competition," in Brad Roberts, ed., *New Forces in the World Economy* (Cambridge: MIT Press, 1996), pp. 15-37.

30. Pierre-Olivier Colleye and Mark Dutz, "Cluster-Based Participation Processes in Emerging Economies," *Firm Connections* 4, no. 6 (1996): 1.

31. Weinberg, "Postwar U.S. Income Inequality."

32. Manuel Pastor and Carol Wise, "The Origins and Sustainability of Mexico's Free Trade Policy," *International Organization* 48, no. 3 (1994): 459-89.

33. "Latinos, Global Change and Latin American Foreign Policy," report of a New American Global Dialogue Conference sponsored by the Stanley Foundation in collaboration with the Tomás Rivera Center, October 7-9, 1994, pp. 14-15.

34. Rosabeth Moss Kanter, *World Class: Thriving Locally in the Global Economy* (New York: Simon & Schuster, 1995).

35. Rebecca Morales, "Role of Mediating Institutions in Matching Hispanics to Employment Opportunities," in the proceedings of the U.S. Department of Labor, Employment and Training Administration Roundtable Discussion on Opportunities for Hispanics in the New Workforce Development System, Washington, D.C., April 18-19, 1996.

36. Morales, "U.S. Urban Policy."
37. Cathryn L. Thorup, "Redefining Governance in North America: Citizen Diplomacy and Cross-Border Coalitions," *Enfoque,* publication of the Center for U.S.–Mexican Studies, University of California at San Diego (Spring 1993): 1, 12-13.

Chapter 2

Acknowledgments: The author wishes to thank Jeffry Frieden, Rebecca Morales, and David Ayon for their comments on his early thoughts on these issues. Thanks also to the participants at the Bellagio conference for their provocative criticisms and suggestions on the first draft.

1. A nonexhaustive list of "trespassers" from the fields of Latin American political economy includes authors in this volume: see, e.g., Rebecca Morales and Paul Ong, "The Illusion of Progress—Latinos in Los Angeles," in Rebecca Morales and Frank Bonilla, eds., *Latinos in a Changing U.S. Economy: Comparative Perspectives on Growing Inequality* (Newbury Park, Calif.: Sage Press, 1993); Edwin Meléndez, "Understanding Latino Poverty," *Sage Race Relations Abstracts* 18 (May 1993): 3-42; and Manuel Pastor, Jr., *Latinos and the Los Angeles Uprising: The Economic Context* (Claremont, Calif.: Tomás Rivera Center, 1993); as well as many others, such as Alejandro Portes and Robert L. Bach, *Latin Journey: Cuban and Mexican Immigrants in the United States* (Berkeley: University of California Press, 1985); Norma Chinchilla and Nora Hamilton, "Central American Enterprises in Los Angeles," *New Directions for Latino Public Policy Research,* working paper no. 6, IUP/SSRC Committee for Public Policy Research on Contemporary Hispanic Issues, Center for Mexican American Studies, University of Texas at Austin (1989). Interestingly, fewer prominent scholars cross from ethnic to area studies; however, many ethnic institutions have done so: note the efforts of the Southwest Voter Research Institute and the National Council of La Raza regarding the North American Free Trade Agreement (NAFTA) and other foreign policy issues.
2. See, for example, Guillermo Gómez-Peña, *Warrior for Gringostroika* (St. Paul, Minn.: Graywolf Press, 1993); Ruben Martinez, *The Other Side: Notes from the New L.A., Mexico City and Beyond* (New York: Vintage, 1992).
3. This view is in line with recent tendencies to broaden the definitions of both area and ethnic studies; on the need to broaden area studies, see Stanley J. Heginbotham, "Rethinking International Scholarship: The Challenge of Transition from the Cold War Era," *Items* (Social Science Research Council) 48 (June-September 1994).
4. See, for example, Paul M. Romer, "The Origins of Endogenous Growth," *Journal of Economic Perspectives* 8, no. 1 (Winter 1994): 3-22.
5. Another factor contributing to rapid growth is investment in human capital and social infrastructure. Such investment is often limited in Latin America because of both fiscal constraints and a lack of political will, a point I return to below.
6. See, for example, Edward E. Leamer, "Wage Effects of a U.S.–Mexican Free Trade Agreement," NBER Working Paper no. 3391 (1992). See also the specific analysis of NAFTA's effects on less skilled workers in Raúl Hinojosa-

Ojeda and Sherman Robinson, "Labor Issues in a North American Free Trade Area," in Nora Lustig, Barry P. Bosworth, and Robert Z. Lawrence, eds., *North American Free Trade: Assessing the Impact* (Washington, D.C.: Brookings Institution, 1992), pp. 69-108. Note that the East Asian experience of rising internationalization and rising wages (see Alice Amsden, "Third World Industrialization: 'Global Fordism'; or a New Model?" *New Left Review* 182 [July-August 1990]: 5-31) was due in part to public investment in education and shifts toward a more skilled labor force. This, however, requires a state that is developmentalist and/or oriented to the economic empowerment of its poorest and least skilled citizens — characteristics of government that are often lacking in Latin America.

7. Manuel Pastor, Jr., and Gary Dymski, "Debt Crisis and Class Conflict in Latin America," *Review of Radical Political Economics* 22, no. 1 (1990): 155-78.

8. Eva Paus, "Capital-Labor Relations and Income Distribution in Latin America in the Eighties," paper presented at the 17th Congress of the Latin American Studies Association, Atlanta, Georgia, March 10-12, 1994.

9. The best recent volume on this process is Morales and Bonilla, *Latinos in a Changing Economy,* which also touches on a variety of domestic explanations for the relatively poor performance of Latinos in the U.S. economy.

10. One of the earliest works on the deindustrialization phenomenon is Barry Bluestone and Bennett Harrison, *The Deindustrialization of America: Plant Closings, Community Abandonment, and the Dismantling of Basic Industry* (New York: Basic Books, 1982).

11. On New York, see Andrés Torres and Frank Bonilla, "Decline Within Decline: The New York Perspective," in Morales and Bonilla, *Latinos in a Changing Economy,* pp. 85-108. On Los Angeles, see Morales and Ong, "Illusion of Progress"; Pastor, *Latinos and the Los Angeles Uprising.*

12. In 1990, for example, Latinos constituted about 35 percent of Los Angeles County's labor force, but over 70 percent of the assemblers and factory operatives and over 60 percent of the laborers; see Goetz Wolff, "The Making of a Third World City? Latino Labor and the Restructuring of the L.A. Economy," paper presented at the 17th International Congress of the Latin American Studies Association, Los Angeles, Calif., September 1992.

13. Los Angeles is also one of the most internationalized regions in the United States and not simply because of labor flows. External trade through the county's ports and airports for 1994 was estimated at nearly $90 billion on the import side and $54.3 billion on the export side (figures provided by Jack Keyser, Los Angeles Economic Development Corporation), with county personal income probably around $170 billion. Of course, much of the port traffic is a "pass-through" from and to other regions, but the degree of openness and the reliance on externally generated jobs are still significant. Southern California's share of U.S. trade has more than doubled since 1967, and it is likely that one in seven jobs depends directly or indirectly on international trade: see *LA 2000: A City for the Future,* Final Report of the Los Angeles 2000 Committee (Los Angeles: LA 2000 Committee, 1988), p. 60.

14. The 1990 county figure of 38 percent Latino is taken directly from the CD-ROM version of the U.S. Census Bureau Summary Tape File 1; if one

factors in the undercount and four years of growth and demographic change, a 40 percent figure seems a safe estimate for 1994. The 1970 Latino figure is from *(Almost) 8 Million and Counting: A Demographic Overview of Latinos in California with a Focus on Los Angeles County* (Claremont, Calif.: Tomás Rivera Center, 1991). The percentage of Latinos in the 1970 population is an estimate, since the Census Bureau did not employ a consistent Hispanic/non-Hispanic distinction until the 1980 count; even the bureau's current inconsistent use makes some calculations by ethnicity difficult, particularly for summary census tracts.

15. A general and early analysis of the rising inequality in Los Angeles is provided by Paul Ong et al. in *The Widening Divide: Income Inequality and Poverty in Los Angeles* (Los Angeles: UCLA Graduate School of Architecture and Urban Planning, 1989). The data in Figure 2.1 came from the Public Use Microdata Sample (PUMS) for Los Angeles County.

16. Kuznets's notion was that income inequality first arose as economic development proceeded, then declined after various measures of such development (for example, per capita GDP) reached a given threshold. For the original argument, see Simon Kuznets, "Economic Growth and Income Inequality," *American Economic Review* 45 (1955): 1–28. For various confirmations, see Montek S. Ahluwalia, "Income Distribution and Development: Some Stylized Facts," *American Economic Review* 66 (1976): 128–35; Felix Paukert, "Income Distribution at Different Levels of Development: A Survey of Evidence," *International Labor Review* 108 (1973): 97–125; and Jacques Lecaillon, Felix Paukert, Christian Morrisson, and Dimitri Germidis, *Income Distribution and Economic Development: An Analytical Survey* (Geneva: International Labour Office, 1984). While Kuznets did not mean to imply that inequality drove growth, the standard interpretation was that altering the regressive pattern could slow economic progress.

17. See, for example, Andrew Berg and Jeffrey Sachs, "The Debt Crisis: Structural Explanations of Country Performance," *Journal of Development Economics* 29 (1988): 271–306.

18. See, for example, Alberto Alesina and Allan Drazen, "Why Are Stabilizations Delayed?" *American Economic Review* 8, no. 5 (1991): 1170–88.

19. See Torsten Persson and Guido Tabellini, "Is Inequality Harmful for Growth?" *American Economic Review* 84, no. 3 (1994): 600–621.

20. See the summary in Romer, "Origins of Endogenous Growth."

21. See, for example, Jeffrey Sachs, "External Debt and Macroeconomic Performance in Latin America and East Asia," *Brookings Papers on Economic Activity* 2 (1985): 523–73; and "Trade and Exchange Rate Policies in Growth-Oriented Adjustment Programs," in Vittorio Corbo, Morris Goldstein, and Mohsin Khan, eds., *Growth-oriented Adjustment Programs* (Washington, D.C.: World Bank, 1987), pp. 291–325.

22. See Berg and Sachs, "Debt Crisis"; Gary Dymski and Manuel Pastor, Jr., "Misleading Signals, Bank Lending, and the Latin American Debt Crisis," *International Trade Journal* 6, no. 2 (1990): 151–91.

23. The fact that the negative impact of inequality on growth is most pronounced in democratic states suggests that "the effect of equality on growth may

indeed operate through a political mechanism" (see Persson and Tabellini, "Is Inequality Harmful," p. 613). The impact of democracy on economic outcomes is also considered in Adam Przeworski and Fernando Limongi, "Political Regimes and Economic Growth." *Journal of Economic Perspectives* 7, no. 3 (Summer 1993): 51-70; and Manuel Pastor, Jr., and Eric Hilt, "Private Investment and Democracy in Latin America," *World Development* 21, no. 4 (April 1993): 489-507; the former find little consistent impact, while the latter argue and provide evidence that more open political systems are conducive to private investment because they provide more avenues for developing a social consensus about appropriate macroeconomic strategies.

24. For more on the emergence of regions, see William R. Barnes and Larry C. Ledebur, "Local Economies: The U.S. Common Market of Local Economic Regions," National League of Cities report, August 1994; Neal R. Peirce, with Curtis W. Johnson and John Stuart Hall, *Citistates: How Urban America Can Prosper in a Competitive World* (Washington, D.C.: Seven Locks Press, 1993); Michael Piore and Charles Sabel, *The Second Industrial Divide: Possibilities for Prosperity* (New York: Basic Books, 1984); David Friedman, "Getting Industry to Stick: Enhancing High Value-added Production in California," mimeo (Los Angeles: Lewis Center for Regional Policy Studies, UCLA, November 1992; Charles Sabel, "Flexible Specialization and the Re-emergence of Regional Economies," in P. Hirst and J. Zeitlin, eds., *Reversing Industrial Decline* (Oxford: Berg, 1988); Allen J. Scott, "The New Southern California Economy: Pathways to Industrial Resurgence," mimeo (Los Angeles: Lewis Center for Regional Policy Studies, UCLA, 1993); and Michael Storper and Allan J. Scott, "The Wealth of Regions: Market Forces and Policy Imperatives in Local and Global Context," Working Paper no. 7, Lewis Center for Regional Policy Studies, UCLA, 1993.

25. See William R. Barnes and Larry C. Ledebur, "Cities' Distress, Metropolitan Disparities and Economic Growth," National League of Cities research report, September 1992; and their "'All in It Together': Cities, Suburbs and Local Economic Regions," National League of Cities research report, February 1993; Richard Voith, "City and Suburban Growth: Substitutes or Complements?" *Business Review,* September–October 1992, pp. 21–33; and H. V. Savitch, David Collins, Daniel Sanders, and John Markham, "Ties That Bind: Central Cities, Suburbs, and the New Metropolitan Region," *Economic Development Quarterly* 7, no. 4 (1993):341-57. For a methodological critique of some of these results, see Edward W. Hill, Harold L. Wolman, and Coit Cook Ford III, "Do Cities Lead and Suburbs Follow? Examining Their Economic Interdependence," mimeo prepared for the conference "Rethinking the Urban Agenda," sponsored by the Sydney C. Spivack Program, American Sociological Association, Belmont Conference Center, Md., May 20-22, 1994.

26. As with the international literature, the exact links between distribution and growth remain somewhat underspecified. For one attempt to formally model the negative impact of inequality on a region, see Marcellus W. Andrews, "On the Dynamics of Growth and Poverty in Cities," draft paper prepared for the "Regional Growth and Community Development" Conference, sponsored by

the U.S. Department of Housing and Urban Development, Washington, D.C., November 18, 1993.

27. For a popular version of these pro-equality arguments, see "Inequality: How the Gap Between Rich and Poor Hurts the Economy," *Business Week,* August 15, 1994.

28. For the underclass model, see William Julius Wilson, *The Truly Disadvantaged: The Inner City, the Underclass, and Public Policy* (Chicago: University of Chicago Press, 1987). For its application to Los Angeles, see James H. Johnson, Jr., Cloyzelle K. Jones, Walter C. Farrell, Jr., and Melvin L. Oliver, "The Los Angeles Rebellion: A Retrospective View," *Economic Development Quarterly* 6 (November 1992): 356–72.

29. I have offered here only a very abbreviated version of a rich and empirically rooted model. For a general critique of the underclass approach, particularly as it applies to Latinos, see Meléndez, "Understanding Latino Poverty"; Joan Moore and Raquel Pinderhughes, eds., *In the Barrios: Latinos and the Underclass Debate* (New York: Russell Sage Foundation, 1993).

30. In addition, 18 percent of Latino households in South Central were female-headed with children, as opposed to 35 percent of non-Latino households. Most data in this paragraph are from the Summary Tape Files, STF1 and STF3, 1990 Census, with the boundaries for South Central taken from the L.A. Office of the Census as previously used in Pastor, *Latinos and the Los Angeles Uprising.*

31. For more on the generational experiences of Latinos, see David E. Hayes-Bautista, "Mexicans in Southern California: Societal Enrichment or Wasted Opportunity?" in Abraham F. Lowenthal and Katrina Burgess, eds., *The California-Mexico Connection* (Stanford, Calif.: Stanford University Press, 1993).

32. See Alejandro Portes, "Latin American Class Structures: Their Composition and Change During the Last Decades," *Latin American Research Review* 20, no. 3 (1985): 7–40.

33. The analysis in Alejandro Portes, Manuel Castells, and Lauren A. Benton, eds., *The Informal Economy: Studies in Advanced and Less Developed Countries* (Baltimore: Johns Hopkins University Press, 1989), draws further parallels.

34. Even though NAFTA accession is unlikely for most other Latin American countries in the near term, their desire to attract capital and lower trade barriers will continue for reasons related to economic growth and stabilization. Moreover, immigration is likely to continue, despite the coming of peace to Central America and a new hostility to immigrants in the United States. Here, however, we are focusing on how the "veto" power of capital reduces the range of government action, and in this arena the enhancement of capital mobility is the most important characteristic.

35. For more on the "Washington Consensus," see John Williamson, "What Washington Means by Policy Reform," in John Williamson, ed., *Latin American Development: How Much Has Happened?* (Washington, D.C.: Institute for International Economics, 1990).

36. See, for example, Theodore Hershberg, "The Case for Regional Cooperation," mimeo (Philadelphia: Center for Greater Philadelphia, University of

Pennsylvania, 1994); and Southern California Association of Governments (SCAG), Draft Regional Comprehensive Plan, December 1993.

37. Some of these general policies were laid out in the mid-1980s by Giovanni Andrea Cornia, Richard Jolly, and Frances Stewart, eds., *Adjustment with a Human Face* (Oxford: Clarendon Press, 1987).

38. The percentages of Latinos in the general population and the poverty population come from the U.S. Census Summary Tape File data for 1990; the voter count is calculated from City Council district-level data from the 1988 presidential elections as made available by the Southwest Voter Registration and Education Project. See Pastor, *Latinos and the Los Angeles Uprising*, for more details.

39. The data for Figures 2.2 and 2.3 are taken from the PUMS (CD-ROM) available from the the U.S. Bureau of the Census.

40. See Jorge G. Castañeda, "Mexico and California: The Paradox of Tolerance and Dedemocratization," in Lowenthal and Burgess, *California–Mexico Connection,* pp. 34–47. These figures probably understate the lack of representation because of the significant undercount of undocumented residents. This means both that the percentage of Latino noncitizens is higher and that their representational difficulties are more acute. Moreover, California's Proposition 187 and other such efforts may cause many who pay taxes to lose access to the services they help fund.

41. We could also consider how political realities limit the abilities of Latin American nations themselves. For example, international financial institutions generally proscribe industrial policy as a legitimate tool for international restructuring. Given the importance industrial policies have played in the economic progress of East Asian manufacturers, these limits may be seen as contributing to inequality between nations and not simply classes within the same nation. Here, however, I focus on empowering the poor *within* Latin America.

42. For an early examination of this trend, see Portes, *Latin American Class Structures,* pp. 7–40.

43. On the civic response to the Mexico City quake, see Elena Poniatowska, *Nothing, Nobody: The Voices of the Mexico City Earthquake* (Philadelphia: Temple University Press, 1995); on Chile, see Cathy Lisa Schneider, *Shantytown Protest in Pinochet's Chile* (Philadelphia: Temple University Press, 1995); on the minimum wage fight, see "A Win for the Working Poor: The Moral Minimum Wage Campaign," released by the Industrial Areas Foundation Network of Southern California, 1988.

44. Moreover, community-level development effectively links political empowerment and economic improvement. For example, one way to improve the distribution of government resources in Latin America is to use nongovernmental organizations to deliver services, which frequently has the side effect of training and enabling communities to press for other sorts of improvements and services. Similarly, in the United States, local community-based organizations can be used for job networking and credit provision (as in credit unions), with the dual effect of promoting growth and enhancing political and policy experience.

45. The most striking case is that of the United Farm Workers. For more on the changing attitudes of Mexican-American organizations toward immigrants, see David G. Gutiérrez, "*Sin Fronteras?* Chicanos, Mexican Americans, and the Emergence of the Contemporary Mexican Immigration Debate, 1968–78," in David G. Gutiérrez, ed., *Between Two Worlds: Mexican Immigrants in the United States* (Wilmington, Del.: SR Books, 1996).

Chapter 3

Acknowledgments: This chapter draws on a previous joint effort, "The Politics of Free Trade in the Western Hemisphere," North–South Agenda Papers, no. 20 (Miami: North–South Center, University of Miami, August 1996).

1. The exception is Chile, which began its liberalization efforts earlier.
2. See Brian Baron and Rick Mendosa, "Healing the Wounds of NAFTA," *Hispanic Business*, January 1994, pp. 16-18.
3. The notion that Latinos would automatically identify with Latin American desires because of past ties also reflects what has been called a "cultural" approach to analyzing the stance of ethnic groups on foreign policy concerns. In contrast, a "structural" approach of the type we take here would consider the specific position of ethnic groups within the labor markets and political opportunity structures of the "host" country. For a review of these perspectives and a general overview of Latino attachment to foreign policy concerns, see Rudolfo O. De la Garza, Jerome Hernandez, Angelo Falcón, F. Chris García, and John García, "Mexican, Puerto Rican, and Cuban Foreign Policy Perspectives: A Test of Competing Explanations," in F. Chris García, editor, *Pursuing Power: Latinos and the Political System* (Notre Dame, Ind.: University of Notre Dame Press, 1997), pp. 401-25.
4. Congresswoman Nydia Velázquez from Brooklyn, New York, explaining her vote against NAFTA, put it most starkly: "I represent one of the poorest districts in the nation, and the jobs that are lost are going to be disproportionately in my district" (see Baron and Mendosa, "Healing the Wounds of NAFTA." *Hispanic Business*, January 1994. Note that such a relatively protectionist stance is consistent with an approach that seeks to protect the rights of immigrants; while discrimination against Latin American immigrants is likely to spill over and hurt U.S. Latinos directly, the spillover effects of goods discrimination are much more limited (on the other hand, some have suggested that opposition to NAFTA was, like anti-immigrant politics, partly driven by racist sentiment; see Howard J. Wiarda, "The U.S. Domestic Politics of the U.S.-Mexico Free Trade Agreement," in M. Delal Baer and Sidney Weintraub, eds., *The NAFTA Debate: Grappling with Unconventional Trade Issues* [Boulder and London: Lynne Rienner Publishers, 1994]).
5. See Robert M. Dunn, Jr., "Winners and Losers from NAFTA," in A. R. Riggs and Tom Velk, eds., *Beyond NAFTA: An Economic, Political and Sociological Perspective* (Vancouver: Fraser Institute, 1993); Raúl A. Hinojosa-Ojeda, "Moving Beyond the NAFTA Debate: The Proposal for a North American Development Bank," statement before the Subcommittee on International Development, Finance, Trade and Monetary Policy of the Committee on Banking, Finance and Urban Affairs, U.S. House of Representatives, July 22, 1993.

6. As one example, see the editorial by Jesse Martinez (financial secretary of the Carpenters Local Union 309), "Latino Leaders Let Down the Latino Worker," *Los Angeles Times,* November 11, 1993; see also Rick Bragg, "Anxiously Looking South," *Los Angeles Times,* November 16, 1993. Opposition was especially strong in Chicago and Los Angeles which have long-settled Latino communities, and many unionized Latino workers tied to industries feeling the NAFTA threat; see "Free Trade: How's That in Spanish?" *The Economist,* August 7, 1993. The latter article also points out that Puerto Ricans were concerned that NAFTA would erode certain trade and tax advantages held by the island; also see the discussion in Baron and Mendosa, "Healing the Wounds of NAFTA." For more on the general divergence in Latino positions, see "Hispanics and NAFTA," *Wall Street Journal,* November 16, 1993.

7. See "Congressional Leaders Warn Clinton About NAFTA," *Trade News Bulletin* 2 (March 12, 1993).

8. The NADBank proposal was supported most forcefully by Congressman Esteban Torres as well as by such prominent Latino groups as the Southwest Voter Research Institute, the National Council of La Raza, and the Mexican American Legal Defense and Educational Fund. See Nancy Zubiri, "¿Qué Pasa? 3 Groups Back Stand on Free Trade Pact," *Nuestro Tiempo* (*Los Angeles Times* section), April 29, 1993.

9. See Sebastian Edwards, "Openness, Trade Liberalization, and Growth in Developing Countries," *Journal of Economic Literature* 31 (1993): 1358–93, for an excellent critique of the econometric work that has provided much of the empirical case in favor of free trade.

10. For an extended discussion of these globalized investment and production dynamics, see Gary Gereffi and Miguel Korzeniewicz, eds., *Commodity Chains and Global Capitalism* (New York: Praeger, 1994).

11. See Helen Milner, "Trading Places: Industries for Free Trade," *World Politics* 40 (1988): 355–76. These trends are not, of course, a complete explanation. Note, for example, that Brazil, which ranks high on intraindustry trade measures, has been the slowest to liberalize, while a country like Chile, with low intraindustry indices, has been eager to open up its trade relations. Understanding the reasons for this requires that we also consider the domestic politics of trade reform.

12. Our view that the favorable Latin American reception of free trade was unexpected is based on confidential interviews conducted in Washington, D.C., from 1990 to 1994 with front line policy-makers in such departments as the U.S. Treasury, the Commerce Department, the State Department, and the Office of the U.S. Trade Representative, an issue explored in the text.

13. For formal models of how the political costs and benefits of open trade are altered by the linkage of free trade with macroeconomic stabilization, see Dani Rodrik, "The Rush to Free Trade in the Developing World: Why So Late? Why Now? Will It Last?" in Stephan Haggard and Stephen B. Webb, eds., *Voting for Reform: Democracy, Political Liberalization, and Economic Adjustment* (New York: Oxford University Press, 1994), pp. 61–88; and Manuel Pastor, Jr., and Carol Wise, "The Origins and Sustainability of Mexico's Free

Trade Policy," *International Organization* 48 (1994): 459-89. Recall that the traditional problem for free trade is that the beneficiaries (consumers) are diffuse, while the losers (selected industries) are concentrated, giving the latter an advantage in organizing for trade barriers. Linking free trade with macroeconomic stability makes its gains more obvious (less overall inflation rather than small price decreases in selected tradables) and prompts certain protectionist interests to shift their calculus of gains and losses, particularly if macro stability results in an expansion of the domestic market.

14. See Sylvia Maxfield, "The Domestic Politics of Mexican Trade Policy," in *North American Free Trade: Proceedings of a Conference* (Dallas: Federal Reserve Bank of Dallas, 1991), pp. 103-8.

15. For more detail see Alejandra Cox Edwards and Sebastian Edwards, "Markets and Democracy: Lessons from Chile," *World Economy* 15 (1992): 203-19; Patricio Meller, "Review of the Chilean Trade Liberalization and Export Expansion Process (1974/90)," *Bangladesh Development Studies* 20, nos. 2-3 (1992): 155-84; Eduardo Silva, "Capitalist Coalitions, the State, and Neoliberal Economic Restructuring," *World Politics* 45 (1993): 526-59. See also an excellent edited collection on the Chilean economyg: Barry P. Bosworth, Rudiger Dornbusch, and Raúl Labán, eds., *The Chilean Economy: Policy Lessons and Challenges* (Washington, D.C.: Brookings Institution, 1994).

16. These fears were compounded by the Mexican peso crisis in late 1994, which triggered an acrimonious debate in the new Republican-controlled Congress over U.S. loan assistance to Mexico, with many members of Congress blaming NAFTA for the peso debacle.

17. Although the Clinton team ultimately was successful in winning the GATT vote, Congress thwarted its attempts to secure the necessary fast-track negotiating authority for expanding NAFTA on the grounds that the environmental and labor stipulations were still not acceptable to all parties involved in the NAFTA debate.

18. This is not to say that these have been an easy alternative: incipient customs unions also have been plagued by fierce fights over how low to set the common external tariff and by differences in macroeconomic policy objectives and management. For details, see Edwards, "Openness"; Luigi Manzetti, "The Political Economy of MERCOSUR," *Journal of Interamerican Studies and World Affairs* 35 (1993-94): 101-41.

19. This arrangement gradually phases in free trade among Colombia, Mexico, and Venezuela over a 10-year period that began in January 1995.

20. See "Brazil Under Cardoso: Returning to the World Stage," dossier no. 52, Instituto de Relaciones Europeo-Latinoamericanas (IRELA) (Madrid: IRELA, 1995), pp. 28-34.

21. See Stephen Lande, "The FTAA Process: Maintaining the Miami Summit Momentum," North-South Center White Paper (Miami: North-South Center, University of Miami, 1996).

22. In the Chilean case, an earlier episode of fixed exchange rates, trade liberalization, and foreign capital dependence (1979-82), resulted in a dramatic economic collapse; macroeconomic policy became more flexible in the 1980s, and the economy grew on the basis of combining this more pragmatic ap-

proach with the earlier accomplishments on trade and domestic liberalization. Colombia, as usual, moved less dramatically on all fronts and boasts a reasonable record with regard to both policy movement and economic performance.

23. Brazil is going its own way: it has declared its allegiance to neoliberal macroeconomic management, toyed with a fixed exchange rate, and seems to be placing its eggs in a non-NAFTA free trade basket. Nonetheless, the initial upshot of its macroeconomic reforms, especially shifts in the trade balance, suggests the same underlying fragility that has characterized the other deficit-ridden reformers reviewed here.

24. Key examples here include the devolution of trade policy to SECOFI (the newly reorganized Ministry of Trade and Industry) in the Mexican case and the creation of an independent currency board in Argentina to manage exchange rate (and hence monetary) policy.

25. For an analysis that incorporates the impacts of rural–urban migration in response to a trade opening, see Raúl Hinojosa-Ojeda and Sherman Robinson, "Labor Issues in a North American Free Trade Area," in Nora Lustig, Barry P. Bosworth, and Robert Z. Lawrence, eds., *North American Free Trade: Assessing the Impacts* (Washington, D.C.: Brookings Institution, 1992), pp. 69-108.

26. For more on industrial concentration under free trade in the Mexican case, see Enrique Dussel Peters and Kwan S. Kim, "From Liberalization to Economic Integration: The Case of Mexico," paper presented at the 17th Congress of the Latin American Studies Association, Los Angeles, September 24-27, 1992.

27. The Gini coefficient, a standard measure of income inequality, rose from 0.46 to 0.51 between 1984 and 1992, with the proportion of national income accruing to the top decile rising from 34.3 to 40.1 percent over the same period. For analysis of these and other trends, see Manuel Pastor, Jr. and Carol Wise, "State Policy, Distribution and Neoliberal Reform in Mexico," *Journal of Latin American Studies* 29 (1997): 419-56.

28. The figures are even worse for heads of households, a pattern suggesting that households were able to keep themselves afloat only by increasing the participation of women and children in labor force activities.

29. Indeed, trade liberalization is likely to have promoted industrial concentration, as larger firms have been better able to achieve the economies of scale necessary to compete in world markets and to obtain the credit necessary to finance adjustment: see Peters and Kim, "Liberalization to Economic Integration."

30. Many small and medium-sized firms could exist successfully in business clusters, but cannot finance the transition given Mexico's segmented credit markets and the relatively high interest rates that banks charge for smaller producers. These latter features are, we believe, also characteristic of other recent reformers.

31. A main criticism of Mexico's compensation scheme, PRONASOL, is that only communities able to organize and articulate demands receive funds, rendering the program little more than a political tool for targeting the country's "hot spots." See Denise Dresser, *Neopopulist Solutions to Neoliberal Problems: Mexico's National Solidarity Program* (La Jolla: Center for U.S.-Mexican Studies, University of California at San Diego, 1991). For an overall view of

safety net compensation schemes, see Carol Graham, *Safety Nets, Politics, and the Poor: Transitions to Market Economies* (Washington, D.C.: Brookings Institution, 1994).

32. While this sort of cluster analysis is now prevalent in urban planning research in the United States, it remains underdeveloped in its applications to Latin America. See Peter B. Doeringer and David G. Terka, "Business Strategy and Cross-Industry Clusters," *Economic Development Quarterly* 9 (1995): 225-37.

33. One hopeful sign is the recent creation of an FTAA working group devoted to the study of competition policy. See "Joint Declaration: Summit of the Americas, Second Ministerial Trade Meeting," Cartagena, Colombia, March 21, 1996, p. 5.

34. See, for example, Alberto Alesina and Allan Drazen, "Why Are Stabilizations Delayed?" *American Economic Review* 81 (1991): 1170-88; Alberto Alesina and Dani Rodrik, "Distributive Policies and Economic Growth," *Quarterly Journal of Economics* 109, no. 2 (1994); Torsten Persson and Guido Tabellini, "Is Inequality Harmful for Growth?" *American Economic Review* 84 (1994): 600-621; Dani Rodrick, "King Kong Meets Godzilla: The World Bank and the East Asian Miracle," in Albert Fishlow et al., eds., *Miracle or Design? Lessons from the East Asian Experience* (Washington, D.C.: Overseas Development Council, 1994), pp. 13-53; Jeffrey Sachs, "Trade and Exchange Rate Policies in Growth-Oriented Adjustment Programs," in Vittorio Corbo, Morris Goldstein, and Mohsin Khan, eds., *Growth-Oriented Adjustment Programs* (Washington, D.C.: World Bank, 1987), pp. 291-325.

35. Barbara Jenkins notes in *The Paradox of Continental Production: National Investment Policies in North America* (Ithaca: Cornell University Press, 1992) that by "ignoring the need to cushion threatened actors, economic liberals in effect sabotage their own projects by guaranteeing that they will not be politically acceptable" (p. 35).

36. See Paul Blustein, "NAFTA's Effects: Pact Hurts U.S. Minorities, Group to Tell Clinton," *Washington Post,* July 16, 1997. For a specific case of NAFTA's negative effects on Latinos in El Paso, see Allen R. Myerson, "Low-Wage Workers Have Been Losing Jobs to Mexico," *New York Times,* May 8, 1997; according to this analysis, El Paso lost nearly six thousand jobs to Mexican trade (most had been held by Latinos), leading to a increase in the unemployment rate of about two percentage points.

37. The key groups declining to support further extension of NAFTA without enhanced federal assistance for displaced Latino and other worker were the Southwest Voter Research Institute (now rechristened the William C. Velazquez Institute) and the National Council of La Raza. See Jim Cason and David Brooks, "Exigen en EU Cambios de Fondo en el TLC," *La Jornada,* July 17, 1997.

38. See Albert Fishlow, Sherman Robinson, and Raúl Hinojosa-Ojeda, "Proposal for a North American Regional Development Bank and Adjustment Fund," in Federal Bank of Dallas, *North American Free Trade: Proceedings of a Conference* (Dallas: Federal Reserve Bank of Dallas, June 1991), pp. 15-29.

39. See the critique in Harry Browne, "NADBank: The BECC's Skinflint Rich Uncle?," *The Workbook* 21 (Winter 1996): 162-64.

Chapter 4

Acknowledgments: This chapter is based on *Immigration Policy in a Global Economy: From National Crisis to Multilateral Management,* a book on immigration policy being written for the Twentieth Century Fund. The author thanks the Fund for its support.

1. See Saskia Sassen, *Losing Control: The Decline of Sovereignty in an Age of Globalization* (New York: Columbia University Press, 1996), a collection of essays first delivered at Columbia University as the 1995 Leonard Hastings Schoff Memorial Lectures.

2. Immigration can be seen as a strategic research site for the examination of the relationship between the idea of sovereignty over borders and the constraints encountered by states in the design and implementation of actual policy on the matter.

3. While there is considerable variation among these countries, there are also important similarities in their fundamental conceptions. A rich scholarly literature documenting and interpreting the specificity of immigration policy in highly developed countries includes Patrick Weil, *La France et ses étrangers* (Paris: Calmann-Lévy, 1991); Wayne A. Cornelius, Philip L. Martin, and James F. Hollifield, eds., *Controlling Immigration: A Global Perspective* (Stanford: Stanford University Press, 1994); Myron Weiner, *The Global Migration Crisis* (New York: Harper Collins, 1995); Yasmin Soysal, *Limits of Citizenship* (Chicago: University of Chicago Press, 1994); Dietrich Thranhardt, ed., *Europe: A New Immigration Continent* (Hamburg: Lit Verlag, 1992); Klaus J. Bade, ed., *Deutsche im Ausland, Fremde in Deutschland: Migration in Geschichte und Gegenwart* (Munich: C. H. Beck Verlag, 1992). See also, generally, Douglas S. Massey et al., "Theories of International Migration: A Review and Appraisal," *Population and Development Review* 19 (1993): 431-66.

4. The sovereignty of the state when it comes to power over entry is well established constitutionally and by treaty law. The Convention of The Hague of 1930 asserted the right of the state to grant citizenship, while the 1952 Convention on Refugees, which declared that the right to leave is a universal right, remained silent on the right to entry.

5. For more information, see Linda S. Bosniak, "Human Rights, State Sovereignty and the Protection of Undocumented Migrants Under the International Migrant Workers Convention," *International Migration Review* 25 (1992): 737-70; James F. Hollifield, *Immigrants, Markets, and States* (Cambridge, Mass.: Harvard University Press, 1992); Rainer Baubock, *Transnational Citizenship: Memberships and Rights in International Migration* (Aldershot: Edward Elgar, 1994); and Sassen, *Losing Control,* part 3.

6. Use of the conventions on universal human rights by national judiciaries can assume many different forms. Some instances in the United States are the sanctuary movement of the 1980s, which sought to establish protected areas, typically in churches, for refugees from Central America; judicial battles, such as those around the status of Salvadorans granted indefinite stays although formally defined as illegal; and the fight for the rights of detained Haitians. It is clear that, notwithstanding the lack of an enforcement apparatus, human

rights limit the discretion of states in how they treat non-nationals on their territory. It is also worth noting in this regard that the United Nations High Commission on Refugees (UNHCR) is the only United Nations agency to enjoy a universally conceded right of access to a country.

7. While such developments in Europe and North America are well known, there is little awareness of similar incipient forms in Japan: see Gregory Shank, ed., *Japan Enters the Twenty-First Century,* a special issue of *Social Justice,* vol. 21 (Summer 1994). In Japan today we see a strong group of human rights advocates for immigrants; efforts by nonofficial unions to organize undocumented immigrant workers; and organizations working on behalf of immigrants that receive funding from individuals or government institutions in sending countries—for instance, the Thai Ambassador to Japan announced in October 1995 that his government would give 2.5 million baht, or about $100,000, to five civic groups that assist Thai migrant workers, especially undocumented ones (*Japan Times,* October 18, 1995). See Saskia Sassen, "The Impact of Economic Internationalization on Immigration: Comparing the U.S. and Japan," *International Migration* 31, no. 1 (1993): 44-102.

8. The growth of immigration, refugee flows, renewed interest in ethnic identity, and regionalism raise questions about the accepted notion of citizenship in contemporary nation-states. And the internationalization of capital and the growing presence of immigrant workers in major industrial countries calls into question the meaning of such concepts as national economy and national work force. See, for example, Baubock, *Transnational Citizenship;* Soysal, *Limits of Citizenship;* Saskia Sassen, *Immigration Policy in a Global Economy,* prepared for the Twentieth Century Fund (forthcoming); John Isbister, *The Immigration Debate: Remaking America* (West Hartford: Kumarian Books, 1996).

9. Jurisdiction over immigration matters in the U.S. Congress lies with the Judiciary Committee, not, as might have been the case, with the Foreign Affairs Committee. Congressional intent on immigration can be at odds with the foreign affairs priorities of the executive, and a tug-of-war over policy frequently results (see Christopher Mitchell, "International Migration, International Relations and Foreign Policy," *International Migration Review* 31 (1989): 681-708. It has not always been this way. In the late 1940s and 1950s there was great concern over how immigration policy could be used to advance foreign policy objectives. When the Department of Labor (DOL) was created in 1914, it was given responsibility for immigration policy. In 1933, President Roosevelt created the Immigration and Naturalization Service (INS) within the DOL. World War II brought a shift in the administrative responsibility for the country's immigration policy: in 1940, Roosevelt recommended that the INS be moved to the Department of Justice because of the supposed political threat represented by immigrants from enemy countries. This shift was meant to last only for the duration of the war, but the INS never was returned to the DOL. The relocation meant that immigration wound up with those congressional committees traditionally reserved for lawyers—the Senate and House Judiciary Committees. It has been said that

this is one reason why immigration law is so complicated—and, I would add, so centered on the legalities of entry at the expense of broader issues.

10. Diverse social forces shape the role of the state, depending on the matter at hand. Thus, in the Third World debt crisis of the early 1980s, the players were few and well coordinated; the state basically relinquished its organizing capacity to the banks, the International Monetary Fund, and a few other actors. The crisis was resolved so discreetly that it seemed as though the government was hardly a player. Public and political deliberation over the passage of the 1986 Immigration and Reform Control Act—a sort of national brawl—offers a marked contrast.

11. Alfred Aman has noted that although political and constitutional arguments for reallocating federal power to the states are not new, the recent reemergence of the Tenth Amendment as a politically viable and popular guideline marks a major political shift since the New Deal in the relations between the federal government and the states (see Alfred C. Aman, Jr., "A Global Perspective on Current Regulatory Reform: Rejection, Relocation, or Reinvention?" *Indiana Journal of Global Legal Studies* 2, (1995): 429–64.

12. In the United States, the costs of immigration are an area of great debate and wide-ranging estimates. The latest study by the Washington-based Urban Institute found that immigrants contribute $30 billion more in taxes than they use in services.

13. States are beginning to request reimbursement from the federal government for the costs of benefits and services that they are required to provide, especially to undocumented immigrants: see Rebecca L. Clark, Jeffrey Passel, Wendy Zimmermann, and Michael Fix, *Fiscal Impacts of Undocumented Aliens: Selected Estimates for Seven States,* Report to the Office of Management and Budget and the Department of Justice (Washington, D.C.: Urban Institute, 1994); General Accounting Office, *Illegal Aliens: Assessing Estimates of Financial Burden on California,* GAO/HEHS-95-22, November 1994; General Accounting Office, *Illegal Aliens: National Net Cost Estimates Very Widely,* GAO/HEHS-95-133, July 1995. In 1994, six states (Arizona, California, Florida, New Jersey, New York, and Texas) filed separate suits in federal district courts to recover costs they claim to have sustained because of the federal government's failure to enforce U.S. immigration policy, protect the nation's borders, and provide adequate resources for immigration emergencies: see Jonathan C. Dunlap and Ann Morse, "States Sue Feds to Recover Immigration Costs," *Legisbrief,* National Conference of State Legislatures, January 3, 1995, p. 1. The amounts of the lawsuits range from $50.5 million in New Jersey for the fiscal year 1993 costs of imprisoning 500 undocumented criminal felons and construction of future facilities, to $33.6 billion in New York for all state and county costs associated with undocumented immigration between 1988 to 1993: see Thomas J. Espenshade and Vanessa E. King, "State and Local Fiscal Impacts of US Immigrants: Evidence from New Jersey," *Population Research and Policy Review* 13 [1994]: 225–56). U.S. District Court judges have dismissed all six lawsuits; some of the states are appealing the decision. President Clinton's 1994 crime bill earmarked $1.8

billion in disbursements over six years to help reimburse states for these incarceration-related costs.

14. See, for example, David M. Reimers, "An Unintended Reform: The 1965 Immigration Act and Third World Immigration to the U.S." *Journal of American Ethnic History* 3 (1983): 9–28; Vernon M. Briggs, *Mass Immigration and the National Interest* (Armonk, N.Y.: M. E. Sharpe, 1992).

15. See, for example, Saskia Sassen, *The Mobility of Labor and Capital: A Study in International Investment and Labor Flow* (Cambridge: Cambridge University Press, 1988); Edna Bonacich, Lucie Cheng, Norma Chinchilla, Nora Hamilton, and Paul Ong, eds., *Global Production: The Apparel Industry in the Pacific Rim* (Philadelphia: Temple University Press, 1994); and *Journal für Entwicklungspolitik, Schwerpunkt: Migration,* special issue on Migration, vol. 11, no. 3 (1995) For a discussion of the literature on the impact of cross-border labor market networks, see Saskia Sassen, "Immigration and Local Labor Markets," in Alejandro Portes, ed., *The Economic Sociology of Immigration: Essays on Networks, Ethnicity, and Entrepreneurship* (New York: Russell Sage Foundation, 1995).

16. See Sarah Mahler, *American Dreaming: Immigrant Life on the Margins* (Princeton: Princeton University Press, 1995).

17. Foreign aid frequently has stimulated, rather than deterred, immigration flows. Take El Salvador in the 1980s: hundreds of thousands of Salvadorans emigrated as U.S. aid raised the effectiveness of the Salvadoran military's aggression against its own people. Or the case of the Philippines, a country that received massive aid and has had high emigration. In both cases, foreign aid, dictated by security concerns, had strong immigration consequences. Flows resulting from U.S. economic and political intervention are also evident in the Dominican emigration in the 1960s. (I have long argued that policy-makers should be required to attach migration impact statements to policies with overseas impacts.)

18. Increasingly, unilateral policy by a major immigration country is problematic. A dramatic example is the case of Germany, which began to receive massive numbers of entrants as other European states gradually tightened their asylum policies, while Germany's remained liberal.

19. The sense in many highly developed countries that an immigration control crisis prevails today is in some respects unwarranted. States may have less control than they would like because immigration is entangled in a web of other dynamics. But when we look at the characteristics of immigrations over time and across the world, it is clear that there are equilibrating mechanisms within these flows; that they have a duration (many immigrations have lasted for fifty years and then come to an end); and that there is more return migration than we generally realize. We also know that in earlier historical periods when there were no controls, most people did not leave poorer areas to go to richer ones, even though there was plenty of opportunity to do so.

20. Globalization has contributed to a massive push toward deregulation across the board in many of the highly developed countries. Aman, "Global Perspective," notes that although not all industries in a nation are equally subject to intense global competition, the existence of such competition in general con-

tributes to an overall political context that encourages domestic regulatory reform in all industries: "Political movements and regulatory trends do not tend to discriminate among industries once the momentum for certain reforms is underway" (p. 433). Thus, the impact of global competition on the domestic politics of regulation goes well beyond the industries in which this competition is most intense. For some recent formulations in a vast literature, see Bonacich et al., *Global Production;* Christine E. Bose and Edna Acosta-Bélen, eds., *Women in the Latin American Development Process* (Philadelphia: Temple University Press, 1995); *Global Crisis, Local Struggles,* special issue of *Social Justice,* vol. 20 (Fall–Winter 1993); and Rebecca Morales, *Flexible Production: Restructuring of the International Automobile Industry* (Cambridge: Polity Press, 1994).

21. This guarantee of the rights of capital is embedded in a certain type of state, a certain conception of the rights of capital, and a certain type of international legal regime—namely, the world's most developed countries, Western notions of contract and property rights, and a new legal regime aimed at furthering economic globalization. The hegemony of the neoliberal concept of economic relations, with its strong emphasis on markets, deregulation, and free trade, has influenced policy in the United States, the United Kingdom, and increasingly in continental Europe. This has contributed to the formation of transnational legal regimes that are centered in Western economic concepts. Through international institutions like the International Monetary Fund, the World Bank, and GATT, this vision has spread to the developing world. Scholars are beginning to examine critically the philosophical premises about authorship and property that define the legal arena in the West; see, for example, Rosemary J. Coombe, "The Properties of Culture and the Politics of Possessing Identity: Native Claims in the Cultural Appropriation Controversy," *Canadian Journal of Law and Jurisprudence* 6 (1993): 249–85.

22. According to some observers, the neoliberalism of the 1980s has redefined the role of states in national economies and in the interstate system. See, for example, James Mittelman, ed., *Globalization: Critical Reflections,* in the annual series *International Political Economy Yearbook,* vol. 9 (Boulder: Lynne Rienner, 1996); Daniel Drache and M. S. Gertler, eds., *The New Era of Global Competition: State Policy and Market Power* (Montreal: McGill-Queen's University Press, 1991); and James N. Rosenau, "Governance, Order, and Change in World Politics," in James N. Rosenau and E. O. Czempiel, eds., *Governance Without Government: Order and Change in World Politics* (Cambridge: Cambridge University Press, 1992), pp. 1–29.

23. There are various sites for governance in the world economy beyond the nation-state. Among these are organizations involved with international economic issues, from the International Chamber of Commerce and the Court of Justice at The Hague to the Single European Market and NAFTA. On a more specialized level, we could add to this list the entities engaged with the formulation of new international accounting and financial reporting standards. These very different kinds of institutions are all engaged in identifying, formalizing, and redesigning components of transnational systems for economic governance. (See Sassen, *Losing Control,* chaps. 1–2).

24. The extent to which international financial markets dictate economic policy for rich and poor countries alike was illustrated by the Mexican financial crisis in 1994-95, and the subsequent fear in Argentina and Brazil that they, too, might lose the confidence of international financial markets. The U.S. response to the crisis—a rescue package designed to restore investor confidence in Mexico—also was shaped by international financial markets. A financial response to this crisis was but one of several options. For instance, there could have been an emphasis on promoting manufacturing growth and protecting small businesses and homeowners from bankruptcy. The U.S. government might have exhorted the Mexican government to give up on restoring confidence in the global financial markets and to focus on the production of real value added in the Mexican economy. Furthermore, this matter, which was presented as a global economic security issue, was handled not by the secretary of state, but by the secretary of the treasury. There are two novel elements here: the Treasury Department's handling an international crisis of this sort, and the fact that the secretary of that agency was a former top partner at Goldman Sachs, a leading global financial firm. The point here is not the potential for corruption but rather the question of what is desirable economically for Mexico.

25. See, for example, Mittelman, *Globalization;* Fred Rosen and Deidre McFadyen, eds., *Free Trade and Economic Restructuring in Latin America: A NACLA Reader* (New York: Monthly Review Press, 1995); and *Competition and Change: The Journal of Global Business and Political Economy* 1, no. 1 (1996).

26. There is an enormous literature on how the evolution of international finance during the 1980s reduced the regulatory control exercised by states over this sector; for a discussion and review see Saskia Sassen, *The Global City: New York, London, Tokyo* (Princeton: Princeton University Press, 1991), part 1. This literature has focused mainly on the loss of regulatory power by single states, rather than the impact on the interstate system.

27. In addition to the extension of the economy beyond the state, new information technologies raise questions of control in the global economy. The best example is probably the foreign currency markets, which operate largely in electronic space. Here, new technologies have increased by orders of magnitude the flow of transactions, leaving central banks incapable of exercising the influence on exchange rates they once had. For details, see Sassen, *Losing Control,* chap. 2.

28. See, for example, Mittelman, *Globalization;* David M. Trubek, Yves Dezalay, Ruth Buchanan, and John R. Davis, "Global Restructuring and the Law: The Internationalization of Legal Fields and Creation of Transnational Arenas," Working Paper Series on the Political Economy of Legal Change, no. 1 (Madison: Global Studies Research Program, University of Wisconsin, 1993).

29. See, for example, Trubek et al. , "Global Restructuring." Globalization restricts the range of regulatory options of national governments, as the Mexico crisis illustrates. Aman, "Global Perspective," shows how a global view of domestic regulatory politics helps explain the absence of radical differences in the regulatory outcomes of different U.S. administrations over the past fifteen

years. The pressures of global competition, the nature of the corporate entities involved, and domestic political pressures to minimize costs and maximize flexibility militate in favor of new, more market-oriented forms of regulatory reform.

30. See Yves Dezalay and Bryant Garth, "Merchants of Law as Moral Entrepreneurs: Constructing International Justice from the Competition for Transnational Business Disputes," *Law and Society Review* 29 (1995): 27-64.

31. See Timothy J. Sinclair, "Passing Judgment: Credit Rating Processes as Regulatory Mechanisms of Governance in the Emerging World Order," *Review of International Political Economy* 1 (1994): 133-59.

32. See Jeswald Salacuse, *Making Global Deals: Negotiating in the International Marketplace* (Boston: Houghton Mifflin, 1991).

33. For instance, we are seeing the formation of an economic complex (finance and corporate services) with properties that distinguish it clearly from other economic complexes, in that the creation of value in this new complex relies much less on the public economic functions of the state than, say, Fordist manufacturing.

34. For further discussion, see Sassen, *Losing Control,* part 3; Isbister, *Immigration Debate;* and Sassen, *Broken Borders.*

35. See Cornelius, Martin, and Hollifield, *Controlling Immigration.*

36. Another instance of the impact of globalization on governmental policy making can be seen in Japan's 1990 immigration law (actually an amendment to an earlier law on the entry and exit of aliens). This legislation opened the country to several categories of highly specialized professionals with a Western background (such as experts in international finance, Western-style accounting, Western medicine, and so on) in recognition of the growing internationalization of the professional world in Japan. The law also made illegal the entry of what is referred to as "simple labor." This can be interpreted as the importing of Western "human capital" and the closing of borders to immigrants: see Sassen, "Impact of Economic Internationalization."

37. Article 1202 contains explicit conditions regarding the treatment of non-national service providers, as do Articles 1203, 1205, 1210 (especially Annex 1210.5), and 1213.2a and b. Chapter Sixteen, "Temporary Entry for Business Persons," covers provisions for those "engaged in trade in goods, the provision of services or the conduct of investment activities" (Article 1608).

38. NAFTA relies on unaccountable panels of "experts" to make economic decisions that elected representatives *should* make, thereby implying a shift of power from states to the representatives of transnational capital.

39. For details, see CEPAL, *Desarrollo reciente de los procesos de integración en América Latina y el Caribe* (Santiago, Chile: CEPAL, 1994); Lelio Marmora, "Desarrollo sostenido y políticas migratorias: su tratamiento en los espacios latinoamericanos de integración," *Revista de la OIM sobre Migraciones en América Latina* 12, no. 1/3 (April–December 1994): 5-50; OIM, *Programa de integración y migraciones para el Cono Sur* (Buenos Aires: PRIMCOS/OIM, 1991); and Ponciano Torales, *Migración e integración en el Cono Sur: la experiencia del Mercosur* (Buenos Aires: OIM, 1993).

40. An Andean Social Charter was created with the participation of trade unions

and the Andean Parliament, as was a basic regulatory framework for regional international migration. In 1992, member countries set up the Committee of Migration Officials of the Andean Group, which includes migration officials of the member countries, to advise the technical and administrative body of the Cartagena Agreement. For more detailed accounts of the Andean Pact, see Acuerdo de Cartagena, Junta (JUNAC), *Acta Final de la 1ra. Reunion de Autoridades Migratorias del Grupo Andino, Bases de Propuesta para la Integracion Fronteriza Andina* (Lima: JUNAC, 1991); *La migración internacional en los procesos regionales de integración en América del Sur* (Lima: JUNAC, 1991); Banco Interamericano de Desarrollo/JUNAC, *Política de integración fronteriza de los países miembros del Grupo Andino: cooperación técnica* (Lima: JUNAC, 1993); JUNAC-OIM, *Integración, migración y desarrollo sostenible en el Grupo Andino* (Lima: JUNAC-OIM, 1993); and Ramón Leon and K. Hermann Kratochwil, "Integración, migraciones y desarrollo sostenido en el Grupo Andino," *Revista de la OIM sobre Migraciones en América Latina* 11 (1993): 5–28.

41. For details see Directores Generales de Migraciones, Centroamérica, "Políticas de control sobre las corrientes migratorias en Centroamérica," in *La migración internacional: su impacto en Centroamerica* (San José, Costa Rica, 1992); CEPAL, "Consideraciones sobre la formación de recursos humanos en Centroamérica," mimeo (Mexico: CEPAL, 1992); Patricia Weiss Fagen and Joseph Eldridge, "Salvadorean Repatriation from Honduras," in Mary Ann Larkin, ed., *Repatriation Under Conflict: The Central American Case* (Washington, D.C.: HMP, CIPRA, Georgetown University, 1991); SIECA, *III Reunión de la Organización Centroamericana de Migración* (Managua, Nicaragua: SIECA, 1991); SIECA, *Antecedentes y acuerdos de la Comisión Centroamericana de Migración* (Guatemala: OCAM, 1991); Eduardo Stein, "Las dinámicas migratorias en el Istmo Centroamericano en la perspectiva de la integración y el imperativo de la sostenibilidad," *Revista de la OIM sobre Migraciones en América Latina* 11, no. 2 (August 1993): 5–51; and OIM, *Proyecto Regional de la Organización Centroamericana de Migración, Políticas e Instrumentos Migratorios para la Integración de América Central* (Costa Rica: PROCAM/OIM, 1991).

42. The U.S. delegation for this group is chaired by the assistant secretary of state for consular affairs and the commissioner of the INS.

43. The Mexican delegation to the February 1995 Zacatecas meeting was headed by the undersecretary for bilateral affairs from the Secretariat of Foreign Affairs, the undersecretary of population and migration services of the Secretariat of the Interior, and the commissioner of the National Migration Institute. The U.S. delegation was headed by the INS commissioner, the U.S. ambassador to Mexico, and the deputy assistant secretary for inter-American affairs of the Department of State. Thus, the meeting was conducted between fairly high-level government officials, not simply technical personnel.

44. This is a complex subject that can be treated only briefly in this chapter. For fuller discussion of the impact of human rights on immigration policy, see David Jacobson, *Rights Across Borders: Immigration and the Decline of Citizenship* (Baltimore: Johns Hopkins University Press), 1996; Martin Heisler,

"Transnational Migration as a Small Window on the Diminished Autonomy of the Modern Democratic State," *Annals* (American Academy of Political And Social Science) 485 (May 1993): 153–66; Soysal, *Limits of Citizenship*, chap. 3; Sassen, *Losing Control;* Sassen, *Broken Borders*.

45. In the early twentieth century there already were several legal instruments that promoted human rights and made the individual an object of international law. But it was not until after World War II that such rights were elaborated and formalized, based on the Universal Declaration of Human Rights adopted by the United Nations in 1948. And only in the late 1970s and 1980s was there a sufficiently large array of instruments and agreements in place that judiciaries, particularly in Europe, would regularly invoke them in their decisions. In the case of the Americas, the system for the protection of human rights is embodied in the Inter-American Commission on Human Rights, which itself is grounded in two distinct legal documents: the Charter of the Organization of American States (OAS) and the American Convention on Human Rights, adopted in 1969 and entered into force in 1978. The human rights regime of the OAS was strengthened markedly in a 1967 protocol that came into force in 1970.

46. Louis Henkin, *The Age of Rights* (New York: Columbia University Press, 1990).

47. Thomas M. Franck, "The Emerging Right to Democratic Governance," *American Journal of International Law* 86, no. 1 (1992): 46–91.

48. Elsewhere I have tried to understand how these changed conditions affect women, and specifically their status in international law and international relations. See Saskia Sassen, "Toward a Feminist Analytics of the Global Economy," *Indiana Journal of Global Legal Studies* 4 (1997): 7–41.

49. The weight of human rights law in many of the Latin American countries is dubious. For a detailed (and harrowing) account of the situation in Mexico, see Andrew Reding, *Democracy and Human Rights in Mexico,* World Policy Papers (New York: World Policy Institute, 1995). See also Kathryn Sikkink, "Human Rights, Principled Issue-Networks, and Sovereignty in Latin America," *International Organization* 47 (1993): 411–41.

50. The growing judicial use of human rights law is suggested by the following statistics: The Universal Declaration on Human Rights was cited in 76 federal cases from 1948 through 1994; over 90 percent of these cases have been heard since 1980, and of these, 49 percent involved immigration issues (rising to 54 percent if refugee cases are included). Jacobson also found that the term "human rights" was referred to in nineteen federal cases prior to the twentieth century, thirty-four times from 1900 to 1944, in 191 cases from 1945 to 1969, in 803 cases in the 1970s, in over 2,000 cases in the 1980s, and in an estimated 4,000 cases in the 1990s. See Jacobson, *Rights Across Borders*.

51. There is an ongoing debate about the notion of citizenship and what it means in the current context; see Soysal, *Limits of Citizenship;* and Baubock, *Transnational Citizenship*. One theme in this debate is a return to notions of cities and citizenship, particularly in so-called global cities, which are partly denationalized territories and have high concentrations of non-nationals from many different parts of the world; see, for example, James Holston, ed., "Cities and

Citizenship," special issue of *Public Culture* (1996); Paul L. Knox and Peter J. Taylor, eds., *World Cities in a World-System* (Cambridge: Cambridge University Press, 1995). The ascendance of human rights codes strengthens these tendencies to move away from nationality and national territory as absolute categories.

52. Peter H. Schuck and Rogers M. Smith, *Citizenship Without Consent: Illegal Aliens in the American Polity* (New Haven: Yale University Press, 1985).

53. See Mitchell, "International Migration."

54. For instance, a change within the state that may have an impact on immigration policy is the ascendance of so-called "soft" security issues. According to some observers, recent government reorganizations in the Departments of State and Defense and the Central Intelligence Agency reflect an implicit redefinition of national security.

Chapter 5

1. See David Hayes-Bautista, Werner Schink, and Jorge Chapa, *The Burden of Support* (Stanford: Stanford University Press, 1988).

2. See William Julius Wilson, *The Increasing Significance of Class* (Chicago: University of Chicago Press, 1980); *The Truly Disadvantaged: The Inner City, the Underclass, and Public Policy* (Chicago: University of Chicago Press, 1987). For those who disagree with Wilson's analysis as it pertains to Latinos, see Joan Moore, "Is There a Hispanic Underclass?" *Social Science Quarterly* 70 (1989): 265; Carlos Vélez-Ibáñez, "U.S. Mexicans in the Borderlands: Being Poor Without the Underclass," in Joan Moore and Raquel Pinderhughes, eds., *In the Barrios: Latinos and the Underclass Debate* (New York: Russell Sage Foundation, 1993).

3. See Wayne A. Cornelius and Philip L. Martin, "The Uncertain Connection: Free Trade and Rural Mexican Migration to the United States," *International Migration Review* 28 (1993): 484.

4. See Philip L. Martin, "Trade and Migration: The Case of NAFTA," *Asian and Pacific Migration Journal* 2 (1993), especially p. 360; and Dolores Acevedo and Thomas J. Espenshade, "Implications of a North American Free Trade Agreement for Mexican Migration into the United States," *Population and Development Review* 18 (1992): 729.

5. See U.S. Bureau of the Census, *Population Profile of the United States, 1995,* Current Population Reports, Series P23-189 (Washington, D.C.: U.S. Government Printing Office, 1995); Steven A. Holmes, "A Surge in Immigration Surprises Experts and Intensifies a Debate," *New York Times,* August 30, 1995.

6. See Riordan Roett, ed., *The Mexican Peso Crisis: International Perspectives* (Boulder: Lynne Rienner, 1996).

7. See Jorge Chapa, "The Question of Mexican-American Assimilation: Socioeconomic Parity or Underclass Formation?" *Public Affairs Comment* 35 (1988): 1–14; "The Myth of Hispanic Progress," *Harvard Journal of Hispanic Policy* 4 (1990): 3–18; "The Increasing Significance of Class: Longitudinal Trends and Class Differences in the Socio-structural Assimilation of Third and Third-plus Generation Mexican Americans," in *The Peopling of the Amer-*

icas (Liege: International Union for the Scientific Study of Population, 1992), vol. 2: 489-521.

8. In addition to the works cited in n. 7, see Frank Bean, Jorge Chapa, Ruth Berg, and Cathy Sowards, "The Educational Incorporation of Hispanic Immigrants in the U.S.," in *Immigration and Ethnicity* (Urban Institute Press, 1994), first published as Texas Population Research Center paper 12.10 (1990-91).

9. See Robert D. Hershey, "Weakness in Jobs Signals Slowing of the Economy," *New York Times,* February 4, 1995.

10. See National Center on Education and the Economy, *Americas Choice: High Skills or Low Wages* (Rochester, N.Y.: National Center on Education and the Economy, 1990); W. B. Johnston and A. H. Packer, *Workforce 2000: Work and Workers for the Twenty-First Century* (Indianapolis: Hudson Institute, 1987).

11. From Frank Levy, "Income and Income Inequality," in Reynolds Farley, ed., *State of the Union: America in the 1990s,* vol. 1: *Economic Trends* (New York: Russell Sage Foundation, 1995), p. 1.

12. Johanne Boisjoly and Greg J. Duncan, "Job Losses Among Hispanics in the Recent Recession," *Monthly Labor Review* 117 (June 1994): 16.

13. Roderick J. Harrison and Claudette E. Bennett, "Racial and Ethnic Diversity," in Reynolds Farley, ed., *State of the Union, America in the 1990s,* vol. 2: *Social Trends* (New York: Russell Sage Foundation, 1995), pp. 202-3.

14. A review of this literature and analysis of the relative importance of these factors can be found in Norton W. Grubb and Robert Wilson, "Trends in Wages and Salary Inequality, 1967-1988," *Monthly Labor Review* 115 (June 1992); David R. Howell and Susan S. Weiler, "Trends in Computerization, Skill Composition and Low Earnings: Implications for Education and Training Policy," paper presented at the Association for Public Policy Analysis and Management Meetings in Chicago, October 1994; Robert Z. Lawrence, "U.S. Wage Trends in the 1980s: The Role of International Factors," *Federal Reserve Bank of New York Economic Policy Review* 1 (January 1995): 18; David A. Brauer and Susan Hickok, "Explaining the Growing Inequality Across Skill Levels," *Federal Reserve Bank of New York Economic Policy Review* 1 (January 1995): 65.

15. Robert D. Hershey, "Bias Hits Hispanic Workers," *New York Times,* April 27, 1995.

16. The following description of San Antonio is based on Gilberto Cárdenas, Jorge Chapa, and Susan Burek, "San Antonio in the World Economy," in Rebecca Morales and Frank Bonilla, eds., *Latinos in a Changing U.S. Economy: Comparative Perspectives on Growing Inequality* (Beverly Hills, Calif.: Sage Publications, 1993).

17. "A Thousand Lives," special report, *San Antonio Light,* November 13, 1990.

18. See John D. Kasarda, *Urban Underclass Database: An Overview and Machine Readable File Documentation (1993 Update)* (New York: Social Science Research Council, 1993).

19. The term "underclass" is a red flag to many researchers, particularly when it is applied to Latinos. Rather than risk a protracted and unproductive debate,

let me suggest that we think of Latinos with all five of these underclass characteristics as "poorly educated, marginally employed, public-aid-receiving, impoverished single parents."

Chapter 6

1. See Nicholas Lemann, *The Promised Land: The Great Black Migration and How It Changed America* (New York: Vintage Books, 1991); Douglas S. Massey, "Latinos, Poverty, and the Underclass: A New Agenda for Research," *Hispanic Journal of Behavioral Sciences* 15 (1993): 449–75; William Julius Wilson, *When Work Disappears: The World of the New Urban Poor* (New York: Knopf, 1996).
2. Gerald R. Adams, Thomas P. Gullotta, and Raymond Montemayor, eds., *Adolescent Identity Formation* (Newbury Park, Calif.: Sage Publications, 1992).
3. Mark Granovetter, "The Old and the New Economic Sociology: A History and an Agenda," in Roger Friedland and A. F. Robertson, eds., *Beyond the Marketplace* (New York: Aldine de Gruyter, 1990).
4. S. Simons, "Social Assimilation," *American Journal of Sociology* 6 (1901).
5. Robert Park, *Race and Culture* (Glencoe: Free Press, 1950).
6. Stanley Lieberson, *A Piece of the Pie: Blacks and White Immigrants Since 1880* (Berkeley: University of California Press, 1980).
7. Alejandro Portes, "Children of Immigrants: Segmented Assimilation and Its Determinants," in Alejandro Portes, ed., *The Economic Sociology of Immigration: Essays on Networks, Ethnicity, and Entrepreneurship* (New York: Russell Sage Foundation, 1995), pp. 1–42.
8. See Robert Blauner, *Racial Oppression in America* (New York: Harper & Row, 1972), on internal colonialism; Alejandro Portes and Robert Bach, *Latin Journey: Cuban and Mexican Immigrants in the United States* (Berkeley: University of California Press, 1985), on ethnic enclaves; Edna Bonacich, "Class Approaches to Ethnicity and Race," *Insurgent Sociologist* 10 (1980), on middleman minorities.
9. Saskia Sassen labels these "transnational labor markets." See Saskia Sassen, "Immigration and Local Labor Markets," in Portes, *Economic Sociology,* 87–127.
10. Philip Kasinitz and Jan Rosenberg, "Missing the Connection: Social Isolation and Employment on the Brooklyn Waterfront," Working Paper, Michael Harrington Center for Democratic Values and Social Change, Queens College of the City University of New York, 1994.
11. M. G. Matute-Bianchi, "Ethnic Identities and Patterns of School Success and Failure Among Mexican-Descent and Japanese-American Students in a California High School," *American Journal of Education* 95 (1986): 233–55.
12. The data are drawn from a 1992 survey of 5,263 children of immigrants and from in-depth interviews conducted with a subsample formed by almost two hundred of those children and their parents. For the original survey, eighth- and ninth-grade students in Dade County (Miami), Broward County (Fort Lauderdale), and San Diego schools were randomly selected among those who met the following definition of second-generation immigrants: those who were born in the United States with at least one foreign-born parent, or those who were born abroad but have resided in this country for at least five

years. Questionnaires were administered to these students in schools selected to include both inner-city and suburban settings and student populations with varying proportions of whites, minorities, and immigrants. In the Miami sample, two predominantly Cuban private schools also were included. The sample was divided evenly between boys and girls; the average age of the youngsters was about fourteen.

Followup interviews were conducted with a subset of those surveyed. The national-origin groups were stratified on the basis of sex, nativity (U.S.-born or foreign-born), socioeconomic status based on father's occupation, and family structure (two-parent families consisting of the biological parents of the child or other equivalent care-providers). In Miami, the Cuban group also was divided between public and private school students. Names within each category were picked randomly by country of origin for the largest groups in the original sample—Cubans, Nicaraguans, Haitians, and West Indians (mostly Jamaicans and Trinidadians) in Dade and Broward Counties; and Vietnamese, Mexicans, Filipinos, Cambodians, and Laotians in San Diego. Here, I focus only on the three Hispanic groups.

13. María Patricia Fernández-Kelly, "Divided Fates: Immigrant Children in a Restructured Economy," *International Migration Review* 28 (1995): 662.

14. Alejandro Portes and Ruben Rumbaut, *Immigrant America: A Portrait* (Berkeley: University of California Press, 1991).

15. Bryan Roberts, "The Effect of Socially Expected Durations on Mexican Migration," in Portes, *Economic Sociology*.

16. Robert N. Bellah et al., *Habits of the Heart: Individualism and Commitment in American Life* (Berkeley: University of California Press, 1985).

Chapter 7

Acknowledgments: The author would like to acknowledge the helpful criticism of Tiffany Manuel, Ben Harrison, and the participants in the Conference on Global Society and the Latino Community, held in Bellagio, Italy, in December 1994.

1. For a comprehensive definition of the neighborhood as an economic unit, see Robert J. Chaskin, *The Ford Foundation's Neighborhood and Family Initiative: Toward a Model of Comprehensive Neighborhood-Based Development* (Chicago: Champion Hall Center for Children, University of Chicago, 1992). The definition of a local community includes several characteristics: a shared space, a range of services and facilities, social institutions and organizations, informal networks of associations, and a degree of common identification.

2. Obviously, there are also numerous examples of organizations and programs that illustrate the limitation of a community-based strategy for promoting economic development. Ultimately, the economic development of any particular area is constrained by the linkages of that area to the regional economy and by the resources, both human and financial, invested in the area.

3. For a review of this literature, see Alejandro Portes, "Modes of Incorporation and Theories of Labor Immigration," in Mary M. Kritz, Charles B. Keeley, and Silvano M. Tomasi, eds., *Global Trends in Immigration: Theory and Research on International Population Movement* (New York: Center for Migration Studies, 1981), pp. 279-97.

4. Peggy J. Levitt, "The Social Aspects of Small-Business Development: The Case of Puerto Rican and Dominican Entrepreneurs in Boston," in Edwin Meléndez and Miren Uriarte, eds., *Latino Poverty and Economic Development in Massachusetts* (Boston: Mauricio Gastón Institute, 1993), pp. 143-58.

5. William Julius Wilson, *The Truly Disadvantaged: The Inner City, the Underclass, and Public Policy* (Chicago: University of Chicago Press, 1987). There is a vast literature on the factors that influence poverty in general and Latino poverty in particular; for an overview see Edwin Meléndez, "Understanding Latino Poverty," *Sage Race Relations Abstracts* 18 (May 1993): 3-42. Most of the debate on the causes of poverty and its concentration in urban areas highlights the interplay of structural and behavioral factors. My intent here is to focus on Wilson's contention that structural factors create the conditions for the appearance and sustainability of the behavioral problems associated with areas of concentrated poverty. I emphasize especially the crucial role that the lack of access to jobs plays in the social dislocation of the inner city.

6. See chapter 6 by Patricia Fernández-Kelly in this volume.

7. Luis Falcón, "Social Networks and Employment for Latinos, Blacks, and Whites," *New England Journal of Public Policy* 11 (1995): 17-28.

8. Robert Putnam, *Making Democracy Work: Civic Traditions in Modern Italy* (Princeton: Princeton University Press, 1993).

9. See Alejandro Portes and Julia Sensenbrenner, "Embeddedness and Immigration: Notes on the Social Determinants of Economic Action," *American Journal of Sociology* 98 (1993): 1320-50; and Chapter 6 in this volume.

10. L. J. D. Wacquant and William Julius Wilson, "The Cost of Racial and Class Exclusion," *Annals* (American Academy of Political and Social Science) 501 (1991): 8-26.

11. See Andrés Torres and Clara Rodríguez, "Latino Research and Policy: The Puerto Rican Case," in Edwin Meléndez, Clara Rodríguez, and Janis Barry Figueroa, eds., *Hispanics in the Labor Force: Issues and Policies* (New York: Plenum Press, 1991), pp. 247-63; National Puerto Rican Coalition, *Public Policy Agenda, 1988-1990* (Washington, D.C.: National Puerto Rican Coalition, 1988); Sonia Pérez and Deirdre Martínez, *State of Hispanic America 1993: Toward a Latino Anti-Poverty Agenda* (Washington, D.C.: National Council of La Raza, 1993).

12. Bennett Harrison, *Building Bridges: Community Development Corporations and the World of Employment Training,* Working Paper Series, H. John Heinz III School of Public Policy and Management, Carnegie Mellon University, 93-60, October 1993.

13. C. Nelson Tienda and Marta Tienda, "The Restructuring of Hispanic Ethnicity: Historical and Contemporary Perspectives," *Ethnic and Racial Studies* 8 (1985): 49-74.

14. See Miren Uriarte, "Contra Viento y Marea (Against All Odds): Latinos Build Community in Boston," in *Latinos in Boston: Confronting Poverty, Building Community* (Boston: Boston Persistent Poverty Project, Boston Foundation, 1993), pp. 1-34; Félix Padilla, "The Quest for Community: Puerto Ricans in Chicago," in Joan Moore and Raquel Pinderhughes, eds., *In the*

Barrios: Latinos and the Underclass Debate (New York: Russell Sage Foundation, 1993), pp. 129-48.

15. Ramón Borges-Mendez, "Migration, Social Networks, Poverty, and the Regionalization of Puerto Rican Settlements: Barrio Formation in Lowell, Lawrence, and Holyoke, Massachusetts," *Latino Studies Journal* 4 (May 1993): 3-21.

16. The labor market status of Latino populations varies greatly depending on the country of origin, region, and many other factors. I have argued elsewhere ("Understanding Latin Poverty") that even though labor market disadvantage explains most Latino poverty, the situations of Mexicans, Cubans, and Puerto Ricans, for example, differ significantly. Mexicans are concentrated in low-wage occupations, Puerto Ricans have a high incidence of unemployment and time spent outside the labor force, and Cubans have a high proportion of self-employed professionals and small businesses.

17. Todd Swanstrom, "Beyond Economism: Urban Political Economy and the Postmodern Challenge," *Journal of Urban Affairs* 15 (1993): 55-78.

18. Thomas R. Bailey, *Immigrant and Native Workers: Contrasts and Competition* (Boulder: Westview Press, 1987).

19. Alejandro Portes and Robert L. Bach, *Latin Journey: Cuban and Mexican Immigrants in the United States* (Berkeley: University of California Press, 1985), p. 203. See also Portes, "Modes of Incorporation."

20. Kenneth L. Wilson and Alejandro Portes, "Immigrant Enclaves: An Analysis of the Labor Market Experiences of Cubans in Miami," *American Journal of Sociology* 86 (1980): 135-60.

21. Silvia Pedraza-Bailey, *Political and Economic Migrants in America: Cubans and Mexicans* (Austin: University of Texas Press, 1985).

22. Roger Waldinger, "The Ethnic Enclave Debate Revisited," *International Journal of Urban and Regional Research* 3 (1993): 444-52.

23. Gilberto Cárdenas, Rodolfo de la Garza, and Neil Hansen, "Mexican Immigrants and the Chicano Ethnic Enterprise: Reconceptualizing an Old Problem," in H. L. Browning and Rodolfo de la Garza, eds., *Mexican Immigrants and Mexican Americans* (Austin: University of Texas, Center for Mexican American Studies, 1986).

24. Alejandro Portes and Alex Stepick, *City on the Edge: The Transformation of Miami* (Berkeley: University of California Press, 1993).

25. Pedraza-Bailey, *Political and Economic Migrants.*

26. Jorge Chapa and Gilberto Cárdenas, *The Economy of the Urban Ethnic Enclave* (Austin: LBJ School of Public Affairs, University of Texas, 1991).

27. Frank Fratoe, "A Sociological Analysis of Minority Business," *Review of Black Political Economy* 15 (Fall 1986): 5-30.

28. Ivan Light, "Immigrant and Ethnic Enterprise in North America," *Ethnic and Racial Studies* 7 (April 1984): 195-216.

29. On educational levels, see "Introduction" in Meléndez, Rodriguez, and Barry-Figueroa, *Hispanics in the Labor Force,* 1-24. On access to capital see Alejandro Portes, "The Social Origins of the Cuban Enclave Economy of Miami," *Sociological Perspectives* 30 (1987): 340-72.

30. Roger Waldinger and Howard Aldrich, "Trends in Ethnic Business in the United States," in Roger Waldinger, Howard Aldrich, Robin Ward, and associates, *Ethnic Entrepreneurs: Immigrant Business in Industrial Societies* (Newbury Park, Calif.: Sage Publications, 1990), pp. 49–78. The argument about the lack of a business tradition in the African-American community is questionable. John Butler eloquently documents entrepreneurship and self-help as long-term aspects of African-American resistance to racial oppression. Many businesses have survived in predominantly black communities despite discrimination and other barriers. See John S. Butler, *Entrepreneurship and Self-Help Among Black Americans: A Reconsideration of Race and Economics* (Albany: SUNY Press, 1993).

31. Roger Waldinger, Howard Aldrich, William D. Bradford, Jeremy Baissermain, Garion Chen, Herman Korte, Robin Ward, and Peter Wilson. "Conclusions and Policy Implications," in Waldinger et al., *Ethnic Entrepreneurs,* pp. 177–98.

32. Levitt, "Social Aspects."

33. Nanette Robicheau, "The Upham's Corner Model: Comprehensive Commercial Revitalization in Multiethnic, Low-Income, Inner-City Communities," in Meléndez and Uriarte, *Latino Poverty and Economic Development,* pp. 159–76.

34. Harrison, *Building Bridges.*

35. Edwin Meléndez and Nilsa Medina, *La Empresa Comunal: lecciones de Casos Exitosos en Puerto Rico* (Boston: Mauricio Gastón Institute, 1996).

36. Michael Porter is the best-known proponent of the small business strategy: see "The Competitive Advantage of the Inner City," *Harvard Business Review* 73 (May–June 1995): 55–82. He argues that minority-owned businesses constitute valuable assets and the most reliable foundation for attracting capital to the inner city. Given the appropriate incentive structure and support system, these entrepreneurs who already have knowledge of poor neighborhoods and a vested interest in their revitalization could capitalize on abundant labor supplies and business opportunities and develop the necessary equity to spark economic growth and job creation. The promotion and support of minority-owned businesses could be even more effective if these businesses were linked to expanding industries in the regional economy. However, he adds, this vision calls for the abandonment of many government programs and traditional community-based organizations.

37. Robicheau, "Upham's Corner Model."

38. Ross Gittell and Margaret Wilder, "Best Practice in Community Revitalization," paper presented at the Annual Conference of the Urban Affairs Association, Portland, Oregon, May 4–6, 1995.

39. Robert Fisher and Joseph King, "Introduction: The Continued Vitality of Community Mobilization," in Robert Fisher and Joseph King, eds., *Mobilizing the Community: Local Politics in the Era of the Global City* (Newbury Park, Calif.: Sage Publications, 1993).

40. Edwin Meléndez, Francoise Carre, and Evangelina Holvino, "Latinos Need Not Apply: The Effects of Industrial Change and Workplace Discrimination on Latino Employment," *New England Journal of Public Policy* 11 (Spring/ Summer 1995): 87–116.

41. Meléndez, "Understanding Latino Poverty."
42. See U.S. Department of Labor, *What's Working (and What's Not): A Summary of Research on the Economic Impacts of Employment and Training Programs* (Washington, D.C.: Government Printing Office, 1995).
43. Harrison, *Building Bridges.*
44. Edwin Meléndez, *Working on Jobs: The Center for Employment Training* (Boston: Mauricio Gastón Institute, 1996).
45. Rebecca Morales, *Project Quest: An Embedded Network Employment and Training Organization* (Chicago: Center for Urban Economic Development, University of Illinois at Chicago, 1995).
46. Harrison, *Building Bridges,* p. 12.

Chapter 8

1. This is a play on the word *comercio* (commerce/trade). By substituting the verb *comer(se)* which would mean "to eat oneself," the phrase can be literally translated as "The Free Eat Yourself Agreement."
2. The dictator Porfirio Díaz ruled Mexico for three decades at the turn of the century.

Chapter 9

1. Quoted in Sumner Welles, *Naboth's Vineyard: The Dominican Republic, 1844–1924* (Mamaroneck, N.Y.: Paul P. Appel, 1966), p. 916.
2. Quoted in George Black, *The Good Neighbor: How the United States Wrote the History of Central America and the Caribbean* (New York: Pantheon, 1988), p. 23.
3. Ibid., p. 61.
4. See John Mollenkopf and Manuel Castells, eds., *Dual City: Restructuring in New York* (New York: Russell Sage Foundation, 1991).
5. Linda Chavez, *Out of the Barrio: Toward a New Politics of Hispanic Assimilation* (New York: Basic Books, 1991), p. 150.
6. Ibid., p. 153.
7. See, for example, the contrasting pictures offered by Patricia Pessar, "The Dominicans: Women in the Household and the Garment Industry," in Nancy Foner, ed., *New Immigrants in New York* (New York: Columbia University Press, 1987), pp. 103–29; and by Ramona Hernández, Francisco Rivera-Batiz, and Roberto Agodini, *Dominican New Yorkers: A Socioeconomic Profile, 1990,* Dominican Research Monographs (New York: CUNY Dominican Studies Institute, 1995).
8. See Silvio Torres-Saillant, "The Construction of the Other in Studies of Dominican Migration," paper presented at the 15th International Congress of the Latin American Studies Association, Miami, Florida, December 3-6, 1989.
9. Otto Schoenrich, *Santo Domingo: A Country with a Future* (New York: Macmillan, 1918), p. 389.
10. Ibid., p. 389.
11. Ibid., p. 390.
12. Fidel Castro, "Second Declaration of Havana" (1962), in Roberto Ramón

Velazco, ed., *Tres documentos de Nuestra América,* Colección Pensamiento de Nuestra América (Havana: Casa de las Américas, 1979), p. 179.

13. Schoenrich, *Santo Domingo,* p. 392.
14. Ibid., pp. 392–94.
15. Ibid., p. 395.
16. W. S. Courtney, *The Gold Fields of Santo Domingo* (New York: Anson P. Norton, 1860), p. 8.
17. Ibid., p. 14.
18. Ibid., p. 132.
19. Ibid., pp. 138, 143, 144.
20. Charles Callan Tansill, *The United States and Santo Domingo: 1798-1873* (Baltimore: Johns Hopkins University Press, 1938), p. 343.
21. Joseph Warren Fabens, *In the Tropics: By a Settler in Santo Domingo,* introduction by Richard B. Kimball (New York: Carleton, 1863), pp. 3–4.
22. Ibid., p. 302.
23. Joseph Warren Fabens, *Life in Santo Domingo: By a Settler,* introduction by Richard B. Kimball (New York: Carleton, 1873), pp. 307–8.
24. See Tansill, *United States and Santo Domingo,* p. 247.
25. Cited in Welles, *Naboth's Vineyard,* pp. 370–71.
26. Ibid., pp. 374–75.
27. Charles Sumner, *Charles Sumner: His Complete Works, Reprinted* (reprint ed., New York: Negro Universities Press, 1969).
28. Deb. Randolph Keim, *San Domingo* (Philadelphia: Claxton, Remsen, and Haffelfinger, 1870), p. 316.
29. U.S. Government, *Report of the Commission of Inquiry to Santo Domingo,* Commissioners B. F. Wade, A. D. White, and S. G. Howe (Washington, D.C.: Government Printing Office, 1871), p. 13.
30. Anonymous, *Santo Domingo: A Brief Sketch of the Island, Its Resources, and Commercial Possibilities with Special Reference to the Treaty Now Pending in the United States Senate* (New York: New York Commercial, 1906), p. 19.
31. Ibid., p. 18.
32. Henry J. Hancock, "The Situation in Santo Domingo," *Annals* (American Academy of Political and Social Science) 463 (1905): p. 50.
33. Frank Bonilla, "Beyond Survival: Por qué seguiremos siendo puertorriqueños," in Adalberto López, ed., *The Puerto Ricans: Their History, Culture, and Society* (Rochester, Vt.: Schenkman Books, 1980), pp. 453–54.
34. Ibid., p. 454.
35. Marian Susann, "María Montez: On and Off Camera," *Latino Stuff Review* 15 (1994): 4.
36. Department of City Planning, *The Newest New Yorkers: An Analysis of Immigration into New York City During the 1980s* (New York: Department of City Planning, 1992).
37. Mike McAlary, "The Framing of a Cop," *New York Post,* October 9, 1991.
38. Mike McAlary, "Washington Heights' Deadly Dominican Connection," *New York Post,* September 16, 1992.
39. Ibid., p. 3.

40. Mike McAlary, "The Tragic Legacy of a 'Narco Village,'" *New York Daily News,* April 20, 1994.
41. Ramona Hernández and Silvio Torres-Saillant, "Marginality and Schooling," *Punto 7 Review: A Journal of Marginal Discourse* 2, no. 2 (1992): 3.
42. Ed Vega et al., "Conversation: The Writers and the Audience," in Silvio Torres-Saillant, ed., *Hispanic Immigrant Writers and the Question of Identity,* Literature/Conversation Series (New York: Ollantay Press, 1989), pp. 71-72.
43. Silvio Torres-Saillant, "El concepto de dominicanidad y la emigración," *Punto y Coma* 4, nos. 1-2 (1992-93): 165-67.

Chapter 10

Note: The term *mestizaje* reflects both the process and the result of the combination of indigenous cultures with European, principally Spanish, cultures during the colonial period. It is a matter of considerable debate whether that process is continual and ongoing or fixed to a specific historical period.

1. Gabriel García Márquez, *The General in His Labyrinth* (New York: Knopf, 1990).
2. Ibid., p. 10.
3. Ibid., p. 105.
4. This is, of course, an old conundrum of political philosophy. Critical legal scholars summed it up as "the fundamental contradiction" in their early work, a position they have largely abandoned. For a statement of the problem and its fuller development, see especially the work of Duncan Kennedy (e.g., "The Structures of Blackstone's Commentaries," *Buffalo Law Review* 28 [1979]: 205) and that of Roberto Unger (see *The Critical Legal Studies Movement* [Cambridge: Harvard University Press, 1986]). Both of these authors take up the problem as one of law and legal analysis and ideology as much as one of political theory.
5. Others may have shared the dream, but Bolívar's name is synonymous with the liberation of Latin America from the Spanish. His dream of a united Spanish America began with the war for the independence of Venezuela and by 1822 was embodied in the battle for the independence of Ecuador and its merger into Colombia.
6. See Michael Omi and Howard Winant, *Racial Formation in the United States,* 2d ed. ((New York and London: Routledge, 1994), pp. 14-23.
7. Ibid., pp. 139, 53-91.
8. See the concluding pages of this chapter. In addition, see Nathaniel Berman, "Economic Consequences, Nationalist Passions," *American University Journal of International Law and Policy* 10 (1995): 620-70, esp. 661-70; "Between 'Alliance' and 'Localization': Nationalism and the New Oscillationism," *New York University Journal of International Law and Politics* 26 (1994): 449-91.
9. Remember here that I am speaking of nationalism in the domestic context. As Iris Young points out, the factionalism of interest group politics functions as a legitimate proxy for the processes of justice where interest groups and social groups occupy the same moral/ethical universe. A rough equality is possible

only where the bonds of affiliation are equivalent to the bonds of filiation. See Iris Marion Young, *Justice and the Politics of Difference* (Princeton: Princeton University Press 1990). See also Gerald Torres, "Critical Race Theory: The Decline of the Universalist Ideal and the Hope of Plural Justice," *University of Minnesota Law Review* 75 (1991): 993.

10. I know that I run the risk of reifying those processes in this discussion, but remember that what I am trying to do here is to *show* that the working out of the processes I describe will produce the results that I suggest.

11. As I discuss below, racial categories have become the defining characteristic of social groupings within identity politics in the United States. See also Young, *Justice and the Politics of Difference,* pp. 122–25.

12. The use of "Latino" or "Hispanic" as a panethnic label is the subject of an ongoing discourse within the Latin American community. For a comprehensive analysis and critique of the various labels, see "The Politics of Ethnic Construction: Hispanic, Chicano, Latino?" a special issue of *Latin American Perspectives* 19 (1992). The people of Florida generally prefer the term "Hispanic," which is largely rejected in California in favor of "Latino" and "Chicano." The people of New York City use both "Latino" and "Hispanic." See Earl Shorris, *Latinos: A Biography of the People* (New York: Norton, 1992); Edward L. Cardenas, "Strength and Unity: Hispanic Heritage Month—Some Favor Term 'Latino' in Battle Over Proper Usage," *Detroit News,* September 15, 1996. "Latino/a" and "Hispanic" also represent the left and the right: Democrats are generally Latinos, Republicans are Hispanic. See Earl Shorris, "Latino, Si. Hispanic, No." *New York Times,* October 28, 1992. The right, or the less confrontational and more market-minded, wing of the panethnic movement, uses "Hispanic" to bring people together without frightening those already in power into barring access. See Geoffrey Fox, *Hispanic Nation: Culture, Politics and the Construction of Identity* (Secaucus, N.J.: Carol Publishing Group, 1996). In the 1970s, the Federal Office of Management and Budget, with the assistance of the king of Spain, created the term "Hispanic," which OMB defined as: "A person of Mexican, Puerto Rican, Cuban or Central American or other Spanish Culture or origin, regardless of race." See *Federal Register* 43 (1978): 19269; see also, Gerardo Marin and Barbara van Oss Marin, *Research with Hispanic Populations* (Newbury Park, Calif.: Sage, 1991), who note that "Hispanic" as an ethnic label is the product of OMB's 1978 decision. Progressives who challenge the use of "Hispanic" generally use "Latino," whose roots are in a nineteenth-century romantic nationalism that dates back to the Second Empire of Napoleon III. The phrase "Latin American" was coined by the Chilean author Francisco Bilbao and, independently, by the contemporary Uruguayan José María Caisedo while both were exiled in Paris. Although "Latino" refers to people from Latin America, the U.S. Census Bureau adopted the term "Hispanic" because "Latino" sounded too much like "Ladino," the ancient form of Castilian now spoken only by descendants of Spanish Jews who went into exile in the fifteenth century, and because "Hispanic" was suggested by the king of Spain. See Shorris, *Latinos.* Coalitions are built from within and should not be created or imposed from the outside. Thus, while the terms "Latino" and "Hispanic" are certainly

imperfect, they have been chosen by various Latin-American communities, even as "Hispanic" has been imposed. Berta Hernández Truyol has criticized the adoption of "Latino" because it is not gender-neutral and thus has the potential to exclude women from political discourse. See Berta Hernández Truyol, "Building Bridges—Latinas and Latinos at the Crossroads: Realities, Rhetoric and Replacement," *Columbia Human Rights Law Review* 25 (1994): 369-433.

13. Omi and Winant, *Racial Formation in the United States,* pp. 14-23, describe the process of ethnic formation in American culture and society.

14. See F. Chris García, John A. García, Rudolfo O. de la Garza, Angelo Falcón, and Clara Abeyata, *Latinos and Politics: A Selected Bibliography* (Austin: University of Texas Center for Mexican American Studies, 1991); Rudolfo O. de la Garza, *Latino Voices: Mexican, Puerto Rican and Cuban Perspectives on American Politics* (Boulder, Colo.: Westview Press, 1993); Shorris, *Latinos.* Fox, *Hispanic Nation.*

15. See Nathaniel Berman, "'But the Alternative Is Despair': European Nationalism and the Modernist Renewal of International Law," *Harvard Law Review* 106 (1993): 1792-1903.

16. Oddly, within the vernacular of American politics Portuguese, Brazilian, and Basque are "Hispanic."

17. She and my father, of course, chose to name me "Gerald."

18. See Omi and Winant, *Racial Formation in the United States,* pp. 139, 53-91.

19. See Tzvetan Todorov, *The Conquest of America* (New York: Harper Perennial, 1984); Anthony Pagden, *Lords of All the World* (New Haven and London: Yale University Press, 1995).

20. "The interpretation of nature's signs as practiced by Columbus is determined by the result that must be arrived at. His very exploit, the discovery of America, proceeds from the same behavior: he does not discover it, he finds it where he 'knew' it would be (where he thought the eastern coast of Asia was to be found. . . . 'I have already said that for the execution of the enterprise of the Indies, reason, mathematics, and the map of the world were of no utility to me. It was a matter rather of the fulfillment of what Isaiah had predicted' (preface to [Columbus's] *Book of Prophecies,* 1501)." In Todorov, *Conquest of America,* pp. 22-23.

21. Notebooks of Christopher Columbus, quoted in ibid., p. 46.

22. Frederick Jackson Turner in many ways invented the idea that the frontier is central to our national self-definition The canonical history of Texas, T. R. Fehrenbach, *Lone Star* (New York: Macmillan, 1980), captures the role that "guns, blood, and guts" played in the "conquest of a nation." There have, of course, been many correctives to this view: see, e.g., David Montejano, *Anglos and Mexicans in the Making of Texas* (Austin: University of Texas Press 1987).

23. The first problem with the notion of discovery was the initial mistaken belief that no new place had been found, but only an old place, "India," a source of wealth, both natural and produced, as well as a source of the exotic.

24. The case of *Johnson v. M'Intosh,* 21 U.S. (8 Wheat.) 543 (1823) involved federal courts' recognition of Indian title to land; see also Philip Frickey,

"Marshalling Past and Present: Colonialism, Constitutionalism, and Interpretation in Federal Indian Law," *Harvard Law Review* 107 (1993): 381.

25. The myth of Pocahontas was preserved in the slave codes of colonial Virginia. See A Leon Higginbotham, *In the Matter of Color: Race and the American Legal Process—The Colonial Period* (New York: Oxford University Press, 1978).

26. The legal debate centered on the character of land. Was it "claimed" by the inhabitants found there in some sense that was legally significant, or was it *terra nullis?*

27. See the discussion of this point in Hugh Thomas, *Conquest: Montezuma, Cortes, and the Fall of Old Mexico* (New York: Simon & Schuster, 1993).

28. Columbus's return from his first voyage was, said David Hume in 1757, "really the commencement of modern History." Quoted in Pagden, *Lords of All the World*, p. 2 .

29. See Todorov, *Conquest of America*, pp. 185-201, where he discusses the journals and essays of Bartolomé de Las Casas and Alvar Núñez Cabeza de Vaca).

30. Ibid., pp. 170-82, 185-201.

31. Columbus initially proposed that those natives who could not be converted to Christianity could be sold into slavery. This would prevent the boat from returning empty and would provide value until gold could be found. See Columbus's notebooks, quoted in Todorov, *Conquest of America*, p. 47. See also Robert Williams, Jr., *The American Indian in Western Legal Thought: The Discourses of Conquest* (New Yokr and Oxford: Oxford University Press, 1990), pp. 81-93.

32. Besides the fear of a Spanish Imperial claim to the entire world, which carried with it the menace of the Inquisition, "the English colonies in America had been founded by men holding a wide variety of religious beliefs. As the English political economist Sir Josiah Child (1630-1699) noted in 1665, the Spanish had already achieved unity between colony and mother country by imposing a rigid code of religious uniformity (although he believed that this had also led to low population growth and excessive indolence among the settler populations), whereas the English who 'vainly endeavor to arrive at a Uniformity of Religion at Home' were prepared to 'allow an Amsterdam of Liberty in our Plantations.' Whatever the nature of these differences, all the British colonists . . . were either Anglicans or Protestants whose religious beliefs might be broadly described as Calvinist. Such men, as Anglicans at home frequently complained, had little real interest in converting Native Americans. 'I would to God,' wrote Richard Eburne in 1624, 'that there among the *Protestants*, that profess and have a better religion than the *Papists*, one half of that zeal and desire to further and dispense our good and sound religion as seems to be among them for furthering theirs.'—Pagden, *Lords of All the World*, p. 36 (footnotes omitted).

33. "In these two respects (colonization as a continuation of already established empire and as a religious mission tied to the Christian *Imperium romanum*) the Spanish empire in America was unique." Ibid., p. 33. In addition, the economic structure of feudal Spanish life, where shipbuilding was the major technological advance, allowed Spain to become the first great conquering

empire. Yet by the time England defeated the Armada and began to compete as an imperial power, it already had a more coherent sense of self and a preindustrial society.

34. The racial notions at the root of national identity are always complex and context-bound, in the context of the colonial plans of the various European powers, the Spanish conquest of the South entailed substantially more mixing of the indigenous and invading populations than did the conquest of the North. The religious motive for imperialism also yielded a different relationship with the indigenous populations in the North and the South.

35. "The Puritan 'Cities on the Hill' were to be *their* cities. They were to contain no aliens. Charles II's charter to settle Carolina characteristically refers to the Native Americans as 'savages' and places them in the same general category as 'other enemies pirates and robbers': persons who are to be displaced, not incorporated." Ibid., p. 37 (footnotes omitted).

36. See Noel Ignatiev, *How the Irish Became White* (New York and London: Routledge, 1995).

37. See Gerald Torres, "The Evolution of American Culture: The Problematic Place of Race and the Right to Have Rights," *Minnesota Law and Inequality Journal* 9 (1991): 457; Higginbotham, *In the Matter of Color.* Of course this debate has its most visible current force in the immigration context.

38. "Mestizo" refers principally to the mixture between Europeans and Indian natives. As Judge Higginbotham points out in his book on race codes, *In the Matter of Color,* most of the legal consequences that flowed from mixture derived from the conception of devolution. Within a hierarchical conception of race, mixture reduced the mixed person to the "lower" classification. For a discussion of the evolution of concepts of race and racial categories, see John G. Mencke, *Mulattoes and Race Mixture: American Attitudes and Images, 1865-1918* (Ann Arbor: UMI Research Press, 1979). Mencke in his introduction distinguishes the mulatto from other new world racial mixtures: "If it is know that an individual is even remotely descended from a black person, he is classified as a Negro. . . . Although words like *mulatto, quadroon,* and *octoroon* have been used on occasion in America, in reality they have little or no social or legal significance. America's racial system recognizes only the dichotomy of black and white, and the mixed-blood is invariably classified as black if his ancestry is known. . . . Unlike Latin America, however, there have never been widely used words to designate people of mixed ancestry" (footnotes omitted).

39. See Young, *Justice and the Politics of Difference,* esp. chap. 6.

40. Some think that this response, however rational it might be, is wrong and relies upon a constellation of faux emotions and faux connections that will prove too fragile to maintain any true vitality in public life. See, e.g., Richard Rodriguez, *Hunger of Memory: The Education of Richard Rodriguez, an Autobiography* (New York: Bantam Books 1982).

41. You might note here that "Puerto Rican" does not have to be hyphenated. Puerto Ricans present an interesting case of a nonimmigrant Latin American subgroup. In many ways Mexican-Americans fill a similar niche by virtue of the porosity of the southern border and the long-time presence of that transborder

commerce. The presence of the border causes some specific permutations in the process of assimilation that I explore elsewhere.

42. Tip O'Neill, *Man of the House: The Life and Political Memoirs of Speaker Tip O'Neill* (New York: Random House, 1987).

43. I explore this idea in Gerald Torres, "Local Knowledge, Local Color: Critical Legal Studies and the Law of Race Relations," *University of San Diego Law Review* 25 (1988): 1043.

44. Laura Lewis is conducting ongoing research on the development of black consciousness in Mexico. She presented a paper on this topic at the 1997 annual meeting of the Latin American Studies Association.

45. I am willfully ignoring the numerous debates lately sprung up in response to multiculturalism about the significance of other nationalities in the creation of the United States. I believe that the existence of that debate merely makes my point. Moreover, one is tempted to say, "English," not "British," but that is merely the starting point of another contemporary debate.

46. I know that this claim is controversial and will be taken by some to be insulting. I do not mean it that way; I am making an empirical point, not a comparative judgmental analysis of native cultures. In the valley of Mexico the Spanish confronted a population ranging from 8 to 30 million. Moreover, the city was said to rival any in Europe and the social organization was substantially advanced in comparison to most in Europe—sufficiently advanced to spark a great ethical debate over the morality of the effort to conquer and colonize. See Thomas, *Conquest*.

47. Brazil is a special case. I am also putting to one side the impact of Catholicism.

48. See Williams, *American Indian in Western Legal Thought*.

49. The systematic attempts to Christianize the Indians would come later.

50. Remember that slaves were originally counted as three-fifths of a person for purposes of congressional representation, and that the Constitution has specific provisions for dealing with Indian tribes. These distinctions, especially the Indian Commerce Clause, are important signifiers of the relation of each group to the dominant political structure of civil society.

51. The situation is very different for Mexican-Americans, as illustrated by a joke that we used to tell: If you were really poor, you were Mexican. If you had a little bit of money you were Mexican-American. If you had a little more, you were American of Mexican descent. If you had a little more, you were Spanish. But if you were really well off, you were Italian.

52. The uprisings in Chiapas, Oaxaca, and Guerrero states point out the continuing instability of this usurpation of Indianness as a constituent of the core identity of Mexicans. Researchers are now exploring the contemporaneous development of "black" racial self-consciousness in Mexican social and political life. The Mexican government has responded to this destabilizing development by funding the folk arts of the various black groups. The goal is to direct their energies into the creation of regional and local identities rather than a racial national identity at odds with the elites' management of racial difference—a management strategy that has been worked out in the context of the colonization of the indigenous people.

53. See Young, *Justice and the Politics of Difference*.

54. See Lani Guinier, *The Tyranny of the Majority* (New York: Free Press, 1993).

55. This dimension is expressed largely in the fact that African-Americans and Indians were allowed the designation of "citizen" only late in our history. For Indians, this is a dual-edged sword, since it permits those who are opposed to Indian sovereignty to argue that citizenship is in derogation of Indian identity.

56. This idea is at the core of the English Only movement, although not all subscribers to that movement would buy into the whole ideological package of its most radical elements.

57. It is important to note here that many feminists claim that nationalist or racialist identity politics are essentially patriarchal.

58. Pagden, *Lords of All the World*, pp. 63–102.

59. See Richard Delgado, ed., *Critical Race Theory* (Philadelphia: Temple University Press, 1995).

60. See, e.g., *Dred Scott v. Sandford*, 60 U.S. (19 How.) 393 (1857); *Plessy v. Ferguson*, 163 U.S. 483 (1954).

61. This is the name the Aztecs gave themselves. See Thomas, *Conquest*, p. ix.

Chapter 11

1. Frank Bonilla, "Migrants, Citizenship, and Social Pacts," in Edwin Meléndez and Edgardo Meléndez, eds., *Colonial Dilemma: Critical Perspectives on Contemporary Puerto Rico* (Boston: South End Press, 1993), pp. 181–88.

2. Douglas B. Klusmeyer, "Aliens, Immigrants and Citizens: The Politics of Inclusion in the Federal Republic of Germany," *Daedalus* 122 (Summer 1993): 84.

3. See, for instance, essays in Laurence Halley, ed., *Ancient Affections: Ethnic Groups and Foreign Policy* (New York: Praeger, 1985); Abdul Aziz Said, *Ethnicity and U.S. Foreign Policy* (New York: Praeger, 1977); Mohammed E. Ahrari, *Ethnic Groups and U.S. Foreign Policy* (New York: Greenwood, 1982).

4. Mervin Holli and Peter d'A. Jones, eds., *Ethnic Chicago* (Grand Rapids: William B. Eerdmans, 1977).

5. See, for example, Rodolfo de la Garza, Robert Winckle, and Jerry Polinard, "Ethnicity and Policy: The Mexican American Perspective," in Chris F. García, ed., *Latinos and the Political System* (Notre Dame: University of Notre Dame, 1988), pp. 426–41.

6. Yossi Shain, *The Frontiers of Loyalty: Political Exiles in the Age of Nation-States* (Middletown: Wellesley University Press, 1992).

7. Juan Gómez-Quiñonez, "On Culture," *Revista Chicano-Riqueña*, 1977, pp. 29–46.

8. See Juan Gómez-Quiñonez, "Notes on the Interpretation of the Relations Between the Mexican Community in the United States and Mexico," and Carlos Zazueta, "Mexican Political Actors in the United States and Mexico: Historical and Political Contexts of a Dialogue," both in Carlos Vasquez and Manuel Garcia y Griego, eds., *Mexican/U.S. Relations: Conflict and Convergence* (Los Angeles: University of California Press, 1983), pp. 417–83.

9. See the work of Tomas Almaguer, "Toward a Study of Chicano Colonialism,"

in *Aztlan: Chicano Journal of Social Sciences and the Arts* 1 (Fall 1970): 7-21; Rudy Acuna, *Occupied America: A History of Chicanos* (New York: Harper and Row, 1988); and Mario Barrera, *Race and Class in the Southwest* (Notre Dame: University of Notre Dame Press, 1979).

10. History Task Force of the Centro de Estudios Puertorriqueños, *Labor Migration Under Capitalism: The Puerto Rican Experience* (New York: Monthly Review Press, 1979); Manuel Maldonado-Dennis, *The Emigration Dialectic: Puerto Rico and the USA* (New York: International, 1980).

11. See, for example, Lourdes Casal, "Cubans in the United States," in Martin Weinstein, ed., *Revolutionary Cuba in the World Arena* (Philadelphia: Institute for the Study of Human Issues, 1979); Lourdes Argüelles, "Cuban Miami: The Roots, Development and Everyday Life of an Emigre Enclave in the National Security State," *Contemporary Marxism* 5 (Summer 1982): 27-44.

12. Carlos Forment, "Caribbean Geopolitics and Foreign State-Sponsored Movements: The Case of Cuban Exile Militancy 1959-1979," in Miren Uriarte-Gastón and Jorge Canas, eds., *Cubans in the United States* (Boston: Center for the Study of the Cuban Community, 1984), pp. 65-102.

13. Marisa Alicea, "Dual Home Bases: A Reconceptualization of Puerto Rican Migration," *Latino Studies Journal* 1, no. 3 (1990): 78-98.

14. Félix Padilla, *Latino Consciousness: The Case of Mexican Americans and Puerto Ricans in Chicago* (Notre Dame: University of Notre Dame Press, 1985).

15. Frank Bonilla, "Brother Can You Paradigm?" Inter-University Program on Latino Research, Milenio Series, 1997.

16. María de los Angeles Torres, "Latinos and U.S. Policies: Foreign Policy Toward Latin America," *Latino Studies Journal* 1 (September 1990): 3-23.

17. David Ayon and Ricardo Anzaldua Montoya, "Latinos and U.S. Policy," in Abraham F. Lowenthal, ed., *Latin America and the Caribbean Contemporary Record* (Baltimore: Johns Hopkins University Press, 1990).

18. Jesús Díaz, *Del exilio a la Patria* (La Habana: UNEAC, 1977).

19. María de los Angeles Torres, "Encuentros y encontronazos: nación y exilio," *Diaspora: A Journal of Transnational Studies* 4 (1995): 211-39.

20. Angelo Falcón, "A Divided Nation: The Puerto Rican Diaspora in the United States and the Proposed Referendum," in Meléndez and Meléndez, *Colonial Dilemma,* pp. 173-80.

21. Gloria Anzaldúa, *Borderlands = La Frontera: The New Mestiza* (San Francisco: Spinster/Aunt Lute, 1987).

22. Cristina García, *Dreaming in Cuban* (New York: Knopf, 1992).

23. Rubén Martínez, *The Other Side: Fault Lines, Guerrilla Saints and the True Heart of Rock 'n' Roll* (New York: Verso, 1992).

24. Richard Rodríguez, *Hunger of Memory: The Education of Richard Rodriguez, an Autobiography* (Boston: D. R. Godine, 1981).

25. Gustavo Pérez-Firmat, *Life on the Hyphen: The Cuban-American Experience* (Austin: University of Texas Press, 1994).

26. Tato Laviera, *AmeRican* (Houston: Arte Public Press, 1985).

27. Madelin Camara, "The Third Option: Beyond the Border," in Ruth Behar, ed., *Bridges to Cuba* (Ann Arbor: University of Michigan Press, 1995).

28. Richard Bernstein, *Dictatorship of Virtue: Multiculturalism and the Battle for America's Future* (New York: Knopf, 1994).

29. Arthur M. Schlesinger, Jr., *The Disuniting of America: Reflections on a Multi-cultural Society* (New York: Norton, 1991).

30. John Rex, "Ethnic Identity and the Nation-State: The Political Sociology of Multi-Cultural Societies," *Social Identities* 1, no. 1 (1995): 21-34.

31. Milton Esman, "The Political Fallout of International Migration," *Diaspora: A Journal of Transnational Studies* 2 (1992): 3-38.

32. For an extensive study of transnational communities, see Linda Basch, Nina Glick Schiller, and Cristina Szanton Blanc, *Nations Unbound: Transnational Projects, PostColonial Predicaments and Deterritorialized Nation-States* (Amsterdam: Gordon and Breach, 1994). See also David Skidmore and Valerie M. Hudson, eds., *The Limits of State Autonomy: Societal Groups and Foreign Policy Formulation* (Boulder, Colo.: Westview Press, 1993).

33. David Lipscomb, "Caught in a Strange Middle Ground: Contesting History in Salman Rushdie's *Midnight's Children*," *Diaspora: A Journal of Transnational Studies* 1 (1991): 163-90.

34. Ellen Dorsey, "Expanding the Foreign Policy Discourse: Transnational Social Movements and the Globalization of Citizenship," in Skidmore and Hudson, *Limits of State Autonomy,* pp. 237-67.

35. Homi Bhabha, "The Third Space," in Jonathan Rutherford, ed., *Identity, Community, Culture and Difference* (London: Lawrence & Wishart, 1990), pp. 207-22.

36. Purnima Mankekar, "Reflections on Diasporic Identities: A Prolegomenon to an Analysis of Political Bifocality," *Diaspora: A Journal of Transnational Studies* 3 (1994): 366.

Chapter 12

1. Brass Workers History Project, *Brass Valley: The Story of Working People's Lives and Struggles in an American Industrial Region,* comp. and ed. by Jeremy Brecher, Jerry Lombardi, and Jan Stackhouse (Philadelphia: Temple University Press, 1982).

2. *Brass Valley,* Brass Workers History Project, distributed by Cinema Guild (1982).

3. *Puerto Rican Passages,* Connecticut Public Television (1995).

4. Robert B. Reich, *The Work of Nations: Preparing Ourselves for Twenty-First Century Capitalism* (New York: Vintage Press, 1992), p. 8.

5. Richard J. Barnet and John Cavanagh, *Global Dreams* (New York: Simon and Schuster, 1994), p. 15.

6. Stephen Viederman, "Ecological Literacy," keynote address to the Associated Colleges of the Midwest Conference on Ecological Education, March 11, 1994.

7. For a fuller discussion of the "race to the bottom," see Jeremy Brecher and Tim Costello, *Global Village or Global Pillage: Economic Reconstruction from the Bottom Up* (Boston: South End Press, 1994), chap. 1.

8. Dan Gallin, "Drawing the Battle Lines," *New Politics* Summer 1994, pp. 109-10.

9. Richard J. Barnet and John Cavanagh, "Just Undo It: Nike's Exploited Workers," *New York Times,* February 13, 1994.

10. On the political origins of the Corporate Agenda, see Thomas Ferguson and Joel Rogers, *The Hidden Election: Politics and Economics in the 1980 Presidential Campaign* (New York: Pantheon, 1981).

11. For an overview of the process by which the Corporate Agenda was incorporated into international institutions, see David Ranney, *The Evolving Supra-National Policy Arena* (Chicago: University of Illinois at Chicago, Center for Urban Economic Development, 1993).

12. For a review of these movements, see Brecher and Costello, *Global Village or Global Pillage,* chap. 5.

13. See, for instance, "North American NGO Computer Networking Against NAFTA: The Use of Computer Communications in Cross-Border Coalition-Building," paper presented at the 17th International Congress of the Latin American Studies Association, Los Angeles, September 24-27, 1994. See also Dan Goldrich, "Report to Activists of the Citizens Trade Campaign: Reflections on the Struggle Over NAFTA and Beyond," manuscript, May 1994.

14. Bruce Rich, *Mortgaging the Earth* (Boston: Beacon Press, 1994).

15. Some of these movements are reviewed in the *American Political Report,* December 17, 1993.

16. See Gay Seidman, "Facing the New International Context of Development," in Jeremy Brecher, John Brown Childs, and Jill Cutler, eds., *Global Visions: Beyond the New World Order* (Boston: South End Press, 1993).

17. See the *American Political Report,* December 17, 1993.

18. See, for example, issues of *Bankcheck Quarterly* for 1993 and 1994.

19. So far as I know, the phrase "globalization-from-below" was first used by Richard Falk. See his "The Making of Global Citizenship" in Brecher et al., *Global Visions,* pp. 39-50.

20. *The International Labor Organization: Backgrounder* (Washington, D.C.: ILO Bureau of Public Information, December 1993).

21. Steve Charnovitz, "International Trade and Worker Rights," *SAIS Review 7* (Winter–Spring 1987).

22. For a summary, see Ian Robinson, *North American Trade As If Democracy Mattered* (Ottawa and Washington, D.C.: Canadian Center for Policy Alternatives and International Labor Rights Education and Research Fund, 1993), pp. 29ff.

23. Jorge Castañeda, *Utopia Unarmed* (New York: Knopf, 1993), pp. 443 ff.

24. Interview with Ron Blackwell, UNITE economist, January 13, 1994.

Chapter 13

1. George W. Landau, Julio Feo, and Akio Hosano, *Latin America at a Crossroads: The Challenge to the Trilateral Countries—A Report to the Trilateral Commission* (New York: Trilateral Commission, 1990), p. 12.

2. Georges Fauriol, ed., *Security in the Americas* (Washington, D.C.: National Defense University Press, 1989), p. 11.

3. Ibid., p. 20.

4. Ronald Takaki, *A Different Mirror: A History of Multicultural America* (Boston: Little, Brown, 1993).

5. The Inter Press Service announced on February 15, 1995, that the United States and Mexico Working Group on Immigration and Consular Affairs had come to an agreement on facilitating the movement of documented workers from border populations by issuing special passports. The agreement cited Mexico's "serious concern about the prevalent tendencies in the United States for local and federal legislative reforms which limit the rights of undocumented immigrants and their access to social service."

6. Quoted in John Tomlinson, *Cultural Imperialism* (Baltimore: Johns Hopkins University Press, 1991), p. 176.

7. Ibid., p. 176.

8. Quoted in E. San Juan, Jr., *Racial Transformations/Critical Transformations* (Atlantic Highlands, N.J.: Humanities Press International, 1992), p. 132.

9. Quoted in Rebecca Morales and Frank Bonilla, eds., *Latinos in a Changing U.S. Economy Comparative Perspectives on Growing Inequality* (Newbury Park, Calif.: Sage Publications, 1993), p. 233.

10. Eugenia Georges, *The Making of a Transnational Community: Migration, Development and Cultural Change in the Dominican Republic* (New York: Columbia University Press, 1990), p. 2.

11. Andrew Hacker in *Two Nations: Black and White, Separate, Hostile, Unequal* (New York: Scribner's, 1992) presents abundant evidence to discredit racist myths about the financial burdens African-Americans place on the state.

12. Jaroslav Pelikan, *The Idea of the University: Reexamination* (New Haven: Yale University Press, 1992), p. 12.

13. For a recent treatment of this topic, see Robert N. Bellah, "Class Wars and Culture Wars in the University Today," *Academe* 8 (July–August 1997): 22-26.

14. See R. C. Lewontin, "The Cold War and the Transformation of the Academy," in Noam Chomsky et al., *The Cold War and the University: Toward an Intellectual History of the Postwar Years* (New York: New Press, 1997).

15. Mark T. Berger, *Under Northern Eyes: Latin American Studies and US Hegemony in the Americas, 1898-1990* (Bloomington: Indiana University Press, 1995), p. 67.

16. Immanuel Wallerstein, "The Unintended Consequences of Cold War Area Studies," in Chomsky et al., *The Cold War and the University*, p. 209.

17. David Dent, *Handbook of Political Science Research on Latin America* (New York: Greenwood, 1990), pp. ix-x.

18. Gilbert Merkx, Editor's Foreword, *Latin American Research Review* 30, no. 3 (1995): 4.

19. Ibid.

20. Joseph S. Tulchin, "Emerging Patterns of Research in the Study of Latin America," *Latin American Research Review* 23 (1983): 87.

21. See Berger, *Under Northern Eyes*, chaps. 3-4.

22. Robert H. Bates, "Area Studies and the Discipline: A Useful Controversy," *PS: Political Science and Politics* 30 (Fall 1997): 166.

23. Wallerstein, "Unintended Consequences," p. 227.

24. San Juan, *Racial Transformations/Critical Transformations*, p. 13.

25. Josephine Nieves, "Puerto Rican Studies: Roots and Challenges," in María Sánchez and Antonio M. Stevens-Arroyo, eds., *Toward a Renaissance of Puerto Rican Studies* (Atlantic Highlands, N.J.: Atlantic Research and Publications, 1987), p. 5.

26. Frank Bonilla, "Puerto Rican Studies: An Interdisciplinary Approach," in ibid., p. 17.

27. Charles Taylor, *Multiculturalism and the "Politics of Recognition"* (Princeton: Princeton University Press, 1992), p. 36.

28. Quoted in Morales and Bonilla, *Latinos in a Changing Economy,* p. 240.

29. Pedro A. Cabán, "Puerto Rican Studies: New Challenges and Patterns," *Centro de Estudios Puertorriqueños Boletín,* Fall 1985, p. 7.

30. Wallerstein, "Unintended Consequences," p. 228.

31. Kelvin Santiago-Valles, *"Subject People" and Colonial Discourses* (Albany: State University of New York Press, 1994), p. 24.

32. William Boelhoer, *Through a Class Darkly: Ethnic Semiosis in American Literature* (New York: Oxford University Press, 1987), p. 140.

33. San Juan, *Racial Transformations/Critical Transformations,* p. 77.

34. Arthur M. Schlesinger, Jr., *The Disuniting of America: Reflections on a Multicultural Society* (New York: Norton, 1991), p. 93.

35. Quoted in San Juan, *Racial Transformations/Critical Transformations,* p. 36.

36. Quoted in Pedro A. Cabán, "The Plebiscite and the Diaspora: The Status Debate on Puerto Rico and Puerto Ricans in the United States," in Gordon Jonathan Lewis, ed., *Puerto Rico and the Proposed Status Referendum and Puerto Ricans in the U.S.* (New York: Columbia University, Institute for Puerto Rican Policy, 1990), p. 14.

37. Richard J. Herrnstein and Charles Murray, *The Bell Curve: Intelligence and Class Structure in American Life* (New York: Free Press, 1994), p. 550.

38. George Black, *The Good Neighbor: How the United States Wrote the History of Central America and the Caribbean* (New York: Pantheon, 1988), pp. xvii-xviii.

39. Morales and Bonilla, *Latinos in a Changing Economy,* p. 235.

40. Tomlinson, *Cultural Imperialism,* p. 175.

41. Jeremy Brecher, John Brown Childs, and Jill Cutler, eds., *Global Visions: Beyond the New World Order* (Boston: South End Press, 1993).

42. Leo Panitch, "Globalisation and the State," in Ralph Milibrand and Leo Panitch, eds., *Socialist Register: Between Globalism and Nationalism* (New York: Monthly Review Press, 1994), p. 64.

43. Frank Bonilla, "Migrants, Citizenship, and Social Pacts," in Edwin Meléndez and Edgardo Meléndez, eds., *Colonial Dilemma: Critical Perspectives on Contemporary Puerto Rico* (Boston: South End Press, 1993), p. 182.

44. Nil Smith and Cindy Katz, "LA Intifada: Interview with Mike Davis," *Social Text* 33 (1992): 19-33.

45. Jeremy Brecher and Tim Costello, "The Lilliput Strategy: Taking on the Multinationals," *The Nation,* December 19, 1994, pp. 757-60.

46. San Juan, *Racial Transformations/Critical Transformations,* p. 133.

47. Ibid., p. 140.

Chapter 14

Acknowledgments: This chapter draws substantially on a paper originally written at the behest of a joint committee of the Social Science Research Council and the Inter-University Program for Latino Research in 1993. An updated version of that work has recently been published by IUPLR in its Milenio series as "Brother, Can You Paradigm?" August 1997.

1. Frank Bonilla and Robert Girling, eds., *Structures of Dependency* (Stanford, Calif.: Stanford University, Institute of Political Studies, 1973).

2. *Open the Social Sciences,* report of the Gulbenkian Commission on the Restructuring of the Social Sciences (Binghamton, N.Y.: Fernand Brandel Center, State University of New York, 1992).

3. David L. Featherman, "What Does Society Need from Higher Education?" *Items* 47, nos. 2-3 (1993): 40-41.

4. Kenneth W. Waltz, *Foreign Policy and Democratic Politics* (Boston: Little, Brown, 1987), 304.

5. Frank Bonilla, "Research and Development Planning: Some Issues for Americans," *Latin American Research Review* 3, no. 1 (1967): 192-200.

6. The following paragraphs paraphrase key passages from Frank Bonilla and José Silva Michelena, eds. *A Strategy for Research on Social Policy* (Cambridge, Mass.: MIT Press, 1967), The Politics of Change in Venezuela series, vol. 1: 384.

7. Jorge Bustamante, Clark W. Reynolds, and Raúl A. Hinojosa Ojeda, *U.S.-Mexico Relations: Labor Market Interdependence* (Stanford, Calif.: Stanford University Press, 1992).

8. Eugene B. Skolnikoff, "Internationalization of the Research Universities," *Daedalus* 122, no. 4 (Fall 1993): 249.

9. Bonilla and Girling, *Structures of Dependency.*

10. Committee for Puerto Rican Studies and Research, "A Proposal for a Center for Puerto Rican Studies and Research at the City University Graduate Center," manuscript.

11. Hisauro Garza, "Origins and Evolution of an Alternative Scholarship and Scholarly Organization," in Tacho Mindiola, Jr., and Emilio Zamora, *Chicano Discourse* (Houston: University of Houston, 1992), pp. 41-42. See also Chicano Coordinating Council on Higher Education, *El Plan de Santa Barbara* (Oakland, Calif.: La Causa Publishers, 1969).

12. Michael B. Katz, ed., *The Underclass Debate: Views from History* (Princeton: Princeton University Press, 1993); Rebecca Morales and Frank Bonilla, eds., *Latinos in a Changing U.S. Economy: Comparative Perspectives on Growing Inequality* (Newbury Park, Calif.: Sage Publications, 1993).

13. Some of the pitfalls of neglecting these complexities are delineated by Walter Stafford, "Political Dimensions of the Underclass Concept," in Herbert Gans, ed., *Sociology in America* (Newbury Park, Calif.: Sage Publications, 1992).

14. See Frank Bonilla, "Circuits and Cycles of Puerto Rican Migration," paper presented at the annual meeting of the Connecticut Humanities Council, Bridgeport, Conn., November 14, 1992; Harriet D. Romo, ed., *Latinos and Blacks in U.S. Cities: Policies for the 1990s* (Austin: University of Texas Press, 1990).

15. *Open the Social Sciences.*

About the Illustrations

FRONTISPIECE
De pico a pico (Beak to Beak), *1993, Bibiana Suárez*
pastel drawing, 74" x 84"

Bibiana Suárez's work focuses on the social, political, and cultural impact of Puerto Rico's status as a colony of the United States, with all the conditions of marginalization and assimilation that status confers. It speaks metaphorically about the dualistic tensions in her transnational existence.

In a recent series titled *De pico a pico (Beak to Beak)*, Suárez uses cockfighting as a metaphor for her resistance to cultural assimilation. In *De pico a pico* (1993), the skeleton of the rooster on the left symbolizes the core and foundation of the Puerto Rican culture within her. On the right is a fighting cock, groomed and prepared to fight as a symbol of the assimilated self. In this image, the core confronts the assimilated self, and the assimilated self confronts the core. The fighting cock's opponent is himself—always vanquished, always triumphant, engaged in an unceasing struggle to maintain and evolve his cultural identity.

PART I
Una cuestión de honor (A Matter of Honor), *1993, Bibiana Suárez*
pastel drawing, 75" x 84½"

Una cuestión de honor (A Matter of Honor) (1993) was the conclusion to Suárez'a *De pico a pico* series. *A Matter of Honor* is how the *galleros,* or trainers, refer to the cockfight. Like the issue of cultural identity, the fighting cock occupies a limitless and timeless space, a kind of cultural limbo, in different states of victory and defeat.

PART II
Green Card, *1992, Iñigo Manglano-Ovalle*
laminated Iris color print, 2" x 3"

The work of Iñigo Manglano-Ovalle, an artist who was born to a Colombian mother and Spanish father and raised in both countries as well as the United States, speaks about immigration and border issues by asking, "Whose entrance into whose nation" *Green Card* (1992) was done to mark the quincentennial of

277

the discovery of the Americas. It is part of a series of works on immigration that examine the contrast between the way identity is constructed by bureaucratic institutions and legislation and the way it is constructed through individual self-perception.

PART III
Portrait of Guillermo Gómez-Peña in performance

Guillermo Gómez-Peña specializes in the transgression of boundaries, whether they are national, cultural, racial, linguistic, or disciplinary. He is an essayist, a poet, and an installation and performance artist whose work is a dizzying interdisciplinary polyglot mix, reminiscent of the movie *Bladerunner* and inspired by the collision of two cultures along *La Frontera*.

PART IV
Detail from Triptych "The South/Missing," panel 3 of 3, 1993, Silvia Malagrino
black and white silverprints, 60" x 40" each

The dissolution and elimination of identity through political terrorism and oppression is the subject of Silvia Malagrino's work. Malagrino is an Argentinian who left her country during the so-called Dirty War (1971–83). In this series of works called *Inscriptions in the War Zone,* she explored the visual and political iconography of *los desaparecidos,* over 9,000 people illegally detained and executed in acts of state-sponsored terrorism. The images in the series use text, photos of the disappeared ones that were carried by Las Madres de la Plaza de Mayo, as well as forensic photos and diagrams.

Malagrino's work references the specific events of that period in Argentina's history, but it also has parallels to a larger history of oppression, terrorism, and genocide around the globe. The killing fields of Cambodia, Nazi concentration camps, and ethnic cleansing in the former state of Yugoslavia are part of the expanded narrative of violence that Malagrino evokes through her examination of the representation of these tragic events in our visual culture.

About the Contributors

Frank Bonilla is Thomas Hunter Professor, emeritus, in the Ph.D. Programs in Sociology and Political Science, City University of New York. Holding a Ph.D. in social relations from Harvard University, he was a founding member and a managing director of the Inter-University Program for Latino Research from 1988 to 1995.

Jeremy Brecher is the author of eight books on labor and social movements, including *Strike!* (San Francisco: Straight Arrow Books, 1972), *Global Visions: Beyond the New World Order* (Boston: South End Press, 1993), and *Global Village or Global Pillage: Economic Reconstruction from the Bottom Up* (Boston: Sound End Press, 1994).

Pedro Cabán is associate professor of political science at Rutgers University, where he was chair of Puerto Rican and Hispanic Caribbean Studies from 1990 until 1997. He has written extensively on political development in Puerto Rico.

Jorge Chapa, a graduate of the University of California, Berkeley, is associate professor of sociology at the Lyndon B. Johnson School of Public Affairs of the University of Texas at Austin. He researches the socioeconomic and social mobility of Mexican-Americans.

Patricia Fernández-Kelly is a faculty associate in the Princeton University Office of Population Research and the Department of Sociology.

Guillermo Gómez-Peña is a performance artist and author. His writings include *Warrior for Gringostroika* (St. Paul, Minn.: Graywolf Press, 1993). One of the founders of the Border Arts Workshop, a politically active artists' collaborative in San Diego, Gómez-Peña was born in Mexico but now lives and works in the United States.

Silvia Malagrino has a master of fine arts degree and is an assistant professor in the College of Art and Design at the University of Illinois at Chicago.

Iñigo Manglano-Ovalle has a master of fine arts degree and is a visiting project coordinator in the College of Art and Design at the University of Illinois at Chicago.

Edwin Meléndez is director of the Mauricio Gastón Institute of the University of Massachusetts in Boston. An economist and graduate of the University of Massachusetts, Amherst, he specializes in issues related to work force development.

Rebecca Morales, a graduate of MIT, is an associate professor at the University of Illinois at Chicago. Her research is in domestic and international economic development.

Manuel Pastor, Jr., is chair of Latin American and Latino Studies at the University of California, Santa Cruz. with a degree in economics from the University of Massachusetts, he has conducted research on Latinos in the United States and on Latin American economic issues.

Saskia Sassen is an urban planner and professor in the Department of Urban Planning and at the School of International and Public Affairs at Columbia University. She has written extensively on international labor migration.

Bibiana Suárez was born and raised in Puerto Rico, but has resided in Chicago since 1980. She has a bachelor of fine arts degree from the School of the Art Institute of Chicago and is assistant professor in the Art Department at DePaul University. Her work explores issues of gender and identity and has been extensively exhibited.

Gerald Torres is H. O. Head Centennial Professor of Real Property Law at the University of Texas Law School. A graduate of the University of Michigan Law School, he is a member of the Critical Race Theory Group and a former acting deputy director of the Department of Justice.

María de los Angeles Torres is associate professor of political science at DePaul University in Chicago. She specializes in the politics and identity of diaspora communities.

Silvio Torres-Saillant, a Dominican-born resident of New York, teaches in the English Department at Hostos Community College of the City University of New York and heads the CUNY Dominican Studies Institute at City College. He holds a Ph.D. in comparative literature from New York University and specializes in Caribbean literature.

Carol Wise is assistant professor of political science at the Johns Hopkins University School of Advanced International Studies in Washington, D.C. She works on Latin American economies.

Index

Acculturation, 171

ACLS. *See* American Council of Learned Societies

African-Americans, 4, 6, 21, 96, 100; and assimilation, 86, 87, 165, 207-8; and citizenship, 269 n. 55; commonalities with Latinos and, 226, 229; and community development corporations, 119; discrimination experienced by, 113, 260 n. 30; as majority in U.S., 204; population and age distributions of, 71; and slavery, 162, 165, 197, 212; and the underclass model of urban poverty, 26, 75; underdevelopment of business among, 113, 260 n. 30; viewed by immigrants, 84, 101-2

African-American Studies, 205, 217, 227

Agency for International Development, 11

Aldrich, Howard, 113

Alfaro, Luis, 131

Alicea, Marisa, 175

Alliance for Progress, 200

Amazon rainforest, 188, 189

American Convention on Human Rights, 253 n. 45

American Council of Learned Societies (ACLS), 200

Andean Group, 62, 251-52 n. 40

Andean Labor Migration Statement, 62

Andean Pact, 44, 62

Anglos, 4, 21, 71, 78; education of, 74, 75, 80; male median income for, (Tab. 5.1, 77)

Angulo family, 94-95, 99

Antonio Maceo Brigade, 174

Anzaldúa, Gloria, 177

Arce, Elia, 131

Areíto, 174

Argentina, 8, 200, 278, 250 n. 24; in-

traindustry trade in, 41, 241 n. 11; and MERCOSUR, 36, 37, 62; trade reform in, 7, 35 (Tab. 3.1, 36-37), 40, 41, 42, 45, 46, 47, 48, 243 n. 24

Arizona, 247-48 n. 13

Artists, 131, 132-33, 135-36, 177-78

Asians, 71, 204

Aspe, Pedro, 46

Assimilation, 83, 103, 105, 175, 211; and African Americans, 86, 165, 207-8; and the border, 267-68 n. 41; demise of theory of, 209, 213; and ethnic identity, 85-89; and Latinos, 204, 207-8; and Mexicans, 86, 165, 171, 173, 267-68 n. 41; and politics and identity, 163, 165, 170-73; and Puerto Ricans, 86, 207, 277

Atman, Alfred, 247 n. 11

Australia, 59

Aztecs, 269 n. 61

Babcock, Orville E., 148

Báez, Buenaventura, 147, 148

Barrio, El, 105, 110, 257 n. 1; and economic empowerment, 106, 107, 111, 125-26

Becton, Dickinson, 191

Belgium, 9

Bell, Daniel, xii

Bell, George, 151

Bellagio conference, ix, xiii, 217, 218, 230

Bellah, Robert, 103

Bernstein, Richard, 180

Bethel New Life, 121

Beveridge, Albert J., 140

Bilbao, Francisco, 264-65 n. 12

Bildner Center for Hemispheric Studies, 142

Binational Study on Migration, 64

Black, George, 209

281